Fiction Beyond Secularism

FLASHPOINTS

The FlashPoints series is devoted to books that consider literature beyond strictly national and disciplinary frameworks, and that are distinguished both by their historical grounding and by their theoretical and conceptual strength. Our books engage theory without losing touch with history and work historically without falling into uncritical positivism. FlashPoints aims for a broad audience within the humanities and the social sciences concerned with moments of cultural emergence and transformation. In a Benjaminian mode, FlashPoints is interested in how literature contributes to forming new constellations of culture and history and in how such formations function critically and politically in the present. Series titles are available online at http://escholarship.org/uc/flashpoints.

1. *On Pain of Speech: Fantasies of the First Order and the Literary Rant,* Dina Al-Kassim
2. *Moses and Multiculturalism,* Barbara Johnson, with a foreword by Barbara Rietveld
3. *The Cosmic Time of Empire: Modern Britain and World Literature,* Adam Barrows
4. *Poetry in Pieces: César Vallejo and Lyric Modernity,* Michelle Clayton
5. *Disarming Words: Empire and the Seductions of Translation in Egypt,* Shaden M. Tageldin
6. *Wings for Our Courage: Gender, Erudition, and Republican Thought,* Stephanie H. Jed
7. *The Cultural Return,* Susan Hegeman
8. *English Heart, Hindi Heartland: The Political Life of Literature in India,* Rashmi Sadana
9. *The Cylinder: Kinematics of the Nineteenth Century,* Helmut Müller-Sievers
10. *Polymorphous Domesticities: Pets, Bodies, and Desire in Four Modern Writers,* Juliana Schiesari
11. *Flesh and Fish Blood: Postcolonialism, Translation, and the Vernacular,* S. Shankar
12. *The Fear of French Negroes: Transcolonial Collaboration in the Revolutionary Americas,* Sara E. Johnson
13. *Figurative Inquisitions: Conversion, Torture, and Truth in the Luso-Hispanic Atlantic,* Erin Graff Zivin
14. *Cosmopolitan Desires: Global Modernity and World Literature in Latin America,* Mariano Siskind
15. *Fiction Beyond Secularism,* Justin Neuman

Fiction Beyond Secularism

Justin Neuman

NORTHWESTERN UNIVERSITY PRESS | EVANSTON, ILLINOIS

the modern language initiative

THIS BOOK IS MADE POSSIBLE BY A COLLABORATIVE GRANT FROM THE ANDREW W. MELLON FOUNDATION.

Northwestern University Press
www.nupress.northwestern.edu

Digital Printing
ISBN 978-0-8101-2989-4

Library of Congress Cataloging-in-Publication Data

Neuman, Justin, author.
Fiction beyond secularism / Justin Neuman.
pages cm. — (Flashpoints)
ISBN 978-0-8101-2989-4 (pbk. : alk. paper)
1. English fiction—20th century—History and criticism. 2. Secularism in literature. 3. Religion in literature. 4. Postsecularism. I. Title. II. Series: FlashPoints (Evanston, Ill.)
PR888.R5N48 2014
820.9382—dc23

2014005101

Contents

Acknowledgments

Before expressing my gratitude to the many people and institutions whose support made it possible for me to write this book, I want to offer an acknowledgment about my relationship to its subject matter. Religiously "unmusical" was Max Weber's preferred self-description. I too have little aptitude for religion, though, while growing up in rural Vermont on the hippie fringe of New York's Jewish diaspora, where the Jewish community shared space with a local church, I made a weekly pilgrimage twenty miles each way on mountain roads for enough religious education to become a bar mitzvah. For my parents, Judaism had more to do with the memory of the Holocaust and with schlepping to High Holiday services than it did either with faith in God or with the practices of *halakha*, or Jewish law. As is the case for many Jews both assimilated and practicing, the commonplace reduction of religion to belief was foreign to my experience of religion, which took its inspiration from my paternal grandfather, a lifelong atheist and a respected Talmudic scholar.

The earliest roots of this project go back to the fall of 2001. I was teaching English at a private school, and my senior English elective on contemporary fiction was in its second week on Salman Rushdie's *The Satanic Verses* at the time of the 9/11 attacks. Over the subsequent weeks a book I had begun to suspect was too challenging for the syllabus became the source of a transformative reading experience for my students and a pivotal one for me. I decided later that year to go back to graduate school in English, with the vague sense that it might be an opportune time to reconsider the relationship between religion, secularism, and the novel on a global scale. At the end of my coursework in the spring of 2004, I had the honor of giving a paper as respondent to French philosopher Alain Badiou at a conference on Saint Paul at the University of Virginia; though his work does not figure directly in this book, our encounter gave it the spark of life.

The thanks I offer here cannot do justice to the debts I have incurred as I worked on the project that has become *Fiction Beyond Secularism*. I am especially indebted to Jennifer Wicke, Peter Brooks, and Michael Levenson, my mentors at the University of Virginia, for their insight, guidance, and generosity. It is they who shaped my sense of the profession, and they who challenged and supported my project and me during a formative phase. Other teachers influenced me substantially in graduate school, among them Eleanor Kaufman, Caroline Rody, Jahan Ramazani, Joseph Davis, James Davidson Hunter, and Eric Lott. I am also grateful to acknowledge the financial assistance of the Institute for Advanced Studies in Culture at the University of Virginia, which provided me with a dissertation fellowship, an office, and an intellectual community including Slava Jakelic, Josh Yates, and Jenny Geddes. My cohort at Virginia were my first readers and continue to be the best of friends; special thanks to Elizabeth Anker, Sean Borton, Bethany Mabee, Chris Nichols, Erich Nunn, Lily Sheehan David Sigler, and Eric Song.

There could be no better place than the English Department of Yale University to complete a book like *Fiction Beyond Secularism*. I am particularly grateful for the generous readings and inspiring guidance of Michael Warner, Amy Hungerford, and Pericles Lewis. The novels analyzed in this study also feature in several courses I have had the privilege to offer at Yale, and I would like to thank my students in several courses, especially "Religion and the Postwar Novel" and "The Novels of J. M. Coetzee," for their vibrancy in the classroom. My extraordinary colleagues Jessica Pressman, R. John Williams, Caleb Smith, and Paul Grimstad have been both stern readers and sources of support in times of need. This book has also benefited immensely from the provocative readings of Rebecca Walkowitz, Akeel Bilgrami, Bruce Robbins, and Simon During; I thank them for their honesty and insight. Many thanks as well to Emily Gum, Rachel Fishkis, Merve Emre, Amanda Crego-Emley, and Elisabeth Magnus for their research, editorial work, expertise, and help preparing the manuscript for publication. I would also like to thank Jody Greene, Ed Dimendberg, and Henry Carrigan at Northwestern University Press for their roles in making *Fiction Beyond Secularism* a reality.

Lectures rooted in this material were presented at Brandeis University, the University of Colorado, the University of the Witwatersrand, Yale University, and the University of Virginia. Early versions, trial balloons, and other adventures were presented at conference meetings of the American Comparative Literature Association, the International Society for the Study of Narrative Literature, and the Modern Language Association. I would like to thank my hosts as well as my audiences on those occasions for their questions, their patience, and their good humor. My thanks to Jonathan VanAntwerpen, Wei Zhu, and others at *The Immanent Frame* for publishing my work and for moderating the best site on the Internet for those interested in secularism, religion, and the public sphere.

Parts of several chapters have appeared in other forms: "Salman Rushdie's Religious Cosmopolitans," in *Cosmopolitanism, Religion, and the Public Sphere*, ed. Maria Rovisco (London: Routledge, forthcoming); "Religious Cosmopolitanism? Orhan Pamuk, the Headscarf Debate, and the Problem with Pluralism," *Minnesota Review* 77 (Fall 2011); "The Novel against God: Questioning the Form's Inherent Secularism," in *Culture* 3.2 (Fall 2009); "The Fictive Origins of Secular Humanism," *Criticism* 50.4 (Fall 2008); "Radical Asceticism: The Turning Away of the Other in J. M. Coetzee's *Life and Times of Michael K*," in *The Camp: Narratives of Internment and Exclusion*, ed. Coleman Hogan (Newcastle: Cambridge Scholars Press, 2007). I am grateful to Routledge Press, Duke University Press, the Institute for Advanced Studies in Culture, and the Cambridge Scholars Press for permission to include the portions of these essays published here.

Preface

In this book I explore the new modes and meanings of secularity that emerge in Anglophone and world literature in the period that begins, roughly, with the Iranian revolution of 1979, picks up speed with the collapse of communism, and gains full legibility in the aftermath of September 11, 2001. I argue that some of the most trenchant and far-reaching critiques of secularist ideologies, as well as the most exciting and rigorous inquiries into the legacies of the religious imagination, take place where we might least expect them: in the pages of contemporary novels composed by a transnational group of writers commonly identified as non- or even antireligious. For the most part, readers assume that when avowedly nonreligious writers like Orhan Pamuk, Salman Rushdie, Ian McEwan, Margaret Atwood, J. M. Coetzee, Nadine Gordimer, Haruki Murakami, and others address religion in their fiction, it will be as the target of energetic critique. Ironically, this response turns out to be equally true of self-identified religious readers who have taken offense at novels like *The Satanic Verses*, *The Handmaid's Tale*, or *Snow* (with or without actually having read the book in question) and of the majority of critics. The latter tend to see the contemporary novel of ideas as an outgrowth of postmodernism antithetical to religions' grand narratives, and the novel *qua* genre as formally and historically antithetical to religion.

Contemporary fiction is not the redoubt of a new atheism, as some have argued, but neither does it portend a "postsecular" return of religion, as others claim. Through a series of case studies, in this book I take a closer look at the ways writers grapple with diverse religious legacies in their work, and I suggest that contemporary fiction is far more systematically and sympathetically interested in religion than has heretofore been acknowledged. After all, the revitalization of religion in recent decades has not implicated believers, theologians, and theorists alone but intellectuals and writers in the United States, South Africa, Turkey, Japan, and across Europe. Transcending geography, this revitalization is very much at stake in the newest forms and latest functions of the novel. For writers like Rushdie, Pamuk, and McEwan, the antagonisms among major world religions and the opposition between avowed secularists and committed believers propel the plots of novels and fuel the controversies that account for much of their notoriety. For the likes of Gordimer, Coetzee, and Murakami, meanwhile, globalization stages a dizzying array of religiously inflected modes of being, knowing, and feeling; this diversity underscores, for them, the need to develop new comparative strategies and broader cultural fluencies. In a wide-ranging set of case studies that frame close literary readings against an interdisciplinary archive of Department of Defense memos, Jewish mysticism, legal cases, continental philosophy, and Islamic theology, *Fiction Beyond Secularism* tracks a shift in literary production and value through which new "religious" novels come into view, revising the dominant accounts of world literatures in this period.

More than any other living writer, Salman Rushdie has come to symbolize the supposed conflict between religious oppression and artistic freedom. In his essays and speeches both before and after the fatwa, Rushdie has consistently styled himself as the champion of personal atheism and political secularism, suggesting that global (and indeed national) citizenship in a world composed of people practicing a multiplicity of faiths—and none—requires either a public sphere distilled of particular religious practices (laicism), or a system that remands religion to a private sphere while remaining formally neutral in religious matters (disestablishment). But, as I argue in my first chapter, "Salman Rushdie's Wounded Secularism," Rushdie's ideological and aesthetic commitments bring him to contradictory conclusions about the nature and meaning of religion and the secular. On the one hand, Rushdie offers a triumphant account of secularization as a progress narrative; on the other, Rushdie tells a set of stories about the way contemporary secularist ideologies produce wounded subjects marked by "God-shaped hole[s]." In Rushdie's recent fiction, the intersections between secularism and cosmopolitanism underscore the importance and the vulnerability of interreligious communities. In the distant mirror of Kashmir in *Shalimar the Clown*—and, in the case of *The Enchantress of Florence*, Mughal India—I argue that Rushdie offers readers a vision of a religiously inflected cosmopolitanism and a reminder of how thin the fabric of pluralism can be.

"J. M. Coetzee's Prophets of Asceticism," my second chapter, turns from Rushdie's maximalist prose to Coetzee's experiments with religiously inflected modes of self-renunciation, starvation, and self-abasement and their relation to minimalist prose forms. Beginning with *Life and Times of Michael K*, Coetzee's most vivid evocation of the human animal at the degree zero of survival, I analyze starvation and self-renunciation as a strategy for escaping the agent/victim dialectic—and, indeed, all human encounter—and thus as a challenge to ethical paradigms rooted in encountering and bearing witness to the pain of others. Moving from the physical asceticism of self-starvation to the ethical realm of sacrifice and care, I evaluate the ways *caritas* comes to serve as a possible corrective for the material disjunctions and injustices of apartheid in *Age of Iron*. I conclude by asking how scenes of erotic self-abasement in *Elizabeth Costello* and *Disgrace* relate to the project of ethical selfhood. Describing Coetzee's giving and suffering protagonists as "prophets of asceticism," I argue that we should read Coetzee as a tragic theologian whose works improvise methods of world renunciation that are highly suspicious of, and sometimes antithetical to, human flourishing.

For billions around the world, the events of 9/11 were experienced as a rupture, a periodizing event that cast the world into a new period of danger and uncertainty. Whether it signified the end of a brief era of optimistic globalism or a bold retaliation against an ungodly global hegemon, and whether it is understood as a deeply historical event or as an apocalypse outside ordinary time, one of 9/11's most salient effects has proved to be temporal in nature. The experience of temporal disorientation and unsettlement has been of paramount importance to the narratives that address the attacks and contend with their unfolding legacy in the subsequent decade. My third chapter, "Time and Terror," asks why and in what ways 9/11 altered time consciousness by tracking the rhetoric of temporality in *The 9/11 Commission Report*, Don DeLillo's *Falling Man*, Ian McEwan's *Saturday*, and Jess Walter's *The Zero*. Beginning with the lexicon of the war on terror, including its temporally overdetermined rhetoric of "the homeland," "preemption," "fundamentalism," and, of course, the name-date "9/11" itself, I consider a few cases of what I call *9/11 chronomania*, the obsession with time and temporal disruption that characterizes representations of 9/11 across a variety of media forms.

In chapter 4, "Messianic Narrative," I analyze historical fiction about encounters with loss through a reinterpretation of Walter Benjamin's "weak messianic power," a concept elaborated upon in his final major work, the "Theses on the Philosophy of History." While strong messianisms refer to belief in a future salvation or in the figure of a particular redeemer, I call attention to a microgenre of historical fiction that credits literature with a weak messianic power: the power to dissolve the current moment and charge the present with the energy of the past. My argument tracks a tradition of weak messianism from its emergence in the Frankfurt School and Judaic theology, through Hannah Arendt's concepts of natality and forgiveness, to Derrida's messianism without a messiah. I stress the resources the messianic offers as an alternate theory of intergenerational trauma and as an orientation toward the past in fictions of encountered loss like Anne Michaels's *Fugitive Pieces*, Haruki Murakami's *The Wind-Up Bird Chronicle*, and Orhan Pamuk's *Snow*.

Chapter 5, "Reading Islam," considers the causes and effects behind the rising popularity of novels in which Islam constitutes a major theme and analyzes the reasons why the production and circulation of such books have, to date, done little to cultivate productive zones of contact and exchange between those of different faiths and of none. By considering representations of Islam in best-selling novels including Khaled Hosseini's *The Kite Runner* and Yann Martel's *Life of Pi*, as well as Nadine Gordimer's *The Pickup* and Alaa al Aswany's *The Yacoubian Building*, I attempt to clarify what, when, and how discourses about Islam circulate in and through world literature and to model strategies for reading across religious difference. Beginning with the lawsuit over the selection of Michael Sells's *Approaching the Qur'an: The Early Revelations* as the summer reading text for incoming first-year students at the University of North Carolina at Chapel Hill in 2002, I analyze how popular fictions like *The Kite Runner* propagate secularized and Protestantized visions of Islam compatible with the political secularity of liberal democratic rule. But the desire to read for questions of religious difference is not merely a new form of Orientalism; situating these works within a project of comparative secularity, I aim to show how a multisited analysis can reshape dialogic approaches to religious difference and national literature alike.

Fiction Beyond Secularism

Introduction

Ka, the protagonist of Orhan Pamuk's novel *Snow*, is an Istanbul-born intellectual who "couldn't see how [he] could reconcile . . . becoming a European with a God who required women to wrap themselves in scarves," and so, dismissively, "kept religion" and its "bearded provincial reactionaries" out of his life (96). In this way, Ka typifies the ideological secularism commonly associated with transnational elites in the late twentieth century, though the particular cluster of beliefs, practices, texts, and communities he has in mind when he thinks of religion are specific to his cultural frame. The suffix *–ism*, attached here to modify Ka's relation to the "secular," signals the doctrinaire, identitarian quality of his unbelief, which borrows its sense of progress and its westward, Europhilic gaze from the legacy of Mustafa Kemal Atatürk. The distinctive tenor and vocabulary of Ka's secularism, parsed carefully throughout by Maureen Freely in her English translation, index the novel quite specifically to the period between the 1979 Iranian Revolution, during which the figure of the bearded reactionary gained global circulation as a mass-mediated symbol of political Islamism, and September 11, 2001, after which not even the most blithely atheistic metropolitan intellectuals would be so confident they could keep "religion" out of their lives.

In the early twentieth century, hoping to cause or accelerate modernization, Atatürk operationalized what nineteenth- and early twentieth-century social theorists like Max Weber and Émile Durkheim took to be an effect or symptom of modernization: the "secularization thesis." This argument, that modernization entails the privatization and inexorable decline of religion, became a theory integral to the self-understanding of Anglo-European modernity for over a century. Non-believers of previous generations or those rooted in different cultural frames might interpret their rupture with normative religious traditions in heroic or tragic modes: as the triumph of reason over superstition on the one hand, or as the painful and devastating loss of meaning or of the sacred on the other. Ka's relatively late arrival in this particular intergenerational trajectory, however, means that he experiences his own unbelief as neither an achievement nor a cause for crisis. His secularism is an uncritical, inherited condition, one peopled with clichéd "reactionaries" projected as its others and structured according to a socially dominant secularist ideology. This ideological secularism fails him, however, when he returns to Turkey and travels to the provincial eastern Anatolian city of Kars, where he experiences new spiritual and creative intensities after a dozen years in Germany as a poet in exile.

Through the eyes of a narrator named "Orhan," the narrative of this double *Künstlerroman* follows Ka to Kars, on a visit screened by a commission to write an article for the secularist Istanbul *Republican* on the local mayoral elections, in which an Islamist candidate is a heavy favorite. Ka is also tasked with investigating a surge of suicides among a group of female Islamic students known as "the head-scarf girls," whose deaths are paradoxically interpreted both as a threat to Islam, which strictly forbids suicide, and as an Islamist assault on the secular state. In this "poorest, most overlooked corner of Turkey"—a city as seemingly peripheral to Istanbul's metropolitan center as the novel's Turks fear they are to an imagined "West"—Ka encounters a Kurdish sheikh, the Islamist mayoral candidate, young men who identify as Islamist radicals and terrorists, and the leader of the head-scarf girls herself, who turns out to be Kadife, the younger sister of Ka's love interest, Ipek (18).

When an Islamist murders an education minister for supporting the head-scarf ban in public universities, shooting him in the very pastry shop where Ka and Ipek are conducting the first rendezvous of their whirlwind courtship, it seems clear that the observant Muslims Ka meets will confirm his worst expectations about the role of religion in the public sphere. The ideological commitments of what Pamuk calls his "political" novel are, readers suspect, sure to lie on the side of the secularists.[1] Instead, in the course of his visit to Kars, Ka gains a new faith in God and recovers his literary gifts, composing a book of inspired poetry that he and various characters in the novel align with Sufi mysticism. "I can't be sure," Ka says to a young Islamist in a confessional moment, thinking of the poems he has written in a green journal, which to the younger man is conspicuous as the color of Islam, "but I think it is God who is sending me the poems" (124). In addition to this newfound openness to religious experience on a personal level, the forms of religious community and modalities of belief Ka finds in Kars are a far cry from the Atatürk-era conception of Islam as the parochial antithesis of modernity that determined the prejudicial tenor of his earlier naive secularism. Though its primary action is set in the early 1990s, the novel was composed between 1999 and late 2001 and was received in 2002 by a Turkish readership (and, within several years, by a global one) primed for its urgency by the landslide victory of the Islamically inflected Justice and Development Party (AKP), the Turkish bid for membership in the European Union, and the emergent "war on terror." What appears peripheral, retrograde, and locally specific is actually globally networked; even the "Islamist" mayoral candidate turns out to be his old friend Mutar, a fellow leftist from his old university days who has become a bourgeois business owner and politician.

It is clear that we—like Pamuk's Ka, the secularist who discovers somewhat belatedly the inadequacy of his own conceptual repertoire—need better ways of talking about the cultural conditions of secularity and what appears to be a worldwide resurgence of religion, both in the public sphere and in literary studies. Empirical data on the continued personal and political salience of religion throughout the twentieth and into the twenty-first century handily disprove prophecies of its imminent decline, and the divergent routes to modernity taken by the nations of Asia, Latin America, and the Middle East, meanwhile (to say nothing of the highly energetic religiosity of politically secular nations like the United States and Turkey), challenge the social-evolutionary assumption that modernization entails secularization or even, in what is only an apparent tautology, that secularism causes secularization. One need not agree with Ashis Nandy's intentionally provocative indictments that secularism has trended toward "ethnocidal" and "authoritarian" governmentality, as he argues in his "Anti-secularist Manifesto," in order to see how "secularism endorses the worldview from within which . . . [sectarian] violence flows" (63). The enduring salience and vitality of public religions around the world reminds us that those who predicted science (or art) would replace religion, or those convinced that modernity would inaugurate a postreligious future, were wrong about the kind of thing religion—and the secular—is.

From a comparative perspective in the second decade of the twenty-first century, it is clear that the tide of secularist iconoclasm, beginning with Nietzsche and cresting by the middle of the twentieth century, has receded. The decline of religion, once posited as an inevitable consequence of modernization, seems better suited to arguments for northern European exceptionalism than as an articulation of a universal rule. And yet, the enduring sense that "the secular" exercises unique claims to universality and that "secular reason" is the hallmark of critical inquiry has left scholars across the academic disciplines ill-equipped to engage the nuances of religious resurgence in their scholarship and hesitant to do so in their classrooms. For scholars of postcolonial and world literatures in particular, the historical complicity between religion and empire and the long shadow of Edward Said's use of the term *secular criticism* to denote privileged modes of inquiry have tended to marginalize rigorous engagements with religiosity. Moreover, it is equally clear that received categories and binaries like religion and the secular, or faith and reason (not to mention nominally unified totalities like Christianity, Islam, and Judaism), tend to conceal what actually involves finer shades of affect and practice, especially when it comes to the dense network of connections that make up our own lives and those brought into being in the fictional worlds of any good book.

To understand what has happened to the cultural conditions of secularity in the past quarter century, the first step is unlearning the habit of conceiving religion and secularity as opposites. A dialectical conception of the relationship between the religious and the secular promises to illuminate little about either term or about the traffic between religion and politics in particular times and places. Pamuk's novel emphasizes how misleading it is to consider the secular as religion's opposite in its repeated satiric riffs on the law of the excluded middle: "There is, after all, only one West and only one Western point of view. And we take the opposite point of view" (228). It also underscores the fact that modes of secularism are not simply neutral remainders left behind after "religion" has been removed from the public sphere, but modes of governmentality prone to violence that produce, maintain, and discipline their own conceptions of religiosity. In *Snow* this process has overt manifestations, like the state-funded *madrasa* attended by Necip and Fasil, and covert ones, such as the clandestine meetings of Sheikh

Saadettin Efendi. The novel's persistent focalization of minorities—Kurds and Sufis, Armenians and Alevis—emphasizes a further distinction: a strong public commitment to religion need not be opposed to, and indeed can work in concert with, politically secular projects, as was the case with the framing of the Establishment and Free Exercise clauses in the US Constitution.

For Ka, taking religion seriously involves revising his attitudes toward the place of Islam in his private life and in the public sphere, but, more importantly, it demands that he reexamine the narrow conceptual armature through which he thinks about religion and secularity in general. In its ideologically driven forms, like the one to which Ka subscribes, secularism becomes a triumphant system denoting, as José Casanova has recently argued, "the phenomenological experience not only of being passively free but also actually of having been liberated from 'religion' as a condition for human autonomy and human flourishing" (60). Instead of marking a self-sufficient immanent sphere, secularism in this sense trends toward the active disavowal and denial that underwrite Ka's image of the religious as a group of "bearded provincial reactionaries." Among other things, thinking beyond secularism means moving toward a more complex account of the social, political, and historical forces that frame both religious and nonreligious modes of being.

In Atatürk's long shadow, to be modern in Turkey has meant looking west. Being a citizen of the republican state, and therefore of the world community, has correspondingly required distancing oneself from the perceived parochialisms and anachronisms of Ottoman and Islamic identities. Atatürk abolished the Caliphate and religious courts in 1924 and, during a long period of single-party rule, instituted a series of sweeping political, economic, and cultural reforms aimed at bolstering Turkish nationalism and achieving parity with Europe. Under the "Six Arrows" of the Kemalist ideology (republicanism, populism, reformism, nationalism, secularism, and statism), Atatürk's top-down initiatives replaced the Islamic calendar with the Gregorian, religious modes of dress with European fashions, Arabic script with the Latin alphabet, *madrasas* with state-run public schools, and a society in which women were at best second-class citizens with one in which women gained the right to vote in 1934, a full decade before similar developments in France. Enshrined in article 2 of the Turkish constitution, which defines the state as "democratic, secular [the Turkish employs the French cognate *laik*], and social," Turkish secularism serves explicitly statist goals; the constitution's preamble mandates that "there shall be no interference whatsoever by sacred religious feelings in state affairs."[2] Modeled on French notions of *laïcité*, the Turkish state presumes to distinguish cleanly between private religious engagement and a public, juridical, and educational sphere entirely purified of religious influence. This Kemalist model depends on strict regulation; all of Turkey's eighty thousand mosques are controlled by the DRA (Directorate of Religious Affairs), and their imams are civil servants.[3]

While the concept of *laïcité* is often translated as "secularism"—and indeed the first article of the French constitution defines it in terms of equality before the law and of the state's respect for all beliefs—in practical terms, *laïcité* has meant that public religions have been viewed with greater skepticism, distaste, and juridical control in France than in the United States.[4] Turkey's history of political laicism stands in stark contrast to the religiosity of its public: according to the 2002 Pew Global Attitudes Project, 99 percent of the Turkish population believes in God and identifies with a particular religion; of these, most Turks are Sunni, the only religion to receive fiscal support from the state (Albright et al., *What the World Thinks*). Sixty-nine percent of the population reports that they attend religious services on a weekly basis, and about three-quarters of Turkish women wear some form of head scarf. Over two-thirds of the population avows that religion plays a "very important" role in their personal lives, though only 41 percent of Turks express a desire for Islam to play a larger role in political life. Indeed, in the countries surveyed in the Pew study, only France exceeded Turkey in the percentage of people (73 percent) who "completely agree" that "religion is a personal matter and should be kept separate from government." A subsequent Pew survey, the 2003 *Views of a Changing World* (Albright et al.), further reports that more than nine in ten Turks maintain that women should have the choice to wear a head scarf or other religious covering, in direct opposition to the official policy prohibiting the practice in certain contexts.

Since the 2002 victory of the Justice and Development Party (AKP) under the leadership of Prime Minister Recep Tayyip Erdoğan and President Abdullah Gül—both committed Muslims and former torchbearers of radical Islam—a party with deep Islamic roots has controlled Turkish politics, garnering a plurality in the 2002 national elections with 34 percent of the vote, a figure that rose to 47 percent in the general elections of 2007. Surprising many, both domestically and internationally, it has been the AKP, often against the will of parties in the

Kemalist tradition, that has supported Turkey's ascension to the EU, championed women's access to education, supported minority rights for Kurds, and called for an end to policies supportive of torture and rendition. Founded from the shards of Islamist political organizations dissolved by Turkey's Constitutional Court for violating the principle of secularism, the AKP treads a fine line, mobilizing Turkey's devout majority through faith-based grassroots activism and projecting the moral values of traditional Islam while simultaneously denying any desire to implement Sharia law. Its party platform contains an extensive section on human rights, and with regard to the issues of the head scarf and the admission of covered women into university the AKP has argued in terms of these rights: rights to higher education, rights to freedom of individual expression, and rights to freedom from discrimination on the grounds of religion. Though the results of its leadership have been mixed, those in Turkey and the West who have accused the AKP of hiding politics of Sharia law within the Trojan horse of multiculturalist rhetoric have overstated their case.[5] Through the AKP, an Islamic political party has challenged hegemonic state secularism by appealing to the rhetoric of human rights usually the exclusive domain of secularists and cosmopolitan humanists.

The plot of Pamuk's novel converges on a series of events that take place at the National Theater in Kars while the town is cut off from the rest of the world by a snowstorm. It is here that Pamuk stages, in a literal sense, the putative conflict between secularism and religion. Before the evening culminates in a revolution staged to upset the imminent mayoral elections, Sunay Zaim, an aging but famous actor, punctuates his variety act routine with a reprise of an Atatürk-era play entitled *My Fatherland or My Head Scarf*. Veiling, as image and practice—and, with it, the female body itself—has become the central symbol of Islamist politics worldwide and a synecdoche for passionate secularist resistance to religion in the public sphere. Given the already extensive commentary on the head-scarf debate, what does Pamuk's *Snow* have to teach its readers about the issues at hand? The play Pamuk describes is a "desperately old-fashioned" production that follows a veiled woman who proclaims her independence by removing her scarf and burning it despite the protests of her family and various "bearded Muslim men"; she is ultimately saved from the reprisals of "prayer-bead-clutching religious fanatics" by Republican soldiers (22). For Ka and the reader, the play's offensiveness and transparent Kemalist statism foreshadow the inadequacy of Ka's own views. Within the action of the novel, the play operates along the lines of Hamlet's mousetrap: by successfully cultivating the ire of the religious high school students in the audience with the symbolic power of a burning head scarf, Sunay intends to provoke a riot among the *madrasa* students and then "save" the secular republic with a fusillade of rifle shots.

Pamuk, however, intends the drama at the National Theater to map the shifting terms of the head-scarf debate and underscore the inadequacy of simplistic understandings of religion and the secular as agonistic opposites. As the narrator notes, the play "was performed frequently in lycées and town halls all over Anatolia [in the Atatürk era], and it was very popular with westernizing state officials eager to free women from the scarf and other forms of religious coercion" (156). Not only did the play once serve as transparent propaganda for Atatürk's secularizing reforms by dramatizing the very act it was written to encourage, its production in civic spaces literally assembled the collectives it attempts to bring into being. The play's author (interviewed by *Snow*'s assiduous narrator, Orhan) describes how "during the thirties, [*My Fatherland or My Head Scarf*] . . . had had the same remarkable effect on lycée girls and state officials alike—it had moved them to tears and standing ovations wherever it was performed" (151). In contrast to the coherence and solidarity generated by these Atatürk-era productions, Sunay's revival of the play occurs in a political landscape in which the cultural coordinates of the head scarf are far more complicated, and a diverse array of cosmopolitical affiliations interrupt the binary modalities on which the drama hinges.

Kadife, the leader of the so-called head-scarf girls, dons her scarf neither out of deep-seated religious conviction nor in pious obeisance to her father, who is a secularist in the Kemalist vein. Instead, Kadife claims she has covered her head "for personal religious reasons but also wears the scarf as an emblem of her faith" and thus as an act of political speech (281). As Kadife notes, "To play the rebel heroine in Turkey you don't pull off your scarf, you put it on" (312). Kadife's claim condenses the convoluted symbolic resonance of the head-scarf debate: in Turkey, where Kemalist legislative reforms have forbidden the wearing of head scarves in government spaces and universities since the 1920s, donning a head scarf indeed constitutes an act of political dissidence. Playing "the rebel heroine," however, asserts claims of individualism, power, and visibility in direct tension with the norms of piety and modesty that the head scarf denotes—pieties Kadife further inverts in her illicit sexual affair with Blue, the novel's cosmopolitan terrorist. For

Ka, who lived outside of Turkey for twelve years before returning to Kars, Kadife represents a new type of Islamic woman whose wearing of the head scarf shatters the myths of female subservience and domesticity associated in his mind with Islamic dress.

Kadife's statement appeals to the same logic employed by Saba Mahmood and others who have noted that the meaning of the head scarf has changed from a sign of subjection, disenfranchisement, and prohibition to an act of political speech and an affirmation of autonomy.[6] In the past, Ka "paid little attention to the head scarves he saw and didn't attempt to distinguish the political kind from any other"—they simply served to demarcate the modern, Western, and the affluent from the retrograde and the poor (23). The narrator continues to explain that Ka "had scarcely been in the habit of noticing covered women. In the Westernized upper-class circles of the young Ka's Istanbul, a covered woman would have been . . . the milkman's wife or someone else from the lower classes" (23). Kadife's head scarf, like the head scarves of women in positions of power or those aspiring to university educations, testifies to the political, religious, and economic shifts that transformed Turkish society between the years of Ka's youth and the narrative present.

In the intervening years, the cultural meanings cathected on the scarf have changed: "Most of the locals in the National Theater were shocked and confused by the first scene," the narrator notes. "No one expected to see an actual woman onstage wearing a head scarf. When they did, they took it to be the sort of head scarf that has become the respected symbol of political Islam" (147). After eighty years of secular rule, the scarf has ceased to function as the symbol of religious and patriarchal traditionalism for which it stood in Kemalist discourse. In fact, persistent attacks on Islamic dress by secular elites and repeated judicial disbandment of opposition political parties on religious grounds have increased the status of the head scarf as a sign of resistance. The head scarf's shifting political signification reflects demographic and economic transformations that have led to what anthropologist Jenny White evocatively terms "the evolution of the Islamist Yuppie," a new class of financially successful, well-educated, politically connected, and pious Turks instrumental in the rise of the AKP and earlier Islamically inflected parties (48). Within Turkey's contemporary Islamic political movements, where women play an increasingly powerful role as activists, Nilüfer Göle argues that the head scarf can constitute "an active reappropriation by women that shifts from traditional to modern realms of life and conveys a political statement" (4).[7]

While Pamuk's readers might expect that "Islam often finds [its] place in Pamuk's work as the antithesis of creative self-expression," as Ian Almond argues it does in his book *The New Orientalists* (2007), in *Snow* we can see that this is emphatically not the case (126). Instead, Pamuk explores alternate modes of religious engagement in ways that are indicative of broader trends in contemporary fiction's focus on the role of religion in global culture. At the level of style and narrative form, one can see how Pamuk draws on theologically inflected accounts of the boundaries between immanent and transcendent, self and other, and being and nonbeing to develop the theme of Ka's lost but inspired poetry, which comes to symbolize the fetish for the sacred word. *Snow* resonates with this desire to refashion both Kemalist laicism and hegemonic conceptions of Islam, so that those who see the novel as exploring the clash between "Islam" and "the West" have mistaken the novel's objects of satire for its earnest subject. This includes the Nobel Foundation, which, in its press release accompanying the announcement of Pamuk's 2006 Nobel Prize, praised him as a writer "who in the quest for the melancholic soul of his native city has discovered new symbols for the clash and interlacing of cultures." By dissolving secularism and religiosity as oppositional discourses, Pamuk reframes the episteme of secularity and recuperates experiences of communalism, inspiration, and revelation aligned throughout the text with Islam in general and Sufi mysticism in particular. This is, of course, a form of secularity, but it is also a reparative religious project that renegotiates the claims of the rigid laicism that is Ka and Pamuk's birthright.

LOSING FAITH IN SECULARISM

Since the early 1990s, a crisis of faith has struck the disciplines once most captivated by the secularization thesis. In an argument that has influenced over a century of thinking on the subject, German sociologist Max Weber contends that modernization entails a tripartite process: the structural differentiation of a once-integrated lifeworld into increasingly autonomous political, economic, familial, and religious sectors; the privatization of religion and a concomitant increase in the emphasis on individual belief; and finally, the decline of religious institutions. The result, as Weber put it in a much-debated passage of *The Protestant Ethic and the Spirit of Capitalism*, is "the disenchantment of the world," a process that emerged out of various reformation movements within Protestant and Catholic traditions and would culminate, it was thought, in the retreat of religion in the face of scientific rationalism (151).[8] Theorists and advocates of secularization, framed in the nineteenth century as a prophecy about the trajectory of modern social development, long expected religious institutions, practices, and communities, like their supposedly discredited ontologies, to attenuate and, eventually, disappear from the public sphere.[9] Objective reason would, it was thought, triumph over superstition when faith came to be seen not as a virtue but as the antithesis of knowledge.[10] In the United States, political theorists have framed questions about secularization through the storied, if misleading, Jeffersonian metaphor of the "wall of separation" between church and state. In its American conception, political secularity prescribes the impartiality of the state in religious matters in order to secure freedom of conscience and practice.[11] As a principle of statecraft in this form, political secularity aims to support the flourishing of diverse religions but problematically presumes to differentiate cleanly between politics and religion, immanent and transcendent, the public sphere and private life.

This book is a part of an energetic and interdisciplinary movement to reconceptualize what it means to live, as Charles Taylor puts it, in a secular age. No longer understood as the simple absence or antithesis of religion, the secular is instead now conceived of as a complex, historically specific set of conditions and practices. As social scientists, political theorists, and anthropologists seek to rethink secularization, the subject has emerged as a major site of academic debate and research.[12] Uncritical ideologies that champion secularism as religion's agonistic opposite have given way to more nuanced approaches to the experience of transcendence and immanence. These views illuminate a spectrum that contains many different shades of experience, ranging from the atheistic and agnostic to the religious and even to those occupying no clear place on this continuum. The ideology, history, and forms of secularity have been subjected to sustained analysis by social theorists like José Casanova, William Connolly, and Jacques Berlinerblau; philosophers such as Jürgen Habermas, Richard Rorty, Jacques Derrida, Slavoj Žižek, and Charles Taylor; theologians like John Milbank and Graham Ward; cultural theorists including Vincent Pecora, Colin Jager, Judith Butler, and Tomoko Matsuzawa; and literary critics like Gauri Viswanathan, Bruce Robbins, and John McClure. Charting a new course in these debates, I argue that in a time of Twitter revolutions and constant connectivity, the long format, the sustained acts of imaginative investment, and indeed the very media form of the novel might seem imperiled, but this study demonstrates why novels remain a vital form at a moment when we have reason to be increasingly skeptical of the short and the flat. As heteroglossic texts, novels are particularly efficient cultural containers; the sustained imaginative investment required to read them, meanwhile, fosters diverse forms of ethical modeling.

In this study, I am concerned primarily with novels in which the idea of what David Damrosch calls an "original culture" loses much of its coherence.[13] Like the idea of hybridity, which depends upon the notional autonomy of diverse groups prior to the moment of amalgamation, the question of original culture runs headlong into the conundrum of scale: for Coetzee, for example, the answer is likely to be either so broad (the Anglophone world) or so narrow (English-speaking Afrikaners of the Western Cape) as to evacuate the coherence of stable fields of knowledge.[14] "Culture," as Rey Chow suggests, "needs to be recognized as always operating *biculturally* or *multiculturally* even when it appears predominantly preoccupied with itself" (301–2). Moreover, as we adopt increasingly flexible and, as Amartya Sen calls them, "robustly plural" senses of our own identity based on multiple, overlapping, and shifting modes of belonging, the illusory nature of unitary source cultures becomes increasingly apparent (19).

Part of what makes theorizing the secular such a difficult enterprise is the way any definition implies that we know what we mean by its putative opposite, namely "religion."[15] Revisionist approaches to secularization and the sociology of religion help us see that the conception of religion as a system of beliefs and propositional statements oriented to the transcendent is a historical construction particular to the Christian West.[16] Pressing a similar point in his book *Semites*, Gil Anidjar quips, "Secularism is a name Christianity gave to itself when it invented religion" (48). Talal Asad's genealogical excavations into the history of the secular over the past quarter century have uncovered the various ways secularism operates as a set of disciplinary and disciplining practices that have produced and policed the modern category of religion. Asad's attentiveness to embodied action and the central role of practice, discipline, and community in religious experience have contributed greatly to efforts to move beyond cognitive and hermeneutic approaches to religion as a cultural system. In addition, Asad's work helps to clarify how attempts to define religion or the secular in terms of transcultural and transhistorical essences are, in their origins and development, a product of a particularly Christian historiography implicitly and explicitly tied to projects of domination.[17] The specifically Christian history of secularization can be identified as part of a strategy for the survival of religious traditions during a time of great unrest in European history. This recognition enables us to see secular pluralism as an epiphenomenon of liberal modes of governance instituted by and for religious reasons, rather than as a purely oppositional force. With a similar emphasis on the importance of embodiment, William Connolly critiques secular ontologies in *Why I Am Not a Secularist,* on the grounds that the articulation of a secular public sphere based on a disembodied model of rational agency neglects the bodily and visceral registers of experience integral to human existence. Like Asad, Nandy, and Connolly, the characters in Pamuk's *Snow* are particularly attentive to the way the values and practices of Christianity determine what counts as religion. Ka is driven by a sense that "in this part of the world faith in God was not something achieved by thinking sublime thoughts and stretching one's creative powers to their outer limits," a sense of religiosity heavy on the individualistic Wordsworthian sublime, and instead that "above all it meant joining a mosque, becoming part of a community" (60–61).

For scholars in many disciplines, Charles Taylor's 2008 opus *A Secular Age* was a much-anticipated book, one that energized Catholics and atheists, historians of the Renaissance and postcolonial theorists alike. Taylor argues against what he calls "subtraction stories," narratives that conceive secularity as the universal substrate of human reason exposed once societies have "lost, or sloughed off, or liberated themselves" from the fetters of religion (22). His work dismantles oppositional conceptions of religion and secularity, replacing them with a narrative in which secularization constitutes a set of developments internal to the history of reform within Latin Christianity. Taylor's sweeping genealogical project attempts to uncover the causes and stages of a deceptively simple transformation: "the shift to secularity," which "consists, among other things, of a move from a society where belief in God is unchallenged and indeed unproblematic, to one in which it is understood to be one option among others, and frequently not the easiest to embrace" (3). As Taylor asserts, in the seventeenth and eighteenth centuries an increasing focus on personal religious commitment and the gradual disarticulation of the immanent and transcendent realms reveal that "secularization went along with an intensification of religious faith," a connection that confounds those who seek to conflate "disenchantment" with secularization.[18] Among other things, Taylor's *A Secular Age* has put to rest the question of temporal progression or "post-ness" in our relationship to secularity—or religion, for that matter—by approaching the secular as the "frame" or condition for both belief and unbelief. This comes at a historical moment when an entirely immanent account of human flourishing is not only widely available but in many ways hegemonic. "Secularity is a condition in which our experience of and search for fullness occurs," he writes, "and this is something we all share, believers and unbelievers alike" (19).[19]

Understood in this way, the idea of a "return" of religion and the myriad speculations about what might come "after" the secular, such as the "postsecular" (Habermas et al.) or "desecularization" (Berger), begin to seem ill conceived. Not only do they reproduce the teleological metanarratives for which they criticize classical secularization theory, but they are also problematically invested in oppositional notions of religion and secularity. Instead, the diverse modes of secularity in specific geopolitical locations require that we pay more attention to the concrete ways in which European and American forms of secularity are indigenized in particular times and places around the globe, as well as to the ways "Western" secularity was shaped by Latin Christendom's colonial and postcolonial encounters with religious difference.[20] If the dominant approach to religion understands it transitively, as denoting a private and self-authenticating belief in *x* or the practice of *y* (from its etymological root in the Latin *religare*, to tie or bind), we might begin by summoning an alternate etymology: *relegere*, to read again. The "second reading" of religion, catalyzed by the critical study of secularism, constitutes both a recovery, like reencountering a novel one has put aside, and a skeptical interrogation—as one would cross-examine a witness.

To read beyond secularism, especially in the work of novelists who self-identify as nonreligious, requires an attentiveness to echoes, intertexts, and genealogies of religiosity often neglected by literary critics. In practice, it also means negotiating between sloganeering on both sides of the political spectrum. This ranges from agonistic models of difference, like the "clash of civilizations" discourse popularized by Samuel Huntington and the self-described "new atheism" of Richard Dawkins and Sam Harris, to multiculturalist models of diversity, which tend to tokenize individuals as representatives of particular groups. The ways the rapid expansion of world trade, untraditional warfare, and market capitalism that we have come to call globalization come to bear on religious experiences, institutions, and collectives—and vice versa—have proven difficult to theorize: the scale of the problem is forbiddingly vast and its contours are obscured by the way global modernity, like commodity capitalism and the multicultural nation-state, has long been seen as both a constitutively and a causally secularizing affair. To travel smoothly along the flows of global culture and public reason one must, in the dominant secularist account, be willing to shed the parochial trappings of religion, or at least relegate such attachments to one's private life—just as in the regnant narrative strong religions bespeak intolerance and violence. The power of religion as a vector of globalization is not unique to this period—religiously inspired pilgrimage, exodus, evangelism, and warfare predate recorded history—but while the rapid expansion and capitalization of an integrated global economy that has characterized the past quarter century were easily predicted and integrated into existing social and geopolitical imaginaries, the apparent resurrection of religion has been more surprising to the academy and destabilizing in terms of geopolitics.

"We develop in multi-cultural and multi-religious societies," writes Cardinal Jean-Louis Tauran. "To say this is to state the obvious. There is no religiously homogeneous society."[21] As president of the Pontifical Council for Interreligious Dialogue, the arm of the Catholic Church established after Vatican II to serve as the site of engagement with the followers of other religious traditions, Jean-Louis Tauran has something of a professional commitment to pluralism. As is more often the case, conversations across boundaries of religious difference tend to be carried out under the flag of interfaith dialogue, whether in the form of direct encounters between people or in hundreds of institutes and nongovernmental organizations around the world.[22] Without discounting the success or intent of programs like John Wallach's "Seeds of Peace" or Tony Blair's "Faith Foundation," the structural premises of interreligious dialogue tokenize individuals as representatives of particular groups, flatten out the internal variety within a given confession, and have difficulty making room at the table for modes of unbelief except in their evangelical atheist forms.[23]

The question of who speaks for a religion, by what right, and chosen by whom is another matter; we need to think more about the processes and systems that legitimate those who speak for a religion. As political scientist James Fearon emphasizes, "It rapidly becomes clear that one must make all manner of borderline-arbitrary decisions" in the process of ethnic categorization, and as a result what he describes as "the contingent, fuzzy, and situational character of ethnicity" is subordinated to a single racial designation (4). If ethnic and linguistic monocultures are always already problematic, claims about religious homogeneity are further complicated by the nature of religious belonging. Even in a hypothetical society where 100 percent of the population might name the same group when asked to state their religion—answering "Christian" or "Muslim" to the question marked "religion" in a Pew Research Center survey, for instance—individuals within the society will differ widely in the intensity, sites, and modalities that define their experience of religion.[24] According to the Pew Research Center's Forum on Religious and Public Life, Afghanistan, Iran, Mauritania, Tunisia, Western Sahara, and Yemen all report that Muslims constitute over 99 percent of the population, but to assume that the result of even this high degree of apparent religious uniformity is a meaningful religious monoculture would be to fall victim to what Nigerian novelist Chimamanda Adichie calls "the danger of a single story." In her 2009 TED talk, Adichie critiques the powers that reduce a society's pluralism to a single story, as European stories forged Africa as "a place of negatives, of difference, of darkness." For Adichie, the problem is not that stereotypes are untrue but that they "flatten [our] experience and overlook the many other stories that inform" our sense of self and that they blind us to the importance of internal diversity.

The collapse of the consensus on secularization presents a unique opportunity to investigate the range of social systems, bodily habits, and ways of knowing that have been inadequately glossed as simply either secular or religious. Doing so entails parsing more subtle distinctions between, for instance, secular*ism*, an ideology held by a secular*ist*, and secular*ity*, a cultural condition that frames both religious and nonreligious beliefs and practices. The sustained imaginative investment that is the lifeblood of literature can, I argue, provide the cultural resources—semantic, narrative, and imagistic—for thinking beyond secularism.

CHAPTER 1

Salman Rushdie's Wounded Secularism

Battle lines are being drawn up . . . Secular versus religious, the light versus the dark. Better you choose which side you are on.
—Salman Rushdie, *The Satanic Verses*

Quoted out of context, as the words of celebrities often are, the epigraph above might easily be taken to betray Salman Rushdie's personal convictions on any question of the "secular versus religious," as the available choices are rendered in this passage of *The Satanic Verses*. Even readers lucky enough to have read the novel during the brief pre-fatwa window—opening with its hardcover publication in the United Kingdom on September 26, 1988, and closing less than five months later with the Ayatollah Khomeini's announcement on February 14, 1989—would be forgiven for assuming that Rushdie had shaped *The Satanic Verses* as the sharp tip of his secularist spear. After all, one of the novel's most conspicuous embodiments of formal religion is a vengeful imam, who appears in Gibreel's dreams with "beard . . . blowing in the wind . . . red eyes . . . [and] fingernails that have grown into long, curved claws" (218). As befits a villain in a novel that owes much to Menippean satire, a tradition that blends carnivalesque parody with a picaresque prose form and epic narrative range, the imam's vision of purity and genocide serves as an antiphonic mirror for the novel's celebration of the hybrid and the new. The first American edition was released a week after the fatwa, and the paperback was delayed by security concerns until 1992; thus, for most readers of the novel, myself included, the dust cloud of the so-called "Rushdie affair" has made it even more difficult to discern the details and implications of what turns out not to be a "battle" of "secular versus religious" in *The Satanic Verses* at all.[1]

In his public pronouncements, Rushdie has often been forced into a pugilistic corner on the subject of religion, from which he echoes the sentiments and confrontational posture of the militant secularism he satirizes in *The Satanic Verses*. "'In God We Trust,'" for instance, an essay published in 1985 and again in revised form after the fatwa, opens with the following assertion, similar in style and form to that of the epigraph: "We stand at a moment in history," Rushdie declares, "in which, as we look around the planet, it appears that God—or, rather, formal religion—has begun once again to insist on occupying a central role in public life. There could scarcely be a more appropriate time to explore the subject of the relationships between politics and religions" (*Imaginary Homelands* 376). In this essay, Rushdie articulates a deeply antagonistic model of the relationship between religion and secularism, one that seems to contain the platform of his thinking throughout the subsequent decades. With its panoptic view of the planet and complicit "we" of insider address, Rushdie's observer of history lays claim to a familiar set of secularist ramparts, rising to defend a public sphere from which God has allegedly once been purged against the incursions of a resurgent "formal religion." Rushdie's primary argument against religion takes as its object textual originalists of various schools—those who believe their sacred texts represent the inerrant word of God—seeing in these modes of reading nothing more than just-so stories and prescientific attempts to explain natural phenomena. In this oft-cited essay, Rushdie communicates the terms and history of his personal convictions in bold tones, espousing an atheism that has become an integral aspect of his public persona, literary voice, and critical reception. If, as he claims, when the subjects of his novels "made it essential for [him] to confront the issue of religious faith," his aim was to "describe" rather than pass "judgment," Rushdie's goals in his essays, in contrast, often seem closer to those of "new atheists" like Christopher Hitchens, Richard Dawkins, Sam Harris, or Daniel Dennett: to bloody noses rather than extend a generous hand.

The combative secularist advocating muscular, evangelical atheism in *The Satanic Verses* turns out to be, not one of the novel's protagonists, but "a tall, thin Bengali woman" named Swatilekha—a minor, unsympathetic figure rendered with an attention to detail that belies her peripheral role in the narrative. Cast as a postcolonial academic whose opinions on the subject are the result of "too much college education," Swatilekha rejects art for what she calls the "crystal clarity" of atheist sloganeering and sees no value in any dimension of religious experience

(551). She appears in a chaotic scene at the end of the novel, as Rushdie struggles to weave a pattern of narrative closure from the many threads of his temporal and geographic canvas. Her demand for a more militant approach to the "problem of religion" nearly derails a political demonstration against communitarian violence for which a group of artists and activists have gathered, joined by Saladin Chamcha and Zeeny Vakil. The event symbolizes the novel's impending resolution: "an unbroken chain of men and women linking hands from top to bottom of the city" (555–56). More damning even than the disunity she fosters is the connection Rushdie draws between Swatilekha's militant secularism and her bad artistic taste. During a metaliterary discussion before the demonstration, Swatilekha ridicules two modes of art that echo the novel's own syncretistic norms and polyphonic form: "a documentary film about communalism, interviewing Hindus and Muslims of all shades of opinion," and the work of a poet who appeals sympathetically to "herds of [Hindu] legends, with sacred cowbells tinkling, grazing on the hillside." In other words, Swatilekha's oppositional paradigm, her "versus," negates the aesthetic of its homophone, Rushdie's "verses." As Zeeny puts it in a bid to hold together a fragile coalition, those who want to prevent "the forces of disintegration" from trending toward bloodshed "must show that there are . . . counterforces at work"—against physical violence motivated by religious sectarianism, and against the systematic exclusions that result from binary conceptions of religion and secularity (522).

By reframing secularity beyond secular*ism* in the conclusion of *The Satanic Verses*, the Swatilekha episode and similar scenes aim to reimagine and redirect some of the novel's animating tensions. Throughout the novel, it appears that secularism operates as a force of almost pure negativity: "What is the opposite of faith?" asks the narrator, concluding that the answer is "not disbelief"—atheism being a position "too final, certain, closed. Itself a kind of belief" in the creed of God's nonexistence—but, simply, "doubt" (94). "To will is to disagree; not to submit; to dissent" (95). Conceived as a labor of scrutiny and critique, secularism in this sense inevitably follows that which it recognizes as religious, as is particularly vivid in exchanges between the novel's butterfly-clad, hadj-leading mystic, Ayesha, and its wealthy, Nietzsche-reading atheist, Mirza Saeed Akhtar:

> He turned to face Ayesha. "There is no God," he said firmly.
>
> "There is no God but God, and Muhammad is His Prophet," she replied.

> "The mystical experience is a subjective, not an objective truth," he went on. . . . "You are leading these people into certain disaster."
>
> "I am taking them into the bosom of God."
>
> "I don't believe in you," Mirza Saeed insisted. "But I'm going to come, and I will try to end this insanity with every step I take." (246)

On a formal level, Mirza Saeed's critical secularism means that what Rushdie calls "the station wagon of skepticism" always follows behind the course of religion (just as Mirza Saeed literally trails Ayesha), lacking a positively framed sense of identity or destination in its own terms.

There is a proliferation of prose—a good deal of it his own—that would have us believe we understood the role of religion in Rushdie's life and fiction. However, the fate of antagonistic conceptions of the "secular versus religious" in scenes like the easily overlooked Swatilekha episode and the uncertain course of the "station wagon of skepticism" help call attention to the way Rushdie's ideological and aesthetic commitments bring him to contradictory conclusions about the nature and meaning of religion and secularism. In this chapter I explore the range of stories Rushdie tells about secularity, identifying two trajectories that emerge in his essays and become increasingly important in his post-fatwa fiction.

On the one hand, Rushdie offers a set of triumphalist accounts in which secularization appears in the guise of a progress narrative of self-actualization. This is framed against the inversely disempowered view of humanity that Rushdie alleges is propagated by religion. Though Rushdie's essays in this mode tend to follow a familiar tradition that self-consciously inherits the Enlightenment's rationalism and faith in progress, I argue that in his fiction Rushdie charts a radically different course, growing increasingly unsatisfied with the assumed connection between secularism and pluralism and with claims about secularization's exclusively Judeo-Christian genealogies.

On the other hand, Rushdie tells another set of stories about the way contemporary secularist ideologies produce people who are wounded, aching, and existentially vulnerable, shot through with what he dubs "a God-shaped hole." In this mode of wounded secularity, Rushdie invokes a vision of the literary as a replacement for religion, an idea rooted, finally, in a benevolent conception of enchantment. My point is not merely to expose a logical contradiction of which Rushdie is well aware: if secularization were the purely utopian project he claims it to be and religion so clearly the manacles of slavery, the loss of religion would produce no psychic wounding. Only if one finds more in the theological, ritual, and mystical dimensions of religious experience than a symbol of human inferiority would anyone mourn religion's loss, let alone maintain that secularization would bring about a void literature might endeavor to fill. Instead, I suggest that the aporias and discrepancies implicit in these triumphant and wounded secularisms that Rushdie articulates in his essays summon him to modify and challenge the connection between religion and enchantment in *Shalimar the Clown* and *The Enchantress of Florence*. The reading of Rushdie's post-fatwa fiction that I offer here thus revises the dominant account of his oeuvre—in which these novels are relegated to the "the late afternoon, perhaps the early evening of his career" (Walkowitz 150)—by arguing that Rushdie's recent work makes a valuable intervention as an analysis of the complex and everywhere entangled modes of religious and secular being.[2] This suggests that his essays are as much a challenge for as an explanation of the aesthetic of his fiction.

RUSHDIE'S SECULARISMS

Born to a Muslim family in Bombay on the eve of Partition, Rushdie describes growing up in a multifaith environment: "I had a Christian ayah," he relates in one essay, "for whom at Christmas we would put up a tree and sing carols about baby Jesus. . . . My friends were Hindus, Sikhs, Parsis" (*Imaginary Homelands* 377). In an episode he describes once from his own perspective in "'In God We Trust,'" and once from Gibreel Farishta's in *The Satanic Verses*, Rushdie tells the story of his own movement away from his Islamic heritage and the syncretistic pluralism of his Bombay milieu and toward a more militant atheism as a Pauline conversion narrative. "God, Satan, Paradise and Hell all vanished one day" when he was fifteen years old, Rushdie writes. "I quite abruptly lost my faith," he maintains, "I recall it vividly. I was at school in England by then. The moment of awakening happened, in fact, during a Latin lesson, and afterwards, to prove my new-found atheism, I bought myself a rather tasteless ham sandwich, and so partook for the first time of the forbidden flesh of the swine" (377). Employing the trope of the sensuous appeal of the forbidden, Rushdie looks back with ironic self-awareness at a rebellion that counts as such only through the valorization of that which it repudiates. In another essay, "In Good Faith," he declares, "To put it as simply as possible: *I am not a Muslim*. It feels bizarre, and wholly inappropriate, to be described as some sort of heretic after having lived my life as a secular, pluralist, eclectic man" (*Imaginary Homelands* 405).

Rushdie has consistently identified as a secular atheist with the exception of a brief period in 1990 when, after being led to think that a public profession of belief and a managed spectacle of contrition might lead to a lifting of the fatwa, he publicly asserted that he had renewed his faith in Islam during an event staged by prominent members of the British Muslim community. The tepid professions made under duress in "Now I Can Say, I Am a Muslim"—"I have been finding my own way towards an intellectual understanding of religion," he manages, "and religion for me has always meant Islam"—feel especially cool in comparison to the blistering attacks against religion that are his usual métier. When his renewal of faith failed to secure Khomeini's annulment of the fatwa, Rushdie quickly repudiated his own claims of religious revival. In *Joseph Anton*, Rushdie refers to his attempted conversion as a "Dreadful Mistake" from which he has only just recovered, for "he was not religious and would never again feign religiosity. He was a proudly irreligious man" (314). Donning the secularist's gloves once more, Rushdie imagines "Religion" on one side and himself "on the other team," fighting against "men in turbans and long beards (or men in frocks pretending to be celibate while molesting young boys)" (315).

As Akeel Bilgrami argues, proponents of exclusive humanism often see the rational space of the secular public sphere as the "end point of a hard-won sequence of struggle against obscurantism and chide the tendencies to obscurantism in our own time as a continuing, infantile dependence," and Salman Rushdie is no exception (146). A secularist political system in particular, Rushdie maintains, "places the human spirit in a position of power over events" and thus expresses "our dreams of improvement, of betterment, of progress" (*Imaginary Homelands* 378). "To such secularists," Ashis Nandy correctly observes, "religion is an ideology in opposition to the ideology of modern statecraft and, therefore, needs to be contained. They feel even more uncomfortable with religion-as-faith claiming to have its own principles of tolerance and intolerance, for that claim denies the state and middle-class ideologies of the state the right to be the ultimate reservoir of sanity and the ultimate arbiter among different religions and communities" (*Politics* 324).

From the perspective of Rushdie's robust atheism, "Religion is the blindfold"—or worse, a false idol urging those of weak will to turn "away from the truth into cosy simplicities" (*Imaginary Homelands* 392). But as Rushdie is no doubt aware, the secular humanism espoused here depends on its own "cosy simplicities" that have themselves come under increasing scrutiny in recent years. As subaltern studies scholar Partha Chatterjee argues, "In the case of the countries of Asia and Africa, secularization is necessarily a normative project formulated and directed by an elite minority" (62); it is thus a "fundamentally coercive" affair (57). Subsequent to the fatwa, Rushdie has been more sensitive to the consequences of secularist norms being used to justify the actions of disciplinary regimes or wielded as a form of coercive power. As Rushdie admits, in India secularism is an elite practice implemented by a minority and imposed upon a deeply religious majority population. It is clear as well that what Rushdie means by "secularism" entails not only the principle of neutrality toward religion but what in other contexts Saba Mahmood describes as "the sovereign prerogative of the state to regulate religious life through a variety of disciplinary practices that are political as well as ethical" ("Can Secularism Be Other-wise?" 293). As Talal Asad argues in *Formations of the Secular*, the modern doctrine of political secularism that arose in European politics as a solution to the wars of religion ensured peace not by eliminating violence but by "shifting the violence of religious wars into the violence of national and colonial wars . . . [a process] closely connected with the rise of a system of capitalist nation-states" (7).[3] By analogy, skeptics of Indian state secularism, like Nandy, have argued that "communalism and secularism" should be seen not "as sworn enemies but as the disowned doubles of each other" ("Twilight" 283). For Nandy and others, the problem with secularism as it is conceived in India has less to do with its alignment with the use of force than with its alleged foreignness to the Indian context and indigenous traditions of religious pluralism.

The triumphant strain of Rushdie's secularism is composed of several themes, the most important of these being a pragmatic or utilitarian defense of political secularity based on arguments about the value of separation between state and religion. Rushdie explains his commitment to a legal structure of disestablishment as the logical and necessary result of his experience of the Partition era in India and utilitarian calculations about the political and physical muscle needed at the time to manage, contain, and prevent sectarian violence. As he observes,

"In independent India, the idea of secular nationalism has a particular importance. . . . After the terrible communal killings of the Partition riots, it was plainer than ever that if India's remaining Muslims, Sikhs, Buddhists, Jains, Christians, Jews and Harijans (untouchables), as well as the Hindu majority, were to be able to live together in peace the idea of a godless State must be elevated above all of the 330 million deities" (*Imaginary Homelands* 385). Writing in a similar vein after the September 11 attacks in an article for *The Guardian*, Rushdie declares, "If terrorism is to be defeated, the world of Islam must take on board the secularist-humanist principles on which the modern is based" ("War"). As Rushdie tells it, secularization, "the restoration of religion to the sphere of the personal—its depoliticization—is the nettle that all Muslim societies must grasp in order to become modern." In this progress narrative, secularization marks a distinct human achievement, but one obtained at great cost; as a form of heroic triumph, this narrative of political secularization resembles the one Rushdie tells about the novelist as a heroic forger of images in a world bereft of transcendent consolation.[4] Rushdie thus recasts the main narrative arc of what Charles Taylor, in *A Secular Age*, describes as inadequate "subtraction stories" that conceive the secular merely as the neutral remnant left behind after the removal of religious illusions. Political secularity requires the extensive exercise of state power and coercion, Rushdie implies, but the goal of preventing sectarian violence—what Rushdie calls "safeguarding the rights of minorities" (*Imaginary Homelands* 385)—justifies the means. In passages such as these, Rushdie unapologetically endorses the rationalist trajectory of cosmopolitan Western modernity and the means of attaining it: a Protestant privatization of faith. For Rushdie, secularist nationalism—not just the promotion of religious freedom, but an ideological commitment to the active exclusion of religion from the public sphere—is necessary to buffer religious communities, viewed as threatened (and potentially threatening) minority groups, from communitarian violence in the postcolonial state: "To be an Indian of my generation was also to be convinced of the vital importance of Jawaharlal Nehru's vision of a secular India. Secularism, for India, is not simply a point of view; it is a question of survival" (*Imaginary Homelands* 404).

The Nehruvian model of political secularity to which Rushdie alludes, negotiated during the independence and Partition period, emphasizes a complex balance between conflicting goals: to establish equality between diverse religious traditions within a pluralistic polity at the national level; to emphasize positive freedoms of practice and worship for individuals; and, exceeding the explicit neutrality toward religious caste divisions characteristic of colonial rule in British India, to mandate state intervention abolishing prejudicial elements of the Hindu caste system.[5] The political framework for this vision is articulated in the preamble to the constitution adopted on November 26, 1947, which establishes the state as a "Sovereign Socialist Secular Democratic Republic" in order to secure "liberty of thought, expression, belief, faith and worship" (India, Ministry of Justice). The adjective *secular*, added to the constitution during the Emergency in 1976, defines the state's official policies of noninterference toward religion as further articulated in clause 25 on the right to freedom of religion, but the lack of a uniform civil code means that most questions of personal and family law remain controlled by the religion of the parties involved rather than by the state.[6]

It is clear that what Rushdie has in mind by secularism goes beyond simple nondiscrimination. The hierarchy upon which Rushdie insists—one nation not "under God" but above 330 million gods—and the deliberately antireligious formulation of a "godless" *laïcité* means that Rushdie anticipates the encounter between state and religion(s) as one marked, not by agnostic and tolerant pluralism, but by an inevitable antagonism. In this essay, "religion," "God," "secularism," and "Islam" are relatively stable categories within and among which one can make precise, often decidedly negative judgments: "The word 'Islam' means submission," Rushdie affirms, "and not only Islam but Christianity and Judaism, too, classically require of believers an act of submission to the will of God" (*Imaginary Homelands* 378). The alternative to religion is "politics," by which Rushdie means something like the processes of public life in North Atlantic democratic states rather than totalitarian governmentality.[7] But even in their most benevolent forms and during times of peace, governments too require acts of submission to the will of the state, an obvious parallel Rushdie ignores or misrecognizes.

Rushdie makes the connection—or lack thereof—between political secularism and a culture of tolerant pluralism the explicit subject of his 2005 revenge tragedy *Shalimar the Clown*, in which Kashmir is portrayed as a lost pluralist paradise for a brief moment in the mid-twentieth century. All the requisites of human flourishing are present in Rushdie's Kashmir —art, fine cuisine, intimate and sustaining networks among people and with the land, relatively stable and transparent forms of local self-determination and governance—except for the very thing that, in his essays, Rushdie has identified as essential to pluralism: a secularist conception of religion and the public sphere. Instead, with novels like *Shalimar the Clown*, and subsequently with *The Enchantress of Florence*, Rushdie sets out to interrogate some of the most axiomatic premises of his secularist commitments, including the necessary relation between cosmopolitan pluralism and the secularization of the public sphere.

The four central characters who occupy the principal roles in *Shalimar the Clown* leave little doubt as to the scale of the novel's ambitions to build the epic of postwar globalization on the scaffold of family romance. Its protagonists include the eponymous Shalimar the clown, born Noman Sher Noman, a Kashmiri Muslim tightrope walker turned terrorist-assassin; Max Ophuls, Jewish survivor of Nazi persecution, hero of the French Resistance, architect of postwar political and economic globalization at Bretton Woods, billionaire, CIA operative, and Don Juan; India Ophuls, Max's globe-trotting illegitimate daughter, born Kashmira Noman; and Boonyi Noman, a Hindu dancer who yearns to escape the narrow confines of village life, wife to Shalimar, mistress to Max, and birth mother to Kashmira.[8]

Published over fifteen years after the fatwa affair marked what many critics retrospectively identify as the close of the most productive and important decade of his novelistic career, *Shalimar* represents Rushdie's return as a writer of important and innovative fiction and also a return to somewhat earlier material, specifically to the days he spent while traveling in India and working on *The Satanic Verses* "with a group of traveling players who performed *bhand pather* or, literally 'clown stories.' . . . Many years later they became the heart of his 'Kashmir novel'" (*Joseph Anton* 83). Like *The Satanic Verses*, *Shalimar the Clown* shuttles between a contemporary narrative present and historical episodes, here focused on the fictional Kashmiri villages of Pachigam and Shirmal, two interfaith communities of Hindus, Sikhs, Muslims, and Jews. The villagers constitute a disparate group of actors and cooks whose idealized valley is ravaged by decades of oppression in struggles between India and Pakistan. Rushdie portrays pre- and post-Partition Kashmir as a world where pluralist religious coexistence is not merely a fact of life but also a source of pride for the inhabitants. As Rushdie tells it, the Hindu/Muslim divide and communitarian violence endemic to the subcontinent in the era of decolonization are largely avoided in Muslim-majority Kashmir because of the syncretistic religious practices of the inhabitants and their robust cosmopolitan norms. Rushdie imagines a form of religious cosmopolitanism in Kashmir—established not by relegating religion to private life but by actively promoting public religions and fostering religiously inflected attachments—that must be parsed more carefully than the novel's tragio-comic tone seems to invite.

Readers of Rushdie's novel enter Kashmir not as a physical traveler would, through the passes of the Himalayan or Pir Panjal mountains that surround the valley like the walls of a deep bowl, but as explorers along the narratives of Vedic astrology, as told by a Hindu pandit to a Muslim boy on the cusp of adulthood. Through a vast and defamiliarizing cosmology, readers access the private spaces of the village, and Shalimar comes to understand his budding love for Boonyi: "The shadow planets [Rahu and Ketu] existed without actually existing. They were heavenly bodies without bodies. They were out there but they lacked physical form. . . . Until he found out about the shadow planets Noman Sher Noman had never understood how to think about love" (*Shalimar* 46). The unstable ontology of the shadow planets, like the novel's engagement with religion and the secular more generally, thwarts any attempt to articulate sharp analytical distinctions between immanent science and transcendental awareness. The young Shalimar, whose love for Boonyi commits him personally to an ideological investment not just in tolerance but in deeper forms of pluralism, imagines that "the words *Hindu* and *Muslim* had no place in their story. . . . In the valley these words were merely descriptions, not divisions. The frontiers between the words, their hard edges, had grown smudged and blurred. This was how things had to be. This was Kashmir" (57; italics in original).

Despite their significant religious, ethnic, economic, and political differences, the valley's individuals sense that they belong to—and feel a normative and ethical obligation to cultivate—a universal community. As Rushdie tells it, the valley experiments with a nonelite and decidedly nonsecular form of cosmopolitanism described in the novel by the valley's historical inhabitants as *Kashmiriyat*: a sense of cultural harmony and of a bond deeper than those of "blood or faith" (47). Exploring material he subsequently develops in *Enchantress of Florence*, Rushdie traces the nonsecular forms of religious pluralism in Kashmir to fifteenth-century origins, when Sultan Zain-ul-abidin, whose father, the Sikander, had waged brutal wars against the Hindu population, adopted religious tolerance as an official policy of statecraft.[9] In a story that echoes Joseph's interpretation of the pharaoh's dream in the Old Testament, Abdullah Noman cites the story of a Hindu doctor who cures an ailing fifteenth-century sultan and is offered a gift of his choice as a reward. Observing that "under the kings who came before you my Brothers were persecuted without end," the doctor seeks an end to the active persecution of Hindus by their Muslim overlords (80). The sultan's actions exceed even the doctor's expectations: "*He* [the Sultan] *made it his Business to see to the Rehabilitation of their devastated and scattered Families, and allowed them to preach and practice their Religion without any Hindrance. He rebuilt their Temples, reopened their Schools, abolished the Taxes that burdened them, repaired their Libraries and ceased to murder their Cows. Whereupon a Golden Age began*" (80; italics in original). In this parable, one of the founding myths in the imagined community of Kashmir, the Hindu doctor approaches his sovereign with a desire familiar to members of religious minorities through the ages: the ambition to live and practice their traditions, free from active discrimination at the hands of the state. But instead of what the doctor imagines as a reward—a political dispensation conceived to promote tolerant coexistence—the Sultan's paradigm involves engaged forms of state sponsorship of religion and public worship that are positively aligned with both national belonging and broader forms of human flourishing.

Abdullah Noman, Shalimar's father and the village *sarpanch* (the elected head of the local Panchayat, or five-member governing council), who plays the character of Zain-ul-abidin in theatrical productions, argues that the sultan represented "everything that was best about the valley he loved, its tolerance, its merging of faiths" (83). Specifically, "the pandits of Kashmir, unlike Brahmins anywhere else in India, happily ate meat. Kashmiri Muslims, perhaps envying the pandits their choice of gods, blurred their faith's austere monotheism by worshiping at the shrines of the valley's many local saints, its pirs. To be a Kashmiri . . . was to value what was shared far more highly than what divided" (83). The day of Shalimar's and Boonyi's birth—just two months after Partition and at the precise moment when violence breaks out between India and Pakistan over conflicting and unresolved territorial claims to Kashmir—constitutes the climax of interfaith convergence in the novel. As his wife goes into the first stages of her labor, Boonyi's father, Pandit Pyarelal Kaul, rhapsodizes about Kashmir's thriving polyculture of public religions:

> Just consider for a moment!" cried Pyarelal. "Today our Muslim village, in the service of our Hindu maharaja, will cook and act in a Mughal—that is to say Muslim—garden, to celebrate the anniversary of the day on which Ram marched against Ravan to rescue Sita. What is more, two plays are to be performed: our traditional *Ram Leela*, and also *Budshah*, the tale of a Muslim sultan. Who tonight are the Hindus? Who are the Muslims? Here in Kashmir, our stories sit happily side by side on the same double bill, we eat from the same dishes, we laugh at the same jokes." (71)

The pluralist ethos praised by Pyarelal is viewed not as the product of protoscientific rationality or the rhetorical gestures of a nonsectarian civil religion but rather as a more dedicated path of religious engagement for Hindus and Muslims in their own terms.

Even the doctor called to attend to the laboring women emphasizes the deep pluralism of the region; a Sufi philosopher as well as a physician, he is "master of medicine both herbal and chemical, traditional and modern, Eastern and Western" (82). The cultural competencies of Pachigam's pre-Partition inhabitants facilitate pluralism through what James Clifford might celebrate as "diverse cosmopolitical encounters, [and] specific, hybrid accommodations with national and transnational forces" (376). Like the *Hamza-nama* tapestries in *The Satanic Verses*—a sixteenth-century series depicting stories in the life of Muhammad's uncle in which "you could see Hindu and Muslim philosophy forming their characteristically late-Mughal synthesis"—the emphasis in Pachigam is not on creating a public sphere purified of particularist commitments but on fashioning a syncretic fusion that, like the tapestries in Saladin's father's art collection, provides "eloquent proof of . . . the eclectic, hybridized nature of the Indian artistic tradition" (*Satanic Verses* 70–71).

Shalimar and Boonyi's marriage marks a second example in which religious cosmopolitanism triumphs over the privatization of religion and public worship reinforces a pluralistic polity. When a spy for the Indian army exposes Shalimar and Boonyi's love affair (assuming he will thereby coerce the disgraced Boonyi to marry him instead of the Muslim Shalimar), the village council and the parents decide to support the interfaith marriage, a move especially surprising for the reader given the quotation from *Romeo and Juliet*, "A plague on both your houses," which serves as a laconic epigraph to the novel. In defense of this decision, Abdullah Noman, Shalimar's father, appeals to the power of a communal, local identity based in the protonationalist notion of *Kashmiriyat*: "the belief that at the heart of Kashmiri culture there was a common bond that transcended all other differences" (110). As he argues, "We have not only Kashmiriness to protect but Pachigaminess as well [with its village council of Hindus, Jews, and Muslims]. . . . There is no Hindu-Muslim issue. Two Kashmiri—two Pachigami—youngsters wish to marry, that's all" (110). Though schismatic bickering inevitably surrounds Boonyi and Shalimar's interfaith wedding (performed twice, first according to Hindu custom and then again in an Islamic ceremony), Rushdie plays the conflict for comic effect—modeling the squabbles over food, ceremony, and schedule on the stock humor of interfaith weddings that have become standard fare in romantic comedies from Bollywood to Hollywood. Rushdie's novel places special emphasis on his characters' public displays of religion and on the region's political dispensation, forged independently of what he elsewhere identifies as distinctly Western conceptions of the separation of church and state.[10]

RELIGIOUS COSMOPOLITANISM

The ideal of *Kashmiriyat* represents both an identity and a conscious normative project: its goal is to forge an ethic of common humanity within a pluralist context that still celebrates its sources of cultural particularity. *Shalimar the Clown*'s sections on Kashmir focus on small-scale, natural ecosystems and domestic rituals of sexual and social reproduction, such as births, marriages, celebrations, festivals, and mourning. Kashmir is a place of roots, to borrow Paul Gilroy's phrase, rather than routes—much in the way that, in *The Satanic Verses*, the sense of place felt by the villagers in Titlipur is metaphorized by the roots of the banyan tree whose growth is coterminous with the settlement. But as Rushdie tells it, in the small, landlocked valley of Kashmir, James Clifford would find what he celebrates as "diverse cosmopolitical encounters . . . [and] hybrid accommodations with national and transnational forces" (376). As I argue here, the ideal of *Kashmiriyat*, with its relationships across religious and ethnic difference rooted in mutual respect and its emphasis on the events of everyday life, enacts many of the distinctive features of the positive, nonelite, and locally sourced recuperations of cosmopolitanism made by social and political theorists since the early 1990s. At the same time, however, Kashmiri public religiosity challenges the latent secularism of cosmopolitan theory.

The secular frame within which cosmopolitanisms have traditionally operated reflects a paradoxically narrow approach to the condition of pluralism when it comes to religion. Current paradigms suggest that global (and indeed national) citizenship in a world composed of people practicing a multiplicity of faiths—or no faith at all—requires either a public sphere distilled of particular religious practices (laicism) or a system that remands religion to a private sphere while remaining formally neutral in religious matters (the storied "wall" of separation). To the extent that religious life and structures have found places in the cosmopolitan imagination, they have done so in this latter sense as valorized modes of private difference, like regional cuisines or architectural styles, which insulate against the charge that globalization produces a McWorld of homogeneous neoliberal consumers. While historically conceived in opposition to the nation-state, cosmopolitan theory has evolved within and become increasingly complicit with nationalism and global capital.[11] Beginning with events like the fatwa affair, strong religions have come to replace nationalisms as cosmopolitanism's foil and ideological antithesis.[12] And yet, precisely because the most prominent boundaries and violent flashpoints of the modern world-system have less to do with nationalism and more to do with religious and economic differences that proliferate both within and beyond the nation-state, any cosmopolitanism worthy of the name must offer a model of inclusivity and universalism that reckons with the substantive differences between a variety of religious and nonreligious modes of life. As cosmopolitan ideals are increasingly predicated on secular subjectivity, it becomes more difficult to recognize religiously inflected transnationalisms as forms of cosmopolitanism; at the same time, by tacitly excluding those with strong beliefs from the pluralist fold, cosmopolitan theorists court the charges of elitism and Eurocentrism that they assiduously seek to avoid.

The return of cosmopolitanism to the center of debate in the humanities has had a great deal to do with Salman Rushdie.[13] Through his prose, his politics, and his persona, Rushdie has played a more pivotal role in shaping new theories of cosmopolitanism than any other living writer. For some, he and his work are symptomatic of the pejorative connotations of cosmopolitanism as synonymous with neoliberal globalism, airport lounges, and transnational elites; for others, they epitomize the positive forms of flexible attachment characteristic of diasporic migrancy. By presenting an exoticized East to the metropolitan reading public of the North Atlantic world, Rushdie's novels can be seen to capitalize on what postcolonial critics have identified as an Orientalist desire for the foreign Other. Timothy Brennan, for example, argues in his monograph on Rushdie that Rushdie's meteoric rise can be attributed to his status as "the third-world writer who . . . plays an intermediary role, the role of ushering in [foreign materials], critiquing the West, usually in acceptable ways, citing strange names, retelling hidden histories, and doing all this pedagogically" (*Salman Rushdie* 41). Aijaz Ahmad agrees, arguing in *In Theory* that Rushdie's assertions of cosmopolitan migrancy reveal more about his own conditions of privilege than they do about the realpolitik of resistance in the worlds from which he has taken flight. Bruce Robbins queries "whether third world fictions and careers (including careers in the making and reading of fictions) that were aimed at and were embraced by the metropolis could ultimately signify anything other than an opportunistic affirmation of the metropolis" (*Feeling Global* 101). Critics like Ahmad, Brennan, and Robbins rightly worry that the very polymorphous hybridity characteristic of Rushdie's prose (with its empowered narrator summoning cultural materials from diverse traditions) replicates the characteristically imperialist failings of a noticeably Eurocentric ideal of cosmopolitan universality.

Alongside rationalist models of cosmopolitan world citizenship associated with the Cynics of Ancient Greece, Kant during the Enlightenment, and Martha Nussbaum in the present moment, a loose coalition of cultural theorists, philosophers, and social scientists have sought to renovate the cosmopolitan ethos by distancing it from rationalism, elite globalism, and juridical culture. Describing these alternate cosmopolitanisms as "rooted," "vernacular," "cosmopolitical," or "discrepant," Kwame Anthony Appiah, Homi Bhabha, Bruce Robbins, James Clifford, and others begin by emphasizing the accuracy of many critiques of cosmopolitanism as it has traditionally been framed—namely that, as Craig Calhoun argues, "cosmopolitanism has been a project of empires, of long distance trade and of cities" ("Class Consciousness" 870).[14] By calling attention to the lives of migrant workers, for example, rather than to the transnational elite, Clifford suggests that the skills, knowledge, and experiences of those often understood as victims of neoliberal capital "can be redeemed under a sign of hope as 'discrepant cosmopolitanisms'" (367).[15] In his influential book *Cosmopolitanism:*

Ethics in a World of Strangers, Appiah argues that "one distinctively cosmopolitan commitment is to *pluralism*. Cosmopolitans think that there are many values worth living by and that you cannot live by all of them. So we hope and expect that different people and different societies will embody different values" (144). In claiming both that cosmopolitanism is an inherently pluralist creed and that this thoroughgoing pluralism is a unique aspect of cosmopolitanism that enables it to be distinguished from other visions of identity, Appiah foregrounds the tension between cosmopolitanism and its antitheses: religious and nationalistic particularism.

The distinction between the new modes of cosmopolitanism imagined by Appiah and others and those hewing closer to the term's philosophical genealogy is readily visible in the way members of the two groups speak of cosmopolitanism's core commitments. As Martha Nussbaum puts it in an influential essay, one's participation in "the worldwide community of human beings" depends upon subordinating national and religious differences to the universals of a common humanity. Nussbaum insists that cosmopolitanism "asks us to give our first allegiance to what is morally good—and that which, being good, I can commend as such to all human beings" (1996, 5).[16] To Diogenes of Sinope, the fourth-century BCE philosopher credited with coining the term *cosmopolitan*, all forms of religious conviction and practice were antithetical to universal citizenship and the edicts of rationalist independence. Among the many anecdotes in *The Lives of Eminent Philosophers* about the man who spurned worldly possessions and appropriated the epithet *kynikos*, or doglike, one recounts that when "asked where he came from . . . [Diogenes] said, 'I am a citizen of the world'"—a *kosmopolitês* (Diogenes Laertius 6.63). Claims to world citizenship erased and superseded local ties and beliefs; for Diogenes, religion appears as a species of particularist commitment to be spurned. In "The Case for Contamination," Appiah suggests in contrast that the primary commitment of cosmopolitanism should be to "individuals": "The right approach, I think, starts by taking individuals—not nations, tribes or 'peoples'—as the proper object of moral concern."

If cosmopolitanism historically offered a rather thinly imagined ideal of world citizenship, proponents of discrepant or rooted cosmopolitanisms seek to invest the concept with greater specificity in order to differentiate it from universalism, and in so doing to increase its ethical and political traction.[17] Because the term has come to mean so much for so many different people, conflicting conceptions of cosmopolitanism, moreover, register opposing reactions to globalization and multiculturalism as phenomena. Some use the term *cosmopolitan* as a gesture of approbation: for instance, to praise how global capital flows, postnational structures like nongovernmental organizations, and the unprecedented interconnectedness of global markets have fostered a more "cosmopolitan" world. Yet cosmopolitanism also names the desire shared by many on the cultural left to forge an ethos of political engagement that navigates a middle path between the particularizing relativism of multiculturalist identity politics on the one hand and managerial globalisms on the other. To do so, new cosmopolitan theorists of various stripes grapple with the two perceived inadequacies of cosmopolitan theory, namely its alleged Eurocentric elitism and the frequent accusation that the ideas of "world" and "humanity" retailed by cosmopolitans are too insubstantial to galvanize the affective attachments necessary for political mobilization.

Most of the thinkers I have mentioned would allow that, in a privatized form, religions are part of what adds tone and definition to cosmopolitanism; religions are part of our rootedness. But strong religions run afoul of what Appiah describes as the second tenet of cosmopolitanism, "what philosophers call *fallibilism*—the sense that our knowledge is imperfect, provisional, subject to revision in the face of new evidence" (*Cosmopolitanism* 144). For Appiah, *The Satanic Verses* serves as a potent example of an aesthetic that positively values "contamination as the name for a counterideal" to cultural preservationists; in *Shalimar the Clown* and *The Enchantress of Florence*, we see Rushdie tackle several of the classic challenges facing cosmopolitan theory. While cosmopolitans embrace pluralism and fallibility, Appiah asserts, "the neofundamentalist conception of a global *ummah*, by contrast, admits of local variations—but only in matters that don't matter. These counter-cosmopolitans, once more like many Christian fundamentalists, do think that there is one right way for all human beings to live" (*Cosmopolitanism* 143).[18] As in Pamuk's *Snow*, where Blue, the terrorist antihero, is the novel's symbol of transnational mobility, the cosmopolitan modalities of contemporary terrorism are Rushdie's central focus in *Shalimar the Clown*. "Study at the Base. You know the Base? Brother Ayman . . . Sheikh Usama. Learn many good thing," a Filipino Muslim advises Shalimar (268). The training he receives in this shadow world is impeccable: after a few years he "had passports in five names and had learned good Arabic, ordinary French and bad English, and had opened routes for himself, routes in the real world, the invisible world, that would take him where he needed to go" (275). Rushdie is keen to emphasize the interconnections between systems of global justice and the organizations dedicated to the destruction of the reigning world order: it is, after all, "Ambassador Max Ophuls who . . . was supporting terror activities while calling himself an ambassador for counterterrorism" in his capacity as a liaison to the Taliban (272).

More than any other figure in Rushdie's novels, Max Ophuls personifies the characteristics associated with deracinated forms of cosmopolitan politics. Born in metropolitan Strasbourg, in the contested border region of Alsace-Lorraine (a territory wrested between France and Germany, making it the analogical twin, in the novel's formulation, of a Kashmir torn between India and Pakistan) the multilingual and dangerously handsome Max epitomizes European cosmopolitanism. Like Joyce's Leopold Bloom, Max's Jewishness enhances rather than detracts from the cultivation of a cosmopolitan ethos; while his affluent family of Ashkenazi Jews falls victim to Nazi persecution, Max's connections to none other than Jean Bugatti allow him to escape capture as "the Flying Jew," piloting Ettore Bugatti's prototype plane to the relative safety of the French Resistance in Clermont-Ferrand.[19] Max, we learn, worked as a forger for the Free French, where he infiltrated the SS and seduced a key operative, a woman known as "the Panther," an event described as "the only known instance in the whole of World War II of a successful 'reverse sting' on a Gestapo infiltration operation" (166).[20] As his infiltration of the SS emphasizes, Max's cosmopolitanism depends upon repudiating—or at least concealing—his religion under an opportunistic facade.

At the close of the war, Max Ophuls's résumé includes his status as the "midwife" to the Bretton Woods Accords, where the institutions of the postwar world were imagined from a small town in New Hampshire.[21] After the war, he turns to writing and a political career, epitomizing the protean subject that Rushdie identifies among globalization's chief victors. Endowed with money, mobility, power, and sexual charisma, Max remakes himself numerous times across three continents. Though we are told that he is a billionaire (and thus more than capable of giving his daughter gifts like a DeLorean sports car or hiring a chauffeur and manservant like Shalimar), Max's wealth is more metaphorical than literal; he made his money, at least in his daughter's assessment, by "selling the future. . . . He had been a dealer in the dangerous, hallucinogenic narcotic of the future, offering it at a price to his chosen addicts" (336). Rushdie's detailed history of Max's life elides any more substantive account of his wealth, his income-producing ventures being limited in the novel to his career as a civil servant and as the author of two popular memoirs.[22] Rather than a careless oversight in the otherwise mimetic texture of his characterization, the missing sources of Max's wealth alert readers to the problematic thinness of cosmopolitan theory and the narcotic effects of capital.

As Rushdie depicts it in Kashmir, the most powerful secularizing force is not militant atheism, separation of state and religion, or the allure of capitalist profits, but rather simple laughter. Playing religiosity for parodic humor, substituting burlesque for ritual, has long been central to Rushdie's critique of orthodoxy and a source of ire for his detractors.[23] At its best, the satiric force of burlesque comedy can subvert the dangerous intensity and easy affiliations of nationalism and religious extremism, as it does in Rushdie's novel. In *Shalimar the Clown,* the forces of carnivalesque satire short-circuit a retributive pogrom. The villagers had heard "legends of the iron mullahs," a "military and miraculous" tale of a new breed of evangelical Islam. Out of the Indian army's abandoned military scrap, "it came to life and took on human form. The men who were miraculously born from these rusting metals . . . were the iron mullahs" (115). In this telling of the rise of al Qaeda, a young mullah arrives in Shirmal and denounces the "neighboring village for its tolerance," and, wielding the power and space of the mosque, "the harsh seductive tongue of Bulbul Fakh," raises a mob with its "powerful hypnotic spell" (125). Having stirred up a mob at the mosque, the iron mullah sends the men against "the enemy within," only to meet Bombur Yambarzal, a respected chef in the village where cuisine is the currency of the realm, who intercepts the Shirmali men galvanized for combat by the iron mullah. Though unambiguously critical of the mullahs' message and their insubstantial claims to religious authority ("The iron mullah never spoke of his origins, never said in what seminary or at the feet of which master he had received religious instruction"), the genesis of the mullahs cleverly implicates secular Indian nationalism as a causal factor in the rise of militant Islam as a political force in Kashmir (117). Specifically, in the golem story of their origins, the mullahs were "born from . . . rusting war metals . . . [and] went out into the valley to preach resistance and revenge" (115). The mullahs, then, are a literal example of using the master's tools to dismantle the master's house; "the truck exhausts, jammed weaponry, and broken tank treads" discarded by secular

India's national army become the very body of resistance. Taken to its conclusion, the novel's logic insists on the more dubious claim that without the presence of the secular military, militant Islam would lack the "soil" in which to grow (115).

Bombur meets the mob as a walking incarnation of the comic grotesque:

> He walked down the main street of Shirmal toward the mosque . . . with kitchen knives and cleavers stuck in his belt, with kitchen kettles and cookpots strewn around his body in place of armor, and with a big kitchen saucepan on his head. The fresh blood of slaughtered chickens dripped from him, he had smeared it over his hands and face and over all the kitchen equipment too and had brought along a small leather wineskin full of even more blood, to make sure the effect wasn't lost ahead of time. He looked simultaneously horrifying and ridiculous. . . . The men of Shirmal poured out of the mosque with zealotry in their eyes. . . . "Look at me," shouted the waza Bombur Yambarzal. "This thick-headed, comical, bloodthirsty moron is what you have all decided to become." (124–25)

Bombur's performance inoculates the men of Shirmal against their own zeal, and humor triumphs over violence.

As a small island of rooted cosmopolitanism, Kashmir is squeezed by an Indian occupation that, while supposedly committed to the defense of Kashmiri Hindus, instead elects to "let two kinds of subversive[s]"—Islamic radicals funded and armed by Pakistan on the one hand, and Hindus who view the army billeted among them as an oppressive burden on the other—"wipe each other out" (132). Likewise, the ideals of "secularism" prove to be a front for India's national interest in Kashmir rather than a support for human flourishing. "The political echelon's decision to declare Kashmir a 'disturbed area'" makes it possible for Boonyi's former spurned lover, (the now general) Kachwaha, to institute a new policy: "*Every Muslim in Kashmir should be considered a militant*" (290–91; italics in original). As the narrator speculates, *Kashmiriyat* as a concept can operate as an idyll only in relation to its own destruction: "Maybe *Kashmiriyat* was an illusion. Maybe all those children learning one another's stories in the panchayat room in winter, all those children becoming a single family, were an illusion.

Maybe the tolerant reign of good king Zain-ul-abidin should be seen—as some bandits were beginning to see it—as an aberration, not a symbol of unity. Maybe tyranny, forced conversions, temple-smashing, iconoclasm, persecution and genocide were the norms and peaceful coexistence was an illusion" (239). Ultimately, the village of Pachigam is destroyed, battered by waves of violence in the broader struggle between Pakistan and India. Shalimar's murder of Max, Kashmira's climactic encounter with Shalimar on the novel's final page—when she combines the high-tech advantage of night-vision goggles with her bow and arrow to kill her parents' murderer—returns crime and punishment to the personal sphere, dismantling *Kashmiriyat* entirely.

If pragmatism buttresses the strident secularism Rushdie espouses in his essays, aesthetics empowers his commitments on an artistic and personal level. "I have thought of myself as a wholly secular person," Rushdie writes, "and have been drawn towards the great traditions of secular radicalism—in politics, socialism; in the arts, modernism" (*Imaginary Homelands* 377). Rushdie explores at length the relationship between personal atheism and aesthetics: "My sense of God ceased to exist long ago, and as a result I was drawn towards the great creative possibilities offered by surrealism, modernism and their successors, those great philosophies and aesthetics born of the realization that, as Karl Marx said, 'all that is solid melts into air'" (417). In this sense, secularism is for Rushdie a testament to the triumph of the human spirit in a journey along the path of a progressive teleology.

Borrowing from an explicitly modernist conception of the literary aesthetic as a substitute for the truth claims of institutional religions, Rushdie asks: "*Can the religious mentality survive outside of religious dogma and hierarchy?* Which is to say: can art be the third principle that mediates between the material and the spiritual worlds; might it, by 'swallowing' both worlds, offer us something new—something that might even be called a secular definition of transcendence? I believe it can. I believe it must. And I believe that, at its best, it does" (*Imaginary Homelands* 420; italics in original). What we might think of as Rushdie's replacement hypothesis involves a series of transpositions, based loosely on Benedict Anderson's account of print nationalism: nonreligious texts take the place of religious ones, communities of readers substitute for church communities, and, finally, an idea of "enchantment" replaces religious belief. Unlike Anderson, who gives an implicitly optimistic account of this process, Rushdie foregrounds wounding and then speculates that literature might provide succor by serving as a substitute for religion: "Perhaps I write, in part," Rushdie avows, "to fill up that emptied God-chamber with other dreams. Because it is, after all, a room for dreaming in" (377). In the essay "The Book Burning," published two weeks after the fatwa, Rushdie gives his most succinct articulation of this narrative of secularization as wounding: "Dr. Aadam Aziz, the patriarch in my novel *Midnight's Children*, loses his faith and is left with 'a hole inside him, a vacancy in a vital inner chamber.' I, too, possess the same God-shaped hole. Unable to accept the unarguable absolutes of religion, I have tried to fill up the hole with literature" ("Book Burning"). Continuing in the same vein, in "Is Nothing Sacred?" Rushdie argues that "literature is, of all the arts, the one best suited to challenging absolutes of all kinds and because it is in its origin the schismatic Other of the sacred (and authorless) text, so it is also the art most likely to fill our god-shaped holes" (*Imaginary Homelands* 423).

The replacement hypothesis and the God-shaped hole have had several major consequences for Rushdie's fiction. Though the heroine of *Shalimar the Clown* cultivates a patina of "disciplined, groomed, nuanced, inward, irreligious, understated calm," Kashmira is another one of Rushdie's characters who finds herself the bearer of a "God-shaped hole." The novel's opening sequence, which follows Kashmira and Max on her twenty-fourth birthday, casts Kashmira as a complex young woman, an atheist who "wanted to inhabit facts, not dreams" and who views "true believers, those nightmarish dreamers," as fanatics who "grabbed at the corpse of the Ayatollah Khomeini" or "in India whose name she bore, had bitten off chunks of the cadaver of St. Francis Xavier" (12). In the fashion proper to the politically correct, she finds her "exoticist, colonial" given name, India, an offensive appropriation. But Kashmira evinces a more ambivalent relationship to secularism, believing herself possessed of "second-sight," a quasi-magical power of perception (5). According to her sexual partners, moreover, she channels strange languages in her sleep: "as if she was speaking Arabic. Night-Arabian, she thought, the dreamtongue of Scheherazade. Another version described her words as science-fictional, like Klingon, like a throat being cleared in a galaxy far, far away" (3). Like Gibreel's channeling of the word of God in *The Satanic Verses*, or Ormus Cama's ventriloquizing of as-yet-unwritten American rock songs through the medium of his dead twin brother in *The Ground beneath Her Feet*, Kashmira's encounters with forces that transcend rationality constitute a mélange of sacred and profane, creating in her a desire for the transcendent that regularly figures in Rushdie's fiction.

Kashmira believes "religion was folly and yet its stories moved her and this was confusing" (18). Quoting a passage from Baudelaire, "*Ton souvenir en moi luit comme un ostensoir*," she tells her soon-to-be-murdered Jewish father that his memory shines in her "like a monstrance," the sunburst-styled holder of the Eucharist in a Catholic mass. Reveling in the ironies of her utterance, the authorial voice intercedes to reflect that "new images urgently needed to be made. Images for a godless world. Until the language of irreligion caught up with the holy stuff, until there was a sufficient poetry and iconography of godlessness, these sainted echoes would never fade, would retain their problematic power, even over her" (19). Combining a satiric dismissal of religion as "the holy stuff" with a sincere analysis of the limitations of secular culture and an appreciation for the literary value of sacred texts, Kashmira's meditations characterize Rushdie's sense that an immanent frame cannot contain the human striving that religion represents, or satisfy the hungers placated by religious practices and rituals.

In his essays of the late eighties and early nineties, Rushdie attempts to resolve this contradiction by aligning the formal qualities and sensibilities of magical realism as a literary mode—in particular, its melding of rationality with myth and the fantastical—with religious belief as a form of life. The argument he makes is one with strong intuitive appeal: "If one is to attempt honestly to describe reality as it is experienced by religious people, for whom God is no symbol but an everyday fact, then the conventions of what is called realism are quite inadequate. The rationalism of that form comes to seem like a judgment upon, an invalidation of, the religious faith of the characters being described" (*Imaginary Homelands* 376). By aligning himself with the stylistic and political norms of the modernists, Rushdie appeals to the idea that literature might serve as a surrogate for religion in a secular world that finds its most potent formulation in the writings of Victorian poet Matthew Arnold, who suggested that "most of what now passes with us for religion and philosophy will be replaced by poetry" (47).[24]

Since one of Rushdie's primary justifications for the literary as a field of knowledge and a mode of inquiry is that it replaces the goods once provided by religion, Rushdie stages the literary as a site of exchange: "A form must be created which allows the miraculous and the mundane to co-exist at the same level—as the same order of event" (*Imaginary Homelands* 376). I see this discourse of enchantment—and with it, the narrative of wounding represented by the God-shaped hole—as the source of Rushdie's distrust of realism and also as the aporia that holds together the apparent contradictions of Rushdie's conflicted secularisms. The problematic idea that religion serves primarily to satisfy desires for "enchantment" repudiated by secular modernity enables him to reposition the notion of literature as a replacement for the goods previously produced through the offices of formal religion.

The use of the term *disenchantment* to denote the apparent retreat of religion and the closure of what Charles Taylor describes as the immanent secular frame can be traced to a dubious translation of Weber's *entzauberung*, advanced by social scientists to describe the process of cultural rationalization that generates the distinctive character of secular Western society.[25] In a coevolutionary development, religion both became more inward, and, following sociological developments in the study of non-Western religions, was increasingly conceived of in terms of a dialectical relationship between the sacred and the profane, which came to dominate social scientific and anthropological discourses on religion. For those who approach the subjects of religion and secularism conditioned by the premises of the secularization thesis in the Weberian tradition, it is commonplace to speak of what was lost in terms of disenchantment's opposite. Jane Bennett, for example, celebrates enchantment as the source of extraordinary moments of "encounter" or "crossing"; enchantment is tantamount to "active engagement with objects of sensuous experience" (5). Bennett pays only the most passing attention to negative aspects of enchantment, focusing instead on its status as "a pleasurable feeling of being charmed by the novel" (5).

As Simon During and Akeel Bilgrami have argued, secularization theorists like Bennett wrongly associate the decline of religion with disenchantment: on the contrary, "The very possibility of agency . . . assumes an evaluatively enchanted world" (Bilgrami 154). For During, "modern enchantments" are precisely located in their rejection of the supernatural; consumers of magic tricks and surprises do not actually want to be the victims of the powers, spells, or enchantments that go under the name of "real" magic (*Modern Enchantments*). As Bruce Robbins has recently argued, "The call for reenchantment cannot help doing precisely the opposite of what it wants to do. It seems to reject the disenchantment story, but it accepts too much of that story, for ordinary life must first be hollowed out and impoverished in order for reenchantment to be granted the contract to fill it up and enrich it again" ("Enchantment?" 92). In an essay called "Enchantment? No, Thank You!" Robbins further explains: "The outline of the story is simple: there is something called enchantment that (1) we once had, but (2) we have since lost, and (3) we are now in dire need of. Opinions differ as to whether it can be retrieved, but everyone agrees that what has been lost is extremely valuable" (74). The problem with enchantment is that it cuts both ways—signaling a life endowed with meaning in an ordered cosmos yet also positing a more porous vision of selfhood vulnerable to a host of unpredictable and often-malicious forces. Much of the attraction of "enchantment" comes down to semantics, as Robbins suggests: "What [a] modern English speaker hears in the word 'enchantment' is the state of being exceptionally charmed, delighted, enraptured, as by an encounter with a person or an artwork. . . . Once upon a time . . . enchantment would have meant, literally, the employment of magic or sorcery. It presumed a situation in which people considered themselves in constant threat of being attacked" by magical entities (74).

THE ENDS OF ENCHANTMENT

Rushdie continues the critique of the myth of secularism's exclusive Western origins in *The Enchantress of Florence*, a globe-traversing prose romance about the vicissitudes of love, power, and storytelling in the guise of an impeccably researched historical novel (complete with an extensive bibliography). The book's opening vignettes transport the reader, along with a golden-haired stranger, by bullock cart into Fatehpur Sikri, the city built by the Mughal emperor Akbar the Great in the sixteenth century. The stranger, who calls himself Mogor dell'Amore—the Mogul of Love—and whose real name is Niccolò Vespucci (cousin of Amerigo and namesake of Machiavelli), has journeyed from the place of his birth in the New World via Florence to Mughal Hindustan with a story he will reveal only to Emperor Akbar. Gaining entry to the court through a series of bold stratagems, feats of linguistic virtuosity, and magic tricks, Mogor dell'Amore discovers an emergent humanist renaissance. Akbar is a man committed to ending sectarian strife in Muslim-ruled Hindustan, someone who "had created a debating chamber in which the adoration of the divine was reimagined as an intellectual wrestling match . . . a revolutionary temple . . . [where] Argument itself—and no deity, however mutilimbed or almighty—would here be the only god" (77–78). An autochthonous atheist who suspects that "it is man at the center of things, not God,"

Akbar "wanted to be able to tell someone of his suspicion that men had made their gods and not the other way around. . . . *Maybe there was no true religion*" (81; italics in original). As he riffs expansively on pre-Socratic relativism in the diction of Renaissance Europe, Akbar circles toward a more properly humanist ambition: to "have no other temples but those dedicated to mankind . . . to found the religion of man" (81).

Rushdie's depiction of the birth of modernity in the budding secular humanisms of Florence and Mughal India severs the link—common to Renaissance self-understanding and to centuries of subsequent scholarship—between the rise of humanist sensibilities and the recovery of classical antiquity (48). According to regnant narratives of the Enlightenment, in fourteenth- and fifteenth-century Florence the pietistic, feudal social matrix of medieval Christianity deformed in the crucible of the city-state under the twin pressures of mercantile capitalism and a revival of classical aesthetics. Individualism, the emergence of linear temporality, and a powerful critique of Christianity depend in no small part on the scholarly methods of textual analysis, hermeneutics, and archival research pioneered by Italian humanists in the fifteenth century—all of which parallel a rapid transformation of the religious world structured by medieval Christendom. No equivalent combination of forces can be found in Mughal India. Rushdie's depiction of Florence, moreover, rejects the disenchantment thesis wholesale, marginalizes classicism and capitalism, and devotes itself instead to the realpolitik of the Medici family and Florentine sexual libertinism. Indeed, though oblique references to the mercantilism and trade that fueled the rise of the Italian city-states register in the interstices of the tale, trade (other than the trade of women) is equally distant from Rushdie's evocation of humanism in Italy and Hindustan. Nor is Rushdie's point the one we might expect him to make, namely that "renaissance" (as the rediscovery of the science, philosophy, and aesthetics of antiquity and the rebirth of Europe) cannot describe an Islamic culture that never "lost" Hellenism in the first place.

What, then, are the nature and status in *The Enchantress of Florence* of ideas like "humanism" and "secularism," refracted as they are by Rushdie's idiosyncratic representation of Mughal Hindustan and Medici Florence? In several important ways, Rushdie's novel conforms to mainstream accounts of secularization (as entailing the retreat of religion from public life paired with the decline of individual belief) and of humanism (epitomized by a commitment to beauty as the ultimate aesthetic value, paired with a recentering of life around worldly affairs and individual reason). None of the novel's principal characters believe in God, whether Christian, Muslim, or otherwise. Instead, religions are an object of scholarly and comparative interest: Akbar establishes a commission to "count and name . . . every worshiped divinity of Hindustan, not only the celebrated, high gods, but all the low ones too" (139). Akbar, like the elite of Florence to whom he is compared, "trusted beauty, painting, and the wisdom of his forebears. In other things, however, he was losing confidence; in, for example, religious faith" (57).

Reflecting dominant theories of secularization, religions in the novel have lost their normative force but retain cultural influence on private life and social structure. Divorced from mercantile capitalism and classicism, secular humanism stands, in *The Enchantress of Florence*, on three equally precarious legs. The first is, ironically, absolute rule: the humanism of Akbar's Mughal empire depends on one charismatic autocrat's pragmatic but hardly necessary response to the demands of administering a multicultural and religiously diverse empire. An emergent humanism is performed in his sovereign decrees, and it achieves its most lyrical evocations in his private meditations. Whereas both Christianity and Islam have wielded the sword of empire and offered transcendental justification for the work and rhetoric of domination, Rushdie's Akbar sees pluralism as an effective structural principle of enduring dominion. The novel's critiques of religion emerge from the relativizing power of this pluralism and from the distancing effect facilitated by a religiously diverse world whose figures travel extensively. When Akbar queries his chief adviser Birbal, an observant Brahmin, regarding philosophical defenses of atheism, Birbal puts the case well: "All true believers have good reasons for disbelieving in every god except their own . . . and so it is they who, between them, give me all the reasons for believing in none" (44).

Not only has *The Enchantress of Florence* divorced humanism from classicism, but by depicting the encounter with fiction through the lens of enchantment, Rushdie's novel severs the links between secularism and its traditional allies: skepticism, reason, and dispassionate analysis. Sikri and Florence are thus humanist and secular in the limited senses described above, but they are strikingly not places where the retreat of religion parallels a fading of what Taylor and others call the enchanted world of a presecular imagination. In fact, these worlds are secular, humanist, and modern to the extent that they are novelistic. The rejection of militant religiosity does not entail or require a commensurate rejection of magic and credulity, nor does it imply an epistemological shift away from an attitude of belief toward one of skepticism. For far too long, scholars of the novel have abetted the project of solidifying a tenuous equivalence between the novel as a genre and secularization as a normative project. *The Enchantress of Florence* presents a decidedly non-Western atheism, a modernity divorced from rationalism, and a political pluralism growing in Islamic soil.

The second enabling condition for a humanist ethos in *The Enchantress of Florence*, and an important site of convergence between Medici Florence and Akbar's Sikri, is an ethos of decadence, sexual licentiousness, and a thriving public culture of prostitution. While Mughal humanism is an epiphenomenon of aesthetic decadence, positing the importance of physical pleasure as a necessary condition for an emergent secular humanism offers a more insightful and enduring commentary. In Rushdie's novel, courtesans and brothels are constitutive elements of the public sphere. The parallel houses of Skanda and Mars in Sikri and Florence sustain unique salon cultures that generate a panoply of visual and literary art while offering an alternative to what Rushdie calls "the stink of religious sanctimony" in sexual permissiveness (146). Men in Rushdie's Florence and Hindustan worship (and purchase) women—indeed, much of the novel is devoted to these activities—who supplant religion and history as the source of inspiration for art and action.[26]

Finally, and most importantly, secular humanism in the novel requires and reflects a certain relationship to narrative that we might call the "novelistic imagination." The successful storyteller in *The Enchantress of Florence* "usurp[s] the prerogative of the gods" in "the creation of a real life from a dream" (47). In this formula, not only does a novelistic imagination foster secularization by substituting worldly stories for those of religion and divinity, but the creative force of authorship casts man—and they are specifically men in Rushdie's novel—in the place of God as creator and sustainer of the world. Humanism and secularism converge within the compass of telling and hearing stories, while the community of auditors describes the limits of public discourse just as surely as political hegemony.

There is a fundamental, unaddressed tension at the heart of *The Enchantress of Florence*—and indeed, in much of Rushdie's prose—between his explicit and implicit endorsements of secularism, humanism, and pluralism on the one hand, and his equally pervasive argument for the power of fiction on the other. In Rushdie's work, fiction and narrative are influential, transformative forces; narrative is less a means of representing the world than a mode of apprehension, a metaphysical hammer he uses to smash certainties of causality, and a forge of the alternate real. For Rushdie, fictions are the world entire. But they are also bound to modes of being and knowing explicitly at odds with the rationalism espoused by regnant theories of secularism, modernity, and humanism. On a personal level, or perhaps a political one, Rushdie is certain that freedom of conscience, belief, and expression are inviolable rights and necessary conditions for human flourishing. But in his novels, Rushdie offers potent reminders that because religious differences are often invoked as the boundaries between peoples, religious reason must inflect cosmopolitan thinking. In practical terms, this means that since exclusive humanism has lost its universality, secularism has shed something of its former worldliness.

CHAPTER 2

J. M. Coetzee's Prophets of Asceticism

Someone should put together a ballet under the title *Guantanamo, Guantanamo!* A corps of prisoners, their ankles shackled together, thick felt mittens on their hands, muffs over their ears, black hoods over their heads, do the dances of the persecuted and desperate. Around them, guards in olive-green uniforms prance with demonic energy and glee, cattle prods and billy-clubs at the ready. They touch the prisoners with the prods and the prisoners leap; they wrestle prisoners to the ground and shove the clubs up their anuses and the prisoners go into spasms. In a corner, a man on stilts in a Donald Rumsfeld mask alternately writes at his lectern and dances ecstatic little jigs.

One day it will be done, though not by me. It may even be a hit in London and Berlin and New York. It will have absolutely no effect on the people it targets, who could not care less what ballet audiences think of them.

—J. M. Coetzee, *Diary of a Bad Year*

When the hunger strikes at the Guantanamo Bay detention facility in Cuba reached an acute stage in the late summer of 2005, a series of widely circulated articles confirmed what many had long suspected: not only were detainees engaging in prolonged and systematic fasts to protest the conditions of their confinement, but the military—following a Department of Defense policy that sanctions "assisted feeding"—was also subduing hunger strikers with head, arm, leg, and torso restraints and feeding them against their wills via nasal intubation, a practice that continues to this day. Imprisoned indefinitely in a legal black hole, Guantanamo detainees, deprived of other options for expression, redress, or resistance, have recurrently used ascetic practices to inscribe the great writ's demand of habeas corpus on the starving body.

A term derived from the Greek *áskēsis*, *asceticism* denotes the arts and exercises of self-discipline practiced by monks or hermits but can be described more generally as any system of world-renouncing beliefs and practices, figuratively or literally enacted through bodily privation. Ascetics, then, reject not only the most basic of worldly goods, often including food, clothing, and shelter, but also what we might call the good of goods as such. Shifting to bodily terms, the slow violence of self-starvation tends to be overshadowed by more spectacular and media-ready forms of self-harm.[1] In the global North, under the lens of scientific rationalism, self-harm is medicalized as a form or symptom of disease or disorder, while deeply sedimented cultural prejudices connect asceticism with a range of negative attributes like victimhood, passivity, and femininity. Especially among anthropologists and ethnographers of what were once called "primitive religions," in contrast, modes of self-harm often associated with initiation rites have traditionally been understood as a technology for linking the human to the sacred, much like the use of psychotropic substances. As a descriptive term, however, the hunger strike emphasizes resistant agency: by weaponizing bodily renunciation, self-starvation enables the weak to take aim at the strong.

The hunger striker exposes a paradox of ascetic protest. Those who starve themselves to protest the conditions of their incarceration would seem to epitomize the ideal of the individual as a rational agent at the center of liberal political theory. To starve oneself, to death if necessary, and to resist the nourishment that the body demands appears to constitute the quintessential act of will, symbolizing the triumph of mind over matter. On the other hand, fasting transforms the mind and body so quickly that the self, conceived as a rational cogito—a slippery subject in the best of circumstances—recedes and shifts. Starvation alters creatural habits, mental states, and even the perception of temporality, troubling the notion that ascetic actions can be attributed to a competent and rational agent. From a neurobiological perspective, only intentionality separates the pain of a hunger striker from that of the tortured or starving. Thinking more philosophically, the positive and communicative valorization of pain implicit in the hunger strike runs counter to what Talal Asad describes as a quintessentially "modern sensibility that recoils from a willing, positive engagement with suffering" (*Formations* 121). Not only does liberal political theory ground its ideological hegemony on its claim to alleviate suffering, as Asad argues; it also tends to cast the body in pain as a passive victim of trauma rather than as an active subject. For Peter van der Veer, who wonders "how much of asceticism can we understand with our modern frame of mind, our modern conceptual apparatus," the ascetic is positioned as modernity's other precisely because the "the nature of ascetic agency . . . can only be understood by the modern observer as 'backward,' pre-modern,' 'magical,' or 'escapist' and thus essentially as powerless, since it does not provide a firm grip on reality and does not contribute to progress" (208–9).

What makes ascetic practices so threatening and destabilizing? The force-feeding of Guantanamo detainees appears to be a clear triumph of biopolitical sovereignty over ascetic agency, and of secularist medical and political understandings of pain over religiously inflected ideas about suffering as a mystical vehicle or technology of self-cultivation. But while it is tempting to see the Guantanamo detainee as an archetype of the figure Giorgio Agamben identifies as *homo sacer*—the killable bare life that constitutes the sovereign's other and double—the hunger strikers are precisely those who must not be allowed to die. While Judith Butler correctly cautions that "it does not follow that if one apprehends a life as precarious one will resolve to protect that life or secure the conditions for its persistence and flourishing," in the case of the Guantanamo hunger strikes, assertions of the precariousness of life have been used in an inverse way to sanction the abrogation of human rights (*Frames* 2). Caught outside the law, where sovereignty's sharpest point presses nakedly against individual bodies, the strikers must not be allowed to make of themselves a sacrifice. Ironically, though the US government fought to exclude "terrorists" from the protections afforded by the Geneva Conventions so that they might be killed by a drone attack in central Asia without legal repercussions, the hunger-striking detainees at Guantanamo have triggered an outpouring of rhetoric about the sacredness of life. According to their captors, the detainees must be protected, their bodies secured from harm and made to flourish.

Two developments—one practical, the other discursive—have enabled Guantanamo administrators to quell the hunger strikes effectively and contain the cultural crises they threaten to expose. First, pragmatic but simple improvements in technology, such as specialized chairs and narrow-gauge, flexible tubing, have helped to screen proponents of force-feeding from the macabre spectacles that such policies produced in the past, such as the images of suffragettes in visible agony being force-fed by prison guards that outraged the British public a hundred years ago. In the media's response to the Guantanamo hunger strikes, in contrast, photographs of implements used during nasogastric intubation—the feeding chair, restraints, plastic tubing, needles, intravenous drip bags, and the blunt and banal cans of Ensure—emphasize the state's efforts to regulate juridical and affective responses to the starving bodies of Guantanamo detainees. Second, against an international consensus that regards force-feeding as a form of torture, an interlocking set of legal, scientific, and ethico-religious discourses centered in the United States have successfully defended force-feeding in the name of protecting the sanctity of the life, health, and safety of the incarcerated. For Coetzee, who dates the "strong opinions" of the aging author in *Diary of a Bad Year*, Señor C, to the period between September 12, 2005, and May 31, 2006, the thought experiment of the Guantanamo ballet indexes the yawning abyss between the spectacle of torture and available modes of apprehending or representing suffering. The time line of Coetzee's composition maps tightly onto the news coverage of the hunger strikes. On September 18, 2005, Neil Lewis of the *New York Times* reported that "as many as 200 prisoners—more than a third of the camp—have refused food in recent weeks to protest conditions and prolonged confinement without trial. . . . While military officials put the number of those participating at 105, they acknowledge that 20 of them, whose health and survival are being threatened, are being kept at the camp's hospital and fed through nasal tubes and sometimes given fluids intravenously." By investigating how we read ascetic bodies in law and literature, this chapter suggests that scenes of self-starvation constitute a crisis point for forms of secularism that positively valorize concepts like progress, agency, human flourishing, and the pursuit of happiness, or those that fall back on rhetoric about the sanctity of life.

J. M. Coetzee writes novels about pain. His growing body of work offers an unflinching exploration of suffering: his spare prose thrusts characters to and beyond human endurance through an astonishing range of limit conditions, including apartheid and its aftermath, torture, starvation, disease, colonial encounter, slavery, rape, and random violence. Using the legal, epistemological, and ethical paradoxes exposed by the hunger strikes in Guantanamo as my fulcrum, this chapter's close readings establish how Coetzee's fiction can be seen as a sustained exploration of a vision of agency beyond the dialectic of active resistance and passive victimhood that draws on religious forms of ascetic self-fashioning. Within the turbulent worlds of his novels,

Coetzee experiments with a series of plots that foreground physical, often specifically sexual, forms of self-abasement. In *Waiting for the Barbarians* (1980), a nameless magistrate on the frontiers of an empire takes a tortured barbarian girl for his bed and invents a ritual of cleansing that is at once sensitive and abusive. At the close of *Life and Times of Michael K* (1983), the starving protagonist returns to Cape Town seeking refuge and finds himself the unexpected recipient—one might even say victim—of the sexual charity of a woman he does not know, who gives him what appear to be the only sexual experiences of his life. In *Age of Iron* (1990), written and set during the nadir of apartheid oppression in 1980s South Africa, Coetzee tells a grim tale of a nation dying of injustice and a woman dying of cancer, in which Elizabeth Curren invites a disfigured vagabond, Vercueil, first into her home and then into her bed. In the dark ethical landscape of sexuality in *Disgrace* (1999), David Lurie begins the novel claiming the "rights of desire" and moves toward forms of ascetic renunciation and erotic charity, offering sexual pleasure to Bev Shaw ("a dumpy, bustling little woman") on a pile of blankets at the Animal Welfare Clinic (72). In *Elizabeth Costello* (2003), Elizabeth recalls that as a young woman she fulfilled the desire of a dying man, Aidan Phillips, to paint her portrait seminude, an act she calls a "blessing"—and then, as his illness advanced, that she took this tableau a step further, removing her clothes for a second time and bestowing on the impotent man the gift of oral sex. In *Slow Man* (2005), the profoundly physical body care needed by amputee victim Paul Rayment leads him to mistake care for charity and physical intimacy for love. Arguing that scenes of renunciation, self-denial, starvation, and *caritas* function as part of an ascetic economy of meaning, I suggest that Coetzee's oeuvre should be understood as the purposeful and systematic articulation of a tragic theology. It is centered on a group of world-renouncing and self-mortifying protagonists I call Coetzee's prophets of asceticism.

WEAPONIZING HUNGER

Though the Guantanamo facility, like the status of "enemy combatant," was devised as a legal sleight-of-hand enabling the Bush administration to dodge the mandates of the Geneva Conventions, hunger strikes expose a fault line that runs through the heart of the convention documents and indeed through much of contemporary political theory.

While the drafters of the Third Geneva Convention's resolutions regarding prisoners of war, executed on August 12, 1949, clearly imagine situations where detaining powers might restrict food and health care as a type of punishment or torture (indeed, the agreement specifically seeks to protect against such forms of coercion), they do not seem to anticipate forms of ascetic agency, such as hunger strikes, initiated by detainees themselves. In Part I, article 3, the core of the document, parties to the convention resolve that in any domestic or international conflict "persons taking no active part in the hostilities" (a category of persons that includes civilians and former combatants) shall be "treated humanely," adding more specific prohibitions on "cruel treatment and torture" along with "outrages upon personal dignity, in particular, humiliating and degrading treatment" (Geneva Convention I.3.1). Adequate food, shelter, and medical care are considered implicit in humane treatment according to the Convention, which specifically prohibits "disciplinary measures affecting food" (II.26) and issues guidelines regarding nourishment and medicine: "The basic daily food rations shall be sufficient in quantity, quality and variety to keep prisoners of war in good health"; moreover, "every camp shall have an adequate infirmary" for administering medical care (II.25, II.33). The reading of the Convention advanced in support of force-feeding considers the imperative to "keep prisoners of war in good health" to sanction, if not require, medical interventions for those whose lives may be endangered by starvation.

As represented in the press, the Guantanamo hunger strikes are understood to operate not primarily or even significantly as religious practice—for example, as a form of fast, or *swam* in Arabic, reflecting a desire to turn the heart and mind away from worldly activities and cultivate personal virtues—but rather as an explicitly nonreligious form of political protest. Indeed, the hunger strikes were accompanied by a formal list of demands addressed to the Guantanamo command, including the request that "we need to see the sunlight" and other bids for "basic human rights" (Center for Constitutional Rights 10). Pragmatically, the Department of Defense during both the Bush and Obama administrations clearly feared that any who starved themselves to death would be celebrated as martyrs by millions on the so-called Arab Street. But the rhetoric employed by defenders of "assisted feeding" focuses on the preservation and, sometimes, the explicit sanctity of life. When confronted about the government's force-feeding policies as a possible violation of the Geneva Convention's prohibition against torture or inhumane treatment, navy lieutenant commander Brook DeWalt, the public affairs director for the Guantanamo camp at the time of the strikes, consistently maintained that the force-feeding policy follows a clear and unquestionable ethical imperative: "To keep somebody alive? . . . We do our best to maintain the safety and security of these individuals. That includes their health" (Shephard). Medical professionals working at the facility, screened in advance to ensure their complicity with DOD policies, have also endorsed the practice and denied allegations of abuse, arguing both that "nothing that we're doing with enteral feeding is cruel or inhumane" and that "the Geneva Conventions don't address enteral feeding" (Shephard).

The force-feeding of hunger strikers exposes significant rifts between international consensus and the regnant legal and social norms governing the war on terror and the US penal system. As is well known, the World Medical Assembly asserts unequivocally that physicians have an ethical obligation not to violate a detainee's will or body. The WMA's 1975 Declaration of Tokyo against the medical support of torture explicitly draws force-feeding into the ambit of torture in paragraph 6: "Where a prisoner refuses nourishment and is considered by the physician as capable of forming an unimpaired and rational judgment concerning the consequences of such a voluntary refusal of nourishment, he or she shall not be fed artificially. The decision as to the capacity of the prisoner to form such a judgment should be confirmed by at least one other independent physician. The consequences of the refusal of nourishment shall be explained by the physician to the prisoner." For the WMA, the challenge for the physician lies not in the apparent conflict between care and torture, as it does in the case of the DOD's defense of force-feeding, but in satisfactorily establishing agency, volition, and intent: the hunger strike must be the product of "the individual's voluntary choice" and must be based on "rational judgment." Expanding on the Declaration of Tokyo to account for the ethical dilemmas that emerge when volition is difficult to identify, the WMA's Declaration of Malta on Hunger Strikers (1991) further elaborates that detainees, like those in Guantanamo, must understand the potential consequences of their actions and be deemed competent by medical professionals before they may be considered to have met the threshold for volition. But while emphasizing the importance of verifying volition and agency, the WMA concludes with a more systemic injunction: "Forcible feeding is never ethically acceptable. Even if intended to benefit, feeding accompanied by threats, coercion, force or use of physical restraint is a form of inhuman and degrading treatment." According to the WMA, physicians must "ascertain the individual's true intention" and "respect individuals' autonomy" while they seek primarily to "benefit" those they treat. For the WMA, this requires balancing the ethical demands of "promoting welfare" and "respecting individuals' wishes." Crucially, for the WMA, "Beneficence does not necessarily involve prolonging life at all costs." More problematically, however, the WMA guidelines systematically replace the authority of the state, as articulated in case law and constitutional documents, with that of the medical professional. Doctors are imagined as having absolute authority, once they have taken care to adequately establish their patient's intentions, to "act in what they judge to be the person's best interest . . . without interference from third parties."

In US law, by contrast, the precedent focuses on a very different set of issues coming to bear on the question of hunger strikes, and the courts have ruled overwhelmingly that the state may intervene to preserve the life of prisoners and other detainees whenever medically necessary or politically expedient. In these cases, as the Supreme Court of Connecticut summarizes in *Lantz v. William Coleman*, feeding a person against his will to preserve his life pits the right of every individual to bodily integrity against the state's fourfold interests: "[In] the preservation of life, the protection of innocent third parties, the prevention of suicide, and the maintenance of security and order of the prison." In *Coleman* and elsewhere, courts have ruled that force-feeding does not abrogate First Amendment guarantees to free speech or those under the due process clause to refuse unwanted medical treatment. On the one hand, citing various precedents, the state supreme court attests that "no right is held more sacred, or is more carefully guarded, by the common law, than the right of every individual to the possession and control of his own person." On the other hand, the limitation of rights inherent to incarceration and the state's desires to maintain control in prisons (its "legitimate penological interest") have been commonly construed, as they are in *Coleman*, to "outweigh those [rights] of the hunger striking inmates."

In questions of legitimate penological interests, even in domestic cases where the suspension of habeas corpus and other constitutional rights is never in question, a great deal of interpretative latitude has typically been accorded to the state. For example, in *In re Joel Caulk* (1984), the state's interest in prosecuting crimes and maintaining prison discipline prevailed over an inmate's right to refuse sustenance and medical treatment. The New Hampshire Supreme Court considered the following question: "Does Joe Caulk, an inmate at the New Hampshire State Prison, have a constitutional right to die, without interference by the State, if he is mentally competent to make such a decision and if he has knowingly and voluntarily decided to die by starvation?" They answered negatively, citing first a procedural technicality—if Caulk succeeded in starving himself to death, he would evade standing trial on two pending indictments in California, unto which he would be delivered at the completion of an estimated thirty years of concurrent sentences in New Hampshire.[2] In order to treat a hunger strike as a weapon wielded by an incarcerated agent, the state must produce a victim. In *In re Joel Caulk* and more recent cases, the government has argued successfully that this victim is a third party: the medical professional administering treatment. A policy that sanctions force-feedings as ethically and constitutionally sound as well as medically necessary will, the state argues, save prison doctors from the conflicting demands of "their constitutional and statutory duty to protect the life that lies precariously in their custody or of honoring a past request that in effect contravenes their legal obligations. Society should not force its servants to make such choices."[3]

Invoking a parallel between the domicile and the body to justify medical intrusion, *In re Joel Caulk* argues that just as the police may "enter a home without a warrant when they have an objectively reasonable basis for believing that an occupant is seriously injured . . . the need to protect or preserve life . . . is justification for what would be otherwise illegal," which in the case of hunger-striking prisoners entails the unauthorized entry of the body by medical professionals (13). The trope of penetration, intrusion, and entry is further elaborated in an appeal of the *Coleman* decision, *Commissioner of Correction v. Coleman*, which argues against the notion of violation in the case of nasal intubation on the grounds that "a nasogastric tube does not require puncturing the defendant's skin or blood vessels and it utilizes the defendant's normal digestive system to process the nutrients administered." *Commissioner of Correction v. Coleman* concludes that force-feeding is a noninvasive medical procedure so long as it is performed for medical, rather than disciplinary, reasons and with the "minimum level of severity." Additionally, in the appeal the court directly addresses the apparent discrepancy between international consensus, which condemns force-feeding as medically unethical, and US law, which often, as in this case, sanctions its use in various contexts of detainment. Against this divergence, the court sided with the plaintiff, claiming that documents like the Declaration of Malta and the Declaration of Tokyo do not reflect a clear consensus in the international community on life-saving interventions. *Coleman* cites the European Court of Human Rights ruling in *Ciorap v. Moldova* (2007), in which it was argued that lifesaving procedures "cannot in principle be regarded as inhuman and degrading."

While the decision in *Boumediene v. Bush* ensures that eventually almost two hundred Guantanamo detainees will have a chance to prove that they are not enemy combatants in proceedings subject to the rules of federal courts, the legality of force-feeding policies remains more or less unchallenged.[4] One of the reasons detainees, both within the ordinary prison system and in untraditional detention facilities like Guantanamo, have had difficulty convincing US courts to issue injunctions against force-feeding is that legal precedent requires plaintiffs to demonstrate that they will suffer significant or irreparable harm if the injunction is not granted. The petitioners in *Al-Adahi v. Obama*, for instance, two individuals detained at Guantanamo whose habeas petitions were then slowly working their way through litigation, fought unsuccessfully in 2009 to seek relief from the force-feeding policies to which they had been subjected on numerous occasions after they began a series of prolonged hunger strikes in 2005. While recognizing that the detainees "have waited many long years (some have waited more than seven years) to have their cases heard by a judge," Justice Kessler of the US district court rejected their petition on the grounds that compared with death by starvation, restrained force-feedings are likely to benefit rather than harm the petitioner. It is, however, precisely to guard against such narrowly corporeal interpretations of harm and injury that article 3 of the Geneva Conventions enjoins more broadly that detainees "shall in all circumstances be treated humanely" and be protected "in particular [from] humiliating and degrading treatment."

Like the absent bodies of hunger-striking detainees at Guantanamo, the haunting and emaciated bodies of literary ascetics serve as fulcrums between being and meaning, speech and the body, imagining and experiencing—tensions endemic to the structure and experience of reading itself.[5] Despite the significant differences between the traditions and practices of Hindu sadhus, Jain ascetics, or the early Christian saints, forms of asceticism in religiously inflected writings share an emphasis on practices of self-restraint and on self-fashioning in pursuit of goals defined against the values normally taken to constitute a flourishing life. Within the contexts of these traditions, restraining and disciplining the body can derive social and individual meaning in relation to religious claims about salvation or transcendence. Coetzee's ascetics, however (with the notable exception of Elizabeth Costello's sister, Blanche, a Catholic nun who devotes her life to serving orphans of the HIV/AIDS epidemic in a Zululand hospital), improvise their ascetic practices in the absence of religious communities, formal theology, or belief in God. Coetzee will never be mistaken for a Christian apologist, though his work reflects a deep preoccupation with concepts like apocalypse and redemption, grace and disgrace, and charity and sacrifice.

When Nietzsche posed the gnomic question "What do ascetic ideals mean," which animates *A Genealogy of Morals*, he saw himself in the vanguard of secularization in a world structured and determined by Christianity. In a cryptic set of answers about the way resentment combines with the will to power, Nietzsche inveighs against the "ascetic ideals" of "Poverty, Humility, Chastity" (146) under which humanity has become a self-subjugated group of "malcontent, conceited and ugly creatures, unable to rid themselves of a deep chagrin at self, at the earth, at all life, and causing each other as much pain as possible" (160). In the well-known anecdote with which Nietzsche begins the third section of *A Genealogy of Morals* about the meaning of asceticism for various types or groups—among philosophers, artists, women, the depressed, priests—ascetic ideals evoke the phenomena and cultural formations Nietzsche most abhorred: a Christian slave morality governed by resentment. Despite the apparently exhaustive taxonomy, Nietzsche is not concerned with the full spectrum of ascetic experience; he focuses, as Foucault does in *History of Sexuality*, on the dichotomy between the asceticism of the ancient (specifically pre-Christian and Greco-Roman) world and that of Christianity. In its Christian form, Nietzsche writes, "It is known that there are three great show-words of the ascetic ideal: Poverty, Humility, Chastity" (146). As preached by the group Nietzsche names the ascetic priests, these values are objects of unqualified derision and scorn, for "the ascetic treats life as a wrong way which man had best retrace to the point whence it starts" (160). The purpose of such a doctrine for Nietzsche—and, as Coetzee represents, the disciplinary regimes of apartheid—is social domination: "*The ascetic ideal offered to mankind a significance*. . . . In it suffering was *interpreted*," Nietzsche writes, but as a form of negativity wielded by a class of ascetic priests, poverty, humility, and chastity merely serve "*the self-protective and self-preservative instinct of degenerating life*,—a life which struggles for existence and seeks to maintain itself by all means" (226, 165; italics in original).[6] But what do ascetic ideals mean for Coetzee, as an Anglophone white South African writing during and after apartheid? In particular, what does asceticism mean for our understanding of Coetzee as an ethical and philosophical thinker?

RADICAL ASCETICS

Coetzee's 1983 Booker Prize–winning novel *Life and Times of Michael K* engages South African history and the legal edifice of apartheid with a directness and specificity notably absent in his previous work. This geographical rootedness belies profound narrative instabilities, however, as the spare prose and compact storytelling characteristic of Coetzee's fiction yield a bleak textual surface largely governed by limited indirect discourse. We witness not K's unmediated subjectivity but rather the reportage of an unspecified narrator closely aligned with K and yet coolly distant in a style reminiscent of Kafka's unsettling prose.[7] Coetzee's novel imagines a near future when the strained apartheid regime—with its restrictive pass laws, inadequate and divided system of "homelands," and controlling white minority sustained by ever-harsher forms of racial oppression—collapses into overt civil war. In the ensuing state of emergency during which most of the book occurs, enemies of the white state are deported to a system of detention and forced labor facilities that evoke the concentration camps of the twentieth century and foreshadow the patterns of extralegal detention in the twenty-first. Along the way, it becomes clear that what is at stake in *Life and Times of Michael K* is not a Levinasian encounter with and respect for otherness, but the impossible fact that the lowest of the low can refuse to be encountered or witnessed for and that this turning away is as powerful and devastating as the turning away of God. The novel has been obscured too long by interpretations that seek a redeeming message about the ethics of alterity and are limited to the work's treatment of apartheid. Instead, I offer a reading that examines the ethics of bare life and its implications beyond the limits of witness and testimony, where it offers a unique twist on the question of sovereign power and the enunciatory space of the victim.

Coetzee goes to great lengths to emphasize Michael K's ambiguity: of mixed racial ancestry and limited cognitive ability, K is an amalgamation whose rough sutures are literalized in the scar of his cleft lip.

Though long a docile subject of apartheid, as the state crumbles in Coetzee's dystopian vision, K abandons his life as a municipal gardener and sets out from Cape Town, pushing his feeble mother Anna in an improvised wheelbarrow in an attempt to reach her birthplace on the rural Eastern Cape. After his mother dies, K completes his pilgrimage to an abandoned farm similar to the one Anna described in her georgic visions of childhood. They set out from Cape Town on their own version of *Die Groot Trek*, inspired by vague concepts of self-determination, to start a new life. Their dream is, ironically, indistinguishable from narratives that have authorized countless colonial settler migrations, including those of the Dutch-speaking Boers fleeing British control in the 1830s and '40s who gave rise to the phrase. Upon his solitary arrival, the barren land, the exigency of eluding military patrols, and the choice of bare life replace the dream of a whitewashed cottage, a homestead (in his case, tended by his mother), and days filled with unspecified work far from oppressive authority (signified by the Cape Peninsula police area). Instead of recreating a lost pastoral or forging a "rival line" to that of the white settlers and building anew on the ruins of their abandoned farm, K progressively disengages from political, social, and material production to become a subsistence farmer (104).[8] Banned simultaneously from travel (by pass laws that restrict his movement), from his previous life in Cape Town (where his lack of a job subjects him to potential deportation), and from the rural land on which he must not be seen for fear of capture, K attempts to eke out an existence beyond the protection of the law and subject to the full force of its violence.

K begins his life as a cultivator by rejecting burial as a fitting end for his mother's ashes. Instead of interring them in the hole he digs for that purpose, the narrator describes how he "[took] the responsibility on himself, and set about clearing a patch a few meters square in the middle of the field. There . . . he distributed the fine grey flakes over the earth, afterwards turning the earth over spadeful by spadeful" (58–59). Sowing his mother's ashes like seeds, he eschews learned cultural rituals and chooses instead to affirm the "impulse to plant," a decision K understands as springing from his "nature" (59). This return to the land, with its problematic juxtaposition of nature and culture, plays out in a riff on Daniel Defoe's *Robinson Crusoe*. K systematically clears land near an irrigation dam, tills the soil, eats birds he kills with a slingshot, and plants his meager cache of pumpkin seeds, corn, and a single bean. "It is because I am a gardener . . . because that is my nature," K muses. Unlike the experience of unease he feels in the farmhouse abandoned by the Visagies, the work of cultivation inspires in K his "deepest pleasure" and "fit[s] of exultation" (59).

Even this life of mere subsistence, however, proves to be too conspicuous, too similar to the lifestyle it replaces, to endure unnoticed beside the crumbling edifice of apartheid. Before even the first of K's seeds have sprouted, the grandson of the farm's owner returns after deserting the army. Though he claims to "have made [his] peace," the boy immediately reintroduces the roles of master and servant: "Do you work here?" he questions K upon first encountering him, adding that he is "boss Visagie's grandson" (60). We are reminded that K has been a gardener before—"municipal services of the city of Cape Town . . . Gardener, grade 3b"—with its implication of the superfluous, of aesthetics over necessity (4). K's subsequent asceticism serves a practical requirement: to survive in a state of exception, one must live without being noticed.

K's tentatively successful foray into subsistence farming is illegible to the apartheid system as anything other than active resistance. K is captured and interrogated by patrolling government soldiers who accuse him of running a staging post for the insurgency and supplying them with food and shelter. "Tell me your story," the officer demands, though the "story" he desires is merely information of a militarily consequential nature (122). "I live in the veld" (120), he answers, and clarifies, "I'm not what you think. . . . I was sleeping and you woke me, that's all" (123). The soldiers' allegations force K's untellable story into the apartheid state's narrative paradigm of racially coded inferiority and insurrection. When the soldiers find him, K is suffering from starvation serious enough that he cannot stand, his gums bleed continuously, and a thunderstorm has flushed him, shivering, from his shelter. The only "supplies" they locate are the few pumpkins K has scattered about the veld; instead of "holes and tunnels . . . [and] storage site[s]" they locate his "house"—the cavelike structure K built into the riverbed—and his meager possessions (121). The soldiers interpret his actions and intentions according to a predetermined script, calling K a monkey, attributing his dizziness to drink, and reading his minimalist existence as evidence of dissimulation: "You see what kind of people they are. . . . You turn your back and they come crawling out of the ground" (121–22). After his capture, K is forced to enter a system of facilities that evoke the Nazi concentration camps of the Second World War and the earlier concentration camps—the first in history known by that name, as Hannah Arendt reminds us at the beginning of *The Origins of Totalitarianism*—established by the British in South Africa during the Boer War of 1889–1902.[9] These are Michael K's life and times, in which K, a man of ambiguously mixed race, "colored" in apartheid terms, chooses to live a life of radical asceticism in an attempt to escape all forms of captivity.[10]

The questions that arise for readers are precisely those that occupy the novel and its characters: Who is Michael K, and how are readers to understand him? How does the docile subject of apartheid we encounter at the beginning of the novel become the man at the novel's end, for whom a skeletal existence at the bare edge of life offers the only possibility of any freedom? Coetzee goes to great lengths to foreground the degree to which K is produced by the repressive ideological forces and social structures in which he is embedded, thus attenuating any appearance of individual agency. Hunger, privation, and pain begin at his birth and on the novel's first page; with his cleft lip and misshapen nose, K cannot nurse and must be fed with a teaspoon.[11] In a succinct series of increasing displacements, Coetzee marks necessity, poverty, and separation: "The child could not suck from the breast and cried with hunger. She tried a bottle; when it could not suck from the bottle she fed it with a teaspoon, fretting with impatience when it coughed and sputtered and cried" (3). This icy progression—note the substitution of *it* where readers expect the pronoun *he*—ruptures the relationship of mother and child spatially and implicates the narrator, whose own disgust we feel in the substitution of pronouns and the cycle of alienation. Nor do relations with other children suture K to a human community: "Because their smiles and whispers hurt her, she kept it [her child] away from other children. . . . Year after year Michael K sat on a blanket watching his mother polish other people's floors, learning to be quiet" (3–4). K is profoundly unwanted, a figure from whom people turn away with disgust, insults, and shame. By implicating his narrator in this aversion, Coetzee immediately dissolves any presumption of sympathetic narrative engagement. This reorientation forces the reader to confront the diverse barriers that surround Michael K, including that of a narrative crafted, not to nurture the reader's sympathy for the protagonist, but to mark precisely a nonrelation. From private exclusions, made under the twin signs of his appearance and limited intelligence, to more pervasive institutional oppressions, K becomes the focal point of these regimes of increasing restriction and segregation.

Huis Norenius, the "institute" for "variously afflicted and unfortunate children" where K grows up as a ward of the state, serves as a potent example of the biopolitical machine that inscribes its marks on

Michael K (4). The narrator's seemingly detached and impartial reportage describes a Foucauldian regime of discipline and surveillance that, combined with instruction in domestic and manual labor, ensures subjugation and produces the submissive laboring bodies required by the apartheid state. In one of the few recollections of the institution that the novel provides, the narrator describes K's memory of a teacher who "used to make his class sit with their hands on their heads, their lips pressed tightly together and their eyes closed while he patrolled the rows with his long ruler" (68). The teacher combines the stereotypical threat of educational corporal punishment (being struck with a ruler) with a simulation of police brutality. The added insistence that students shut their eyes further enhances the panoptic asymmetry of power between the divided population of students in their separated rows and the central authority. Again, Coetzee implicates the testimony of the narrator in the structure of discipline and control through the ruse of impartiality and the parodic content and diction of the scene. Coetzee's narrator glosses years of narratable events in K's life in a style that echoes apartheid's hollow self-justification as a necessary and impartial system based on innate inequalities: K spent "his childhood in the company of variously afflicted and unfortunate children learning the elements of reading, writing, counting, sweeping, scrubbing, bedmaking, dishwashing, basketweaving, woodworking, and digging" (4). With this bare, indifferent description, Coetzee's narrative performs the very subjection, isolation, and reduction it purportedly details.

For Michael K as an adult in the state of exception, everyone is sovereign. K can be arrested, deported, forced into servitude, surveilled, schooled in an institution, and interrogated until his testimony conforms to the preexisting assumptions of his white captors regarding "rebel" activity. His race and even his name are explicitly artifacts of another's performance.[12] K's repeated captivity in the system of concentration camps serves as final confirmation of the state of exception that holds him in its grasp as a mere biological life unwanted by and entrapped in the apartheid regime.

THE DOUBLE STRUCTURE OF EXCEPTION

Coetzee's K is caught in a double structure of exception: first, internal to the narrative, as his life is seized by concentration camps and the state of emergency; and second, by the text itself, where K, though produced by and included in the fiction, constantly escapes its emotional and mimetic world. In this context, K can be seen as a literal embodiment of Agamben's *homo sacer*, or sacred man, "the person whom anyone could kill with impunity" but whom "it is not permitted to sacrifice," the "limit figure . . . [and] radical crisis of every possibility of clearly distinguishing between membership and inclusion, between what is outside and what is inside, between exception and rule" (*Homo Sacer* 25).[13] If it were simply that the totalitarian violence presented in Coetzee's novel produced the biopolitical subject we recognize as *homo sacer*, then we could say that Coetzee raises and anticipates contemporary theories of power, subjection, and the supposed sacredness of life. Although he is clearly engaged in this project, Coetzee focuses more on the tactics of passivity and self-imposed starvation to explore modes of ascetic agency that challenge state power and secularist conceptions of progress and the flourishing life. Through Coetzee, we see the state of exception as an auto-imposed assertion of agency and encounter: we see *homo sacer* not merely as an effect but also as a source of power.

In a scene that falls at the midpoint of the text and marks its emotional core, Michael K escapes the Jakkalsdrif labor camp and walks through the night without stopping. He emerges at dawn at the abandoned farm he had earlier fled upon the return of its white owner's grandson. Capture, escape, return: these events recur with archetypal persistence in the novel, a cycle K ruptures by altering the form of his creatural existence. Upon his arrival at the farm, K articulates a vision of a consciously chosen bare life that involves extreme physical asceticism and the rejection of political and social engagement—even shunning active resistance to the apartheid state and thus withdrawing from the pale of victim discourse. The passage is one of the novel's most resistant and haunting: "I want to live here, he thought: I want to live here forever. . . . What a pity that to live in times like these a man must be ready to live like a beast. A man who wants to live cannot live in a house with lights in the windows. He must live in a hole and hide by day. A man must live so that he leaves no trace of his living. That is what it has come to" (99).

K's escape from the camp stages some of the novel's rare glimpses of unalloyed personal desire ("I want") contrasted against a backdrop of necessity and echoing void ("he must live in a hole"). The deliberately vague "times like these," which leaves open both an interpretation restricted to a local socio-temporal context and one of a more universal reach, contrasts sharply with the geographical specificity of K's desire to dwell in a particular place, albeit a place only accidentally determined. In a scene of great physical and emotional strength, where "he walked all night, feeling no fatigue, trembling sometimes with the thrill of being free," he speaks in the first person with clear declarations and claims his status as a human being, as "a man," with great vehemence (97). Yet it is also this scene that articulates the need to erase the traces or signature of his humanity—and even of his animal being—during his longest and most profound period of starvation.

Under the ascetic regime outlined above, K experiences a rapid physical and psychological transformation that shatters the categories and limits of human experience. In the intensity of his starvation, K's body becomes a physical index of pain: "There was a throbbing that would not leave him; lances of light pierced his head. Then he could keep nothing down; even water made him retch. There was a day when he was too tired to get up. . . . He shivered continually" (69). Coetzee figures the pains of the body through movements, such that eating is keeping something "down," exhaustion is the inability to rise, and shivering is an uncontrollable convulsion. Alongside the connection between pain and control of movement, the narrative suggests that time's movement, like that of the body, is altered by the experience of pain. Time advances in uncontrolled surges, giving the impression of a temporal progression whose precise content remains unmarked. After this series of bodily descriptions, the narrator offers K's own interpretation of his suffering: "It came home to him that he might die, he or his body, it was the same thing, that he might lie here till the moss on the roof grew dark before his eyes, that his story might end with his bones growing white in this faroff place" (69). The description of K's awareness of death through the trope of homecoming intersects with the novel's repeated problematization of the notion of home. Home is something "we must all leave," linked both to the maternal and to the corporeal drives of instinct (124).

Although he insists throughout the text on his identity as a "cultivator," K rejects even subsistence farming as too conspicuous a lifestyle. Instead of recreating a lost pastoral, K endures day after day of fasting while he constructs a makeshift burrow in which to live. Unlike the elaborate system of protective tunnels and chambers filled with provisions constructed by the paranoid protagonist of Kafka's short story "The Burrow," the critical feature of K's shelter is its ephemeral nature and its illegibility as a human construct. To live in a hole is, for Coetzee's K, not a defensive gesture but a way of living that seeks to escape from the ethical costs Walter Benjamin sees as the price of civilization: since "there is no document of civilization which is not at the same time a document of barbarism," K's lesson is to live a life without documents ("Theses" 256). K's radical asceticism can be seen as an attempt to reject "history" in the biological, anthropological, or Hegelian-materialist senses of the term and thus to withdraw from the barbaric as such. When K ponders the perspective of something akin to Benjamin's historian who cannot contemplate without horror the material evidence of a prior culture, he finds solace in the fact that his form of life invalidates the question of civilization by negating not only all aspects of material culture but also the dignity assigned to human creation. He has no use for civilization: "If ever they find this place or its ruins, and shake their heads and say to each other: What shiftless creatures, how little pride they took in their work!, it will not matter" (101). As a figure of bare life, K now becomes the anti-Crusoe who does "not turn his cave into a home or keep a record of the passage of the days" (68).

As a radical ascetic, K calls into question the problematic nexus of human and animal being in the conjunction of man and beast, a theme that becomes central to Coetzee's later fiction. Though he describes the need to "live like a beast," he does not have hunting in mind (99). Although K was successful at hunting small game before he was captured and taken to the labor camp, subsistence activities fade from his repertoire when he returns to the farm, and the "animal" nature that guides him to certain shrubs and berries becomes more and more attenuated. Nor does K's conception of living like a beast include the connotative characteristics of either domesticated "beasts of burden" or threatening "wild beasts." If K lives as a "beast," it is not as a Yeatsian messianic figure that wakes the earth from its stony sleep as it slouches toward Bethlehem, but rather as the smallest, most inconsequential of phenomena. K withdraws from biological life, the life he shares with animals, nearly as completely as he does from a political and social life shared with other humans. If material production promises only suffering, sexual reproduction possesses even less appeal: "How fortunate that I have no children, he thought: how fortunate that I have no desire to father. I would not know what to do with a child out here in the heart of the country" (104).[14] Similarly, animal being and human nature blur in his self-conception as a cultivator of the land. In K's view, gardening—an aesthetic and cultural practice with strong overtones of British colonial labor—collapses with human identity and animal natures of the "lowest" variety: "I am . . . like an earthworm, he thought. Which is also a kind of gardener. Or a mole, also a gardener, that does not tell stories because it lives in silence" (182). The "trace" of the human that endures in cultivation thus replaces the trace of the story K refuses to tell and that of the witness for whom the mole and the worm go unnoticed.

Michael K becomes a liminal zone of indistinction where animal being, human nature, and inanimate matter pass through one another: "He thought of himself not as something heavy that left tracks behind it, but if anything as a speck upon the surface of an earth too deeply asleep to notice the scratch of ant-feet, the rasp of butterfly teeth, the tumbling of dust" (97). In this passage, self-consciousness begins with the human subject ("he thought of himself") but is transposed across the threshold of K's consciousness to the very earth, which takes on a slumbering sentience. This traversal works in the opposite direction as well, with inanimate material proving indistinguishable from the sentient: "Perhaps I am the stony ground," K reflects (48), and later, "I am becoming smaller and harder and drier . . . If I were to die here . . . I would be dried out by the wind in a day, I would be preserved whole, like someone in the desert drowned in sand" (67–68). Here we see K as a vector along which animate and inanimate, living and dead, conscious and unconscious, transition across the threshold of bare life. The "I" persists, though not as a site of enunciation.

Not only does Coetzee's resistant text maintain the rupture between the narrated and lived experiences of suffering, it also records repeated attempts by figures on both sides of apartheid's violence to pry K's story from its unwilling source. As the narrative of the medical officer demonstrates, "testimony" is compulsory and subjugates the witness to a sovereign power, exposing the hidden connection between the controlling desire of Coetzee's liberal multiculturalist audience to hear about apartheid and physical violence. Interrogation, violence, and compulsion cast a shadow over the privileged confessional mode of witness and linear testimony, as well as over attempts to understand others across boundaries of power, implicating Coetzee in a similarly exploitative dynamic through his own efforts to engage his character. As the medical officer explains to Michael K:

> We give you a nice bed and lots of food, you can lie in comfort all day . . . but we expect something in return. It's time to deliver, my friend. You've got a story to tell and

> we want to hear it. Start anywhere. Tell us about your mother. . . . Tell us your views on life. . . . Tell us what we want to know. . . . You want to live, don't you? Well then, *talk*, make your voice heard, tell your story! We are listening! Where else in the world are you going to find two polite civilized gentlemen ready to listen to your story all day and all night, if need be, and take notes too? (140; italics in original)

In this case, the expressed desire for personal narrative ("I want to know your story") masks the primary militaristic motivation behind the interrogation, namely that "you're in the shit, Michaels. . . . Your friends from Prince Albert have been misbehaving. . . . We need to catch them. . . . We want you to tell us about your friends" (151, 138). "They want me to open my heart and tell them the story of a life lived in cages," K reflects (181).

Instead of celebrating narrative's ability to bear witness to injustice, the novel addresses a more radical paradox by linking mimetic narrative to an economy of interrogation, violation, and retribution. Other contexts and scenes of captivity repeat this initial paradigm of narration as interrogation that predetermines the content ultimately produced. From K's first experience with government bureaucracy in his failed attempt to procure the necessary permits to leave the Cape Peninsula police area to his time in the hospital in which his mother dies, narrative and its meanings are externally enforced. The second section of the novel, which is narrated by the medical officer who oversees K's recuperation and interrogation in the Kenilworth rehabilitation and detention camp, constitutes an extended attempt on the part of a white narrator to make sense of K's story. However sympathetic the medical officer is at times, his task remains the extraction of information about the resistance: "Tell us the truth, tell us the whole truth and . . . we won't bother you any more" (138). The medical officer's desire for narrative enacts the fundamental biases of a privileged liberal audience coded by a culture of confession and watered-down Freudian psychology. K's mother (whom the medical officer believes, in good Freudian fashion, to be the cause of K's problems) figures strongly in the story he wants to hear, the story of a life that, by this account, emerges as valuable and permanent only in its documentation. The association between confession and the preservation of life in this preceding quotation functions in two ways: first to insinuate that refusal can be punishable by execution, and second to suggest that life actualizes itself through confession.

The narratives the medical officer constructs out of the fragments Michael K reveals in conversation—and those which he simply extrapolates and imagines—fall into two dominant trajectories: the first is loosely clinical in nature, while the second is inflected by ideas of religiosity and transcendence. To his credit, the medical officer questions the official account in K's file; he cannot reconcile the story that K is an "arsonist . . . escapee from a labour camp . . . and the manager of a flourishing garden . . . feeding the local guerrilla population" with K's physical and mental condition (131). Instead, the medical officer experiments with the registers of religiosity in failed attempts to narrate his own story and his relationship to K. As I argue here, the medical officer's failed imaginative project clarifies the inadequacies of received secularist and religious discourses alike.

In the process of identification, the medical officer moves incrementally closer to K, relinquishing interrogation as the mode of address. The medical officer's narrative reads like a journal with its series of nearly daily entries recording events in the camp, which are interrupted when a letter addressed to K appears. Remaining obviously undelivered, the letter's presence exemplifies the medical officer's contradictory imaginative trajectories, one toward violence and the other culminating in a fantasy of discipleship and imagined dialogue. The narrative voice in the document similarly slips between an extractive logic of power and interrogation and an alternate pole marked by tropes of salvation and forgiveness. "I want to know your story," he begins, but becomes increasingly pedantic, condescending, and self-congratulatory: "I am the only one who sees you for the original soul you are. I am the only one who cares for you. I alone see you as . . . a human soul above and beneath classification, a soul blessedly untouched by doctrine, untouched by history" (151). The rhetoric of care, recognition, and the human soul ultimately deteriorates into a primitivist mode, in which the medical officer recasts K as a specimen of the "noble savage," fit for interrogation and display: "We ought to value you and celebrate you, we ought to put your clothes on a maquette in a museum . . . with a label. . . . I appeal to you, Michaels: *yield*!" (152; italics in original).

Ultimately, the medical officer reveals a crypto-religious compulsion to identify K as the messiah and become his disciple, following the call of his ascetic saint: "If one dark night I were to slip into overalls and tennis shoes and clamber over the wall . . . I have chosen you to show me the way. . . . You were not a hero and did not pretend to be, not even a hero of fasting" (162–63). The overall problem lies in his attempt to derive meaning from K as more than an individual: "Michaels means something, and the meaning he has is not private to me . . . a privileged site where meaning erupted into the world. . . . Your stay in the camp was merely an allegory, if you know that word. It was an allegory—speaking at the highest level—of how scandalously, how outrageously a meaning can take up residence in a system without becoming a term in it" (165–66). More important than whether Michael K is a site of allegorical meaning, the medical officer's narrative establishes conclusively the impossibility of his bearing witness to K's experience without reducing him to a victim or, as K laments, "an object of charity" (181). By the end of this trajectory of radical asceticism, K has become a nocturnal figure weighing less than eighty pounds. Upon his recapture, even one of the camp administrators is forced to admit "he looked like someone out of Dachau" (146).

In stark contrast to the role testimony plays in concentration camp narratives, K sees relating his experiences at the horizons of radical asceticism as an unfeasible and potentially irrelevant task: "Always, when he tried to explain himself to himself, there remained a gap, a hole, a darkness before which his understanding baulked, into which it was useless to pour words. The words were eaten up, the gap remained. His was always a story with a hole in it: a wrong story, always wrong" (110). In Nazi Germany's death camps, on the other hand, the *muselmann* testifies to the site where the biopolitical power of the state creates a class of life, a "grey zone" in Primo Levi's terms, that ruptures all distinction between human and inhuman and shatters in advance any question of agency or freedom.[15] For Agamben as for Levi, the "actively passive" survivor speaks for and on behalf of the *muselmann*, the true, mute witness to the starvation and violence of the camps who is driven into a state of abjection so profound that observers would no longer recognize one as human (*Remnants* 111). To see K as a *muselmann* figure that turns away and refuses to be witnessed for is simply not possible within Agamben's theorization, or in any mode that valorizes empathy, testimony, and witness. Choice and desire, as signs of the fullness of subjectivity, collapse for the *muselmann*, as do all modal categories. The minimal difference between these two instances of bare life—one inside the camps, unwilled, the other a willed choice beyond the camps, yet superficially indistinguishable from passive exposure to violence—suggests that Coetzee envisions some remnant of agency emergent at the threshold of asceticism where one can still choose and even desire the necessary. Where Arendt claims that "the destruction of a man's rights, the killing of the juridical person in him, is a prerequisite for dominating him entirely" ("Total Domination" 132) and "precisely because man's resources are so great, he can be fully dominated only when he becomes a specimen of the animal-species man," K reveals that this destruction, while perhaps necessary for domination, is not necessarily causal or externally imposed (137). Through this initial choice, bare life can be seen to constitute a form of sovereignty as well as an abyss, a line of flight through which K preserves the spectral marks of agency and desire.

K's starvation involves not only a physical but also a social asceticism, as his choice signals the failure of egalitarian or ethical interpersonal relations and more radically questions the very possibility of reciprocity between human beings. In this rejection of the interpersonal, K's asceticism deviates radically from the forms of sociality that Michel Foucault argues are framed by ascetic modes of self-fashioning. Foucault's central insight in his extensive meditations on Greco-Roman asceticism is that socially productive forms of asceticism structure ancient bodily practices and modes of self-understanding. As Foucault explains, crafting the proper self requires both a systematic practice of self-regulation and an interpersonal encounter involving two actors, one active and one passive, the latter made up of a group "sometimes referred to as a way of designating the objects of possible pleasure: 'women, boys, slaves" (*Use* 47).[16] One of the lessons we are supposed to learn from his analysis of sexual practices in the Greco-Roman world is the way the love of boys created an ascetic libidinal and textual discourse very different from that of Christian Europe, which Foucault characterizes, following Nietzsche quite closely, as a culture governed by a juridical and clerical system devoted to sexual austerity. The key aspect of asceticism thus conceived as fundamentally interpersonal and socially constructive in nature is what Foucault later identifies as its other-directed qualities: "The interplay of the care of the self and the help of the other blends into preexisting relations, giving them a new coloration and a greater warmth. The care of the self . . . appears then as an intensification of social relations" (*Care* 53).

While this interpersonal asceticism is clearly operative in the collective hunger strike, a different dynamic is at play in Coetzee's novel. The passage in which K articulates his vision of radical asceticism proves crucial in calling attention to the vexed distinction between self and other, both within the text and across the problematic boundaries of reader and novel, writer and subject. The narrative as a whole registers and wrestles with the desire to speak of and for K as the figure of bare life, the true witness to the violence of apartheid, by a writer who does not share his experience. Nearly everything about K—from the resistance of his actions to interpretation, to his profound starvation, his race, his physical appearance, his minimal mental capacity, and the ceaselessly allusive letter of his name—seems designed to cast him as an unknowable figure of vulnerable alterity in Levinas's sense of the term.[17] But if we subscribe too quickly and uncritically to a Levinasian reading of K, we threaten to obscure Coetzee's distinctively antihumanist contribution to ethical thought and to erase the specific characteristics of K's experience at the limits of human endurance.

For Levinas, the other is both ontologically prior and hierarchically superior to the self, an encounter embodied by what Levinas calls the face-to-face.[18] Articulating the stakes of this encounter most vividly in *Alterity and Transcendence*, Levinas writes, "The face facing me, in its expression—in its mortality—summons me, demands me, requires me: as if the invisible death faced by the face of the other—pure alterity, separate, somehow, from any whole—were 'my business'" (24). This encounter with others constitutes the very condition of the emergence of subjectivity, since we are interpolated as subjects through the other's unconditional call, a summons "that is presupposed in all language" (*Alterity* 97). Though our relation to the other always maintains its a priori character for Levinas—ethics precedes ontology—the centrality of the demand of the other who holds us hostage raises the question of what happens when the other turns away and issues no call, a possibility Levinas never considers. The turn away in effect denies any chance of the face-to-face encounter.

With his usual poignant intensity in "Neighbors and Other Monsters: A Plea for Ethical Violence," Slavoj Žižek reflects on the *muselmann* as a challenge to Levinasian ethics: "The figure of the Muselmann signals the limitation of Levinas: when describing it, Primo Levi repeatedly uses the predicate *faceless*, and this term should be given here its entire Levinasian weight. When confronted with a Muselmann, one cannot discern in his face the trace of the abyss of the Other in his/her vulnerability, addressing us with the infinite call of our responsibility. . . . Maybe the Muselmann is thus the zero-level neighbor, the neighbor with whom no empathetic relation is possible" (161–62). Žižek argues that the *muselmann* represents the real of monstrous otherness, a traumatic encounter with the inhuman for which the model of otherness offered by Levinas is a gentrification and an insufficient defense. Ultimately, Žižek seeks to supplement or perhaps even supplant Levinas's account of ethics with one of justice conceived as choosing *against* the neighbor whose face we see and in favor of the countless faceless multitudes. Contrary to what Žižek implies here and in his more recent *Parallax View*, empathy is neither necessary nor sufficient for an ethical relation with the other as Levinas construes it. In fact, the radically asymmetrical nature of the relationship Levinas describes renders the premise of equivalence and mutuality suspect, because mutuality depends on the self as a measure for the experience of the other. Rather, as Michael Marais rightly notes, Levinas's account of the work of ethics foregrounds the rejection of this use of the self to understand the other; ethics, in contrast, is "a departure with no return" (162). Nevertheless, Žižek correctly identifies that the condition of the *muselmann* constitutes a limit condition of the Levinasian face-to-face, though not simply because, as he argues, "One could say that the Muselmann is precisely the one who is no longer able to say 'Here I am!' (and in front of whom I can no longer say 'Here I am')" ("Neighbors" 161). The *muselmann*'s challenge to Levinasian ethics, and likewise the challenge posed by Coetzee's K, is ultimately far more profound: the bare life of radical asceticism as he enacts it (starving and living in a hole) maintains its ethical content as a tactic of resistance even as it rejects the very premise of the Levinasian face-to-face.

When Levinas speaks of hunger as the motivating principle of secularization in "Secularization and Hunger," he has in mind a process that commenced thousands of years ago, when the attitude of those gazing at the stars began to shift from wonderment (an attitude proper to the sacred) to analysis. Hunger as a corporeal phenomenon secularizes in that it turns us from concepts and "spirit" to an immanent caloric materialism: "The hunger which no music pacifies secularizes all this romantic eternity" (10). For Levinas, who spent the duration of the Second World War as a Jewish prisoner of war in a German camp, "We are not astonished enough by the force of transference which goes from the memory of my own hunger to the suffering and the responsibility for the hunger of the neighbor" (11).

The problematic status of bearing witness and giving testimony in Coetzee's novel derives instead from its implication in structures of sovereignty and power. Although Agamben attempts to dislodge the concepts of "witness" and "testimony" from their juridical contexts in

Remnants of Auschwitz and *Homo Sacer*—and this is precisely what is at stake in Levi's insistence on the impossibility of judgment—they remain enmeshed in the very structures of modern sovereignty that Agamben, following Foucault, sees as contiguous with the biopolitical regimes of modernity. Felman more readily acknowledges testimony's inextricable bond to the juridical realm: "To bear witness is to take responsibility for truth: to speak, implicitly, from within the legal pledge and the juridical imperative of the witness's oath. . . . To testify is always, metaphorically, to take the witness stand" (204). It requires no great leap, however, to see the figure of the witness summoned or compelled to deliver testimony as a traumatic inversion of the Levinasian subject. There can be neither witness nor testimony outside of the juridical realm, the realm of sovereign power. If bare life can be seen as the turning away of the other and serves as a site of resistance, Coetzee seems to suggest it does so categorically: if radical asceticism is a tactic of resistance, it must act against both violence and testimony, both camps and texts.

At the end of the novel, K returns, not to internment camp captivity or to his burrow in the veld, but to the storage closet that was once his mother's servant quarters in a Cape Town seaside apartment building. The space is one of raw foreclosure: windowless, airless, barred by a skull and crossbones "Danger" sign stenciled on its door. His mother's former room, looted and abandoned during the state of emergency, allows neither the georgic consolations of farming, however close to the edge of subsistence, nor the tragic pathos of internment. The closet—with its empty bottle, cardboard bed, and blanket bespeaking a companion he only imagines but never sees—enforces a structural circularity to a narrative that has moved geographically outward from this space of claustrophobia that is full of the material evidence of apartheid labor relations. Though K's final vision imaginatively recuperates the very teaspoon that signified his near starvation and physical deformity as a child, its status as dying vision forecloses in advance the imagined return to the veld that constitutes the novel's last words: "He would clear the rubble from the mouth of the shaft, he would bend the handle of the teaspoon in a loop and tie the string to it, he would lower it down the shaft deep into the earth, and when he brought it up there would be water in the bowl of the spoon; and in that way, he would say, one can live" (184). If Coetzee's novel has an ethical message, it is a particularly caustic and demanding one, grounded on this vision of ascetic sainthood rather than on a flourishing life.

REDEEMING CHARITY

In *Age of Iron*, Coetzee aligns hope for racial rapprochement—and literary production—with the unfinished project of restoring reciprocity to embodied acts of giving and receiving, based on an economy not of desire but of mutual self-abasement. Beyond the pale of theistic certainties and in the midst of state-sanctioned injustice, the suffering and comforted bodies of Elizabeth Curren and Vercueil open a space of ascetic sustenance mirrored in acts of reading and authorship. In the novel's first pages, readers encounter the protagonist, Elizabeth, a retired classics professor and the novel's narrator, returning to her home in Cape Town from a doctor's appointment during which she learned that she is dying of cancer. She arrives to find that a homeless black man, who gives his name as Vercueil, has taken up residence on her property.

The ways of knowing and ordering the world that surround and infuse the text—namely apartheid, classicism, and Christianity—appear as failures or distant echoes. From the very start, the man's arrival and that of her cancer are linked in the novel's episteme, and Elizabeth accepts both. As the writer of her own story, she uses her body's breakdown as a heuristic device to help her understand her ethical place within a disintegrating apartheid system, much as Coetzee appears to be using Elizabeth herself as a narrator. Drawing variously on the deconstructive discourse of the gift and a terminology appropriated from Christian revelation, she describes Vercueil as an "annunciation," a "derelict," a "messenger," and a "visitor, visiting himself upon me" (5, 4). In many ways, Vercueil serves as an unlikely hybrid of *muselmann* and angel, in the tradition of Michael K. Political disintegration and Elizabeth's own imminent death produce a moment of openness in which Coetzee and Elizabeth evaluate possibilities for ethical action across boundaries of racial, sexual, and economic difference through narratological and theological improvisations.

The economies forged by charity on the one hand and apartheid capitalism on the other contrast with those that might occur in imagined social relations predicated on gift exchange. This is modeled on the unique "gift," delivered after her death, to Elizabeth by Vercueil. In the conceit on which the novel rests, we learn that Elizabeth, the narrator, plans to entrust her manuscript to Vercueil with instructions to post it to her daughter in the United States after her death. Though Elizabeth (presumably) does not create the echo intentionally, when she leaves her manuscript with the indigent, alcoholic, vagrant Vercueil upon her death, Coetzee stages an inversion of the moment when, along with instructions to burn everything, a dying Franz Kafka entrusts his papers to Max Brod, the one man most likely to refuse this wish. Of all men, Coetzee suggests, Elizabeth has chosen the one least likely to perform the task required of him. To frame it differently, the fact that we are readers of Elizabeth's story provides evidence of a promise kept from beyond the grave. As such, the novel attempts to implicate its readership, however geographically distant from the site, within the compass of its ethical address.

When Vercueil and Elizabeth begin their cohabitation, Vercueil repeatedly spurns Elizabeth's requests for him to join her bed. Coetzee describes the slow process through which they become neighbors, then figurative spouses, in the language of religious parable: Elizabeth must "love him because . . . [she does not] love him . . . because he is the weak reed [she] lean[s] upon him" (131). The linguistic and cultural meanings of charity—particularly the problematic status of charity as an economic concept—constitute one of the novel's central concerns, first as Elizabeth attempts to forge a relationship with Vercueil and then as she endeavors, in her words, to "redeem" herself from the guilt of her complicity with apartheid.

At the beginning of the novel, Elizabeth attempts to frame her relationship with Vercueil within a racialized economics of privilege. In this context, Elizabeth believes she unequivocally occupies the role of the giver of charity or, more damningly, of the employer who regards herself as generous for deigning to honor a laborer with the therapeutic value of work. As becomes clear in her narration of the event, Elizabeth is aware the pose is a ruse: "Do you want a job of work?" she enquires, after giving him a cup of coffee (8). In answer he spits next to her foot and hands the coffee back. "We can't proceed on a basis of charity," Elizabeth explains to Vercueil as she pays him for an afternoon of haphazard gardening, "because you don't deserve it. And he, smiling, keeping his smile to himself: 'Deserve . . . Who deserves anything?'" (21). An entrenched ideology, to which Elizabeth gives voice here, sees charity as alms given to the poor, a system that reifies divides of race and gender. Elizabeth is performing a caricature, and she seems to know it, as the text's double consciousness emphasizes. Elizabeth has missed the point, however, as Coetzee's emphasis on Christian rhetoric emphasizes: charity as an expression of agapic love is entirely undeserved and is modeled on God's unconditional love for imperfect humanity. As Timothy Jackson, a scholar of religious ethics and one of the foremost contemporary thinkers on the subject of *agape* and charity, argues in *Love Disconsoled*, "*Agape* as adoration is due the Holy Other as a matter of strict justice, since God is utterly lovable; but as passionate service to other creatures *agape* is ultimately an unmerited gift, since creatures are fallen and continuously sinful" (28). While Vercueil's smiling response to Elizabeth's assertion that he does not deserve her charity stresses foremost the material injustices of apartheid, the exchange simultaneously suggests that it is Elizabeth, not Vercueil, who may not "deserve" care.

Neither Coetzee nor Elizabeth sets out to be a systematic theologian, and both are painfully aware of the strategic alignment between Calvinism and apartheid, as well as of the central role liberation theology played in overturning it.[19] "Are there not still white zealots preaching the old regime of discipline," she muses, "the spirit of Geneva triumphant in Africa. Calvin, black-robed . . . victorious" (51). Instead, the novel follows a rather haphazard series of theological associations that Elizabeth describes as a "cruciform logic, [one] which takes me where I do not want to go!" (137). The novel's epistolary form emphasizes the discrepancies between its audience as a text (the readers), the audience of address (the daughter), and the vehicle of transmission (Vercueil). Elizabeth realizes that her story is predicated on Vercueil not just for its delivery but also for its very articulation: "In the look he gives me I see myself in a way that can be written," she notes, adding that "when I write about him I write about myself," a doubling that confirms the suggestions implicit in Vercueil's ambiguous name: "Verskuil" in Afrikaans loosely translates as "alter ego" (9).[20]

Seeing herself in the mirror of the other's gaze is more than a clever exposé of the mutually constitutive nature of apartheid's masters and slaves. Shedding irony, Elizabeth encounters Vercueil's gaze as a gift, and thus the distance between their subjectivities begins a halting process of disintegration. This ambivalent gift constitutes the novel's seminal moment, establishing a distinction between a horizontal axis of the material and embodied relationship that connects Elizabeth and Vercueil and the vertical axis of their spiritual or ethical connection. Coetzee, like Paul Ricoeur, sees the possibility of ethics and religion arising out of an unceasing process of interpretation and rearticulation. Moments of erotic charity and their narrative mediation possess what Ricoeur calls a "logic of superabundance, which flows directly from the economy of the gift" (300). Ricoeur comes to this conclusion within the context of the contrast between an ethics of the golden rule and one governed by what he calls the "logic of equivalence" (300). These vertical movements are, however, transient and proposed under erasure. Elizabeth and Coetzee warn the reader against the pleasures of recognition: "Do not read in sympathy with me. Let your heart not beat with mine" (104). Elizabeth's warning against physical and textual intimacy belies the central acts of her relationship with Vercueil.

At first, attempting to justify to herself and her reader why she has accepted Vercueil's presence and offered him food, Elizabeth appeals with savage irony to maternal instinct: "Why do I give this man food? For the same reason I would feed his dog (stolen, I am sure) if it came begging. For the same reason I gave you [her daughter] my breast. To be full enough to give and to give from one's fullness: what deeper urge is there? Out of their withered bodies even the old try to squeeze one last drop. A stubborn will to give, to nourish. Shrewd was death's aim when he chose my breast for his first shaft" (7–8). Linking the projection of her pain as cruelty and the reduction of love (filial, agapic, maternal, and erotic) to an inverted Nietzschean will to sacrifice, the passage above both naturalizes the desire to give and removes the act of giving from any possible reciprocity. At the same time, in casting herself as the ultimate source of the gift—the withered body providing for all in need—Elizabeth elides the gravity of her own equally stubborn desire for life and nourishment. In strong terms, by naturalizing charity to an instinctual and almost vicious response, Elizabeth repudiates the ethical primacy accorded to charity in Christian traditions while ironically affirming one of the central tenants of agapic love—namely, its equal regard for others over and against the selective criteria of erotic, maternal, and filial love.[21]

But Elizabeth sees herself as a nonbeliever living in purely immanent terms, drawing on the rhetoric and lexicon of a borrowed Christianity. Elizabeth's nihilistic rejection of "ethics" as a motive or measure for her actions exposes what we might call the paradox of charity when it is articulated beyond the pale of Christian metaphysics. Within a theological canopy supported by a conception of God as love, "charity is the métier of everyone made in God's Image" (Jackson 4). While there are likely to be as many theological positions about an idea as there are theologians, most would argue that charity as an ethical mandate derives from the causally and ontologically prior love of God for humanity. For Christians who believe that *agape* is the highest good, "*Only* because God first loves us gratuitously are we commanded *and enabled* to love God unreservedly and to love fellow human beings as (we ought to love) ourselves" (Jackson 12; italics added). While this concept of *caritas* confirms the unmerited nature of *agape* and grace, it simultaneously binds the obligation of charity to a transcendental metaphysics and a distinctly Judeo-Christian conception of divinity. *Agape* depends on God in the dominant Christian account. If there is no God, however, or if we are mistaken about the nature of divinity, the obligation to perform acts of charity, as well as the epistemological primacy of charity as such, would seem to evaporate. Elizabeth's approach to this cluster of problems serves as the novel's theological fulcrum: "God cannot help me. God is looking for me but he cannot reach me. God is another dog in another maze. I smell God and God smells me. I am the bitch in her time, God the male. . . . But he is lost as I am lost" (138).[22]

In passages such as this, Coetzee is engaged in many levels of narrative play. Intentionally haptic, corporeal, and vulgar, Elizabeth's troping fashions an immanent and antihumanist tradition. Outside a protective transcendental canopy, defenses of charity tend to be coded through the language of altruism or, in political theory, grounded on values like egalitarianism or modeled on the premise of economic redistribution. In a world conceived without God, as Elizabeth's clearly is, both charity and love remain horizontal filiations deprived of the vertical dimension she is invoking. It is important, then, that Coetzee has not staged anything like a deathbed conversion narrative in which a lifetime nonbeliever "returns" to the fold of a once-abandoned tradition.

At the center of Elizabeth's conflicted engagement with charity lie the injustices of apartheid and unanswerable questions common to conflict and postconflict zones. How much responsibility do individual members of a society bear for injustices to which they have objected but of which they are nonetheless beneficiaries? The novel's address to Elizabeth's daughter in her comfortable American home, meanwhile, reminds its readers of complicities that extend to all those who occupy positions above the station of those like Michael K and Vercueil. When Elizabeth contemplates suicide (for which Vercueil offers his assistance several times), she reflects on the nature of her culpability: "Why should I be expected to rise above my times? Is it my doing that my times have been so shameful? Why should it be left to me, old and sick and full of pain, to lift myself unaided out of this pit of disgrace?" (117). Economic restitution on an individual level clearly falls far short of remedying the systematic oppression of apartheid, while the diseased polity it has produced interrupts the possibility of forgiveness. Has Elizabeth just missed the point that charity as an expression of agapic love is an entirely undeserved gift modeled on God's unconditional love for imperfect humanity? The conflicted logic of her argument exposes not the incoherence of charity as a system but rather her own profound ambivalence about her individual responsibility as an objector to apartheid who is nevertheless a member of the minority white ruling class. Circumstance has dealt a deadly blow to systemic theory. Vercueil, meanwhile, rejects not only the particular system of apartheid's distributive (in)justice but the very idea of inherent human worth that would authorize rights claims beyond those given by contingent, social systems.

As a concept, charity occupies an unstable position in relation to economic exchange: while charity necessarily evokes the economic redistribution of alms giving, its broader meaning encompasses its status as the preferred Latin translation of the Greek *agape*.[23] As a classics professor, Elizabeth is well aware of the etymology that links charity as alms giving to *caritas* and *agape* as God's pure love for humanity. Elizabeth, however, insists on making a false, embittered etymological argument to Vercueil: "*Charity*: from the Latin word for the heart. It is as hard to receive as to give. It takes that much effort. I wish you would learn that. I wish you would learn something instead of just lying around" (22; italics in original). She continues, privately, "A lie: charity, *caritas*, has nothing to do with the heart. . . . Care: the true root of charity. I look for him to care, and he does not. Because he is beyond caring. Beyond caring and beyond care" (22; italics in original). While in this passage Elizabeth may believe she looks "for him to care," it would be more accurate had she reversed the prepositions: Elizabeth looks to Vercueil *for* care. Ironically, even Elizabeth's private confession that she has lied about the etymology of *charity* contains equally spurious details: asserting that "care" is the "root" of charity elides the term's etymological roots in the Old English *cearu*.[24]

The intimacy and proximity of the evolving relationship between Vercueil and Elizabeth, meanwhile, exceed or supplement the Christian parameters of neighbor love. As Elizabeth muses, it is "easy to give alms to the orphaned, the destitute, the hungry. Harder to give alms to the bitter-hearted . . . but the alms I give Vercueil are hardest of all. What I give he does not forgive me for giving. No charity for him, no forgiveness. . . . Without his forgiveness I give without charity, serve without love. Rain falling on barren soil" (131). In Elizabeth's comments on alms giving, she clings to the notion of charity as articulated within the structures of economic and racial difference: "alms" as the religious duty of giving material relief to the poor. The word derives from the Old English *aelmysse* and the Greek *elemosyna* (compassion or mercy) according to the *OED*; conceived as such, charity sustains a position of relative privilege for the giver. Read symptomatically, Elizabeth's insistent deployment of theologically loaded terms, like *love*, *forgiveness*, and *gift*, alongside a seemingly immanent account of human relations, expresses the unstable relationship between the horizontal and vertical implications of charity.[25] For Elizabeth, human charity is constituted by a performance and a reception that refuse reciprocal materialism. Indeed, Coetzee seems to give voice to the concerns of political scientist Romand Coles, who writes that "insofar as generosity does not understand itself to be deeply rooted in a receptive encounter with others, it will proliferate a blindness, theft, and imperialism despite its best efforts" (3).[26]

Confession offers a paradigm for approaching the salvation Elizabeth desires, but though the text is replete with moments in which she admits her complicity with apartheid directly to black South Africans, it is to no great effect. As is also the case for David Lurie, for Elizabeth the problem with confession as a paradigm arises not simply because of the lack of juridical context in which it can be framed (an absence that would be remedied by the Truth and Reconciliation Commission in 1995), but rather because absolution requires the intercession of a transcendental agent and, in the absence of transcendental reward, reifies self-abasement as an end in itself.[27] "I want to be saved," Elizabeth admits, but "how shall I be saved? By doing what I do not want to do. This is the first step: that I know. I must love, first of all, the unlovable" (136). "The unlovable" in this case refers to an adolescent foot soldier in the resistance to apartheid who is shot and killed by the police in Elizabeth's home shortly after this revelation, effectively foreclosing the a priori love Elizabeth seems to offer.

Another possibility for salvation that the text explores is a variation on the theme of charity as commerce: "I want to sell myself, redeem myself, but am full of confusion about how to do it," Elizabeth explains (117). In the arithmetic of self-abasement she pursues, Elizabeth abandons the position of privilege that makes possible a *caritas* of alms giving. She becomes, like Vercueil, a vagrant sleeping on the street, smelling of urine, at the mercy of the casual violence of those who would violate an old and helpless woman. Just as charity without forgiveness serves only to emphasize the racial divides enforced by apartheid, Elizabeth's self-abasement as such cannot, in consequentialist or utilitarian terms, pay her debt in shame. In *Age of Iron*, *caritas* is unmoored from its Christian foundations and therefore from the economics of heavenly reward.

A profound act of care interrupts Elizabeth's willful renunciation and vagrancy when Vercueil discovers her and brings her home and the two begin an unlikely period of mutual companionship. As Elizabeth describes it, "We share a bed, folded one upon the other like a page folded in two, like two wings folded: old mates, bunkmates, conjoined, conjugal," and likewise, "It is not he who fell under my care when he arrived, I now understand, nor I who fell under his: we fell under each other, and have tumbled and risen since then in the flights and swoops of that mutual election" (189; 193). While the theological implications of a "mutual election" reject the norms of Calvinist Protestantism, the phrase stresses a vision of charity rearticulated within the bounds of a reciprocal relationship. Similarly, Elizabeth and Vercueil's bond shatters the constraints of the social conditions in which it is articulated.[28] The solace Vercueil offers, which Elizabeth describes in the novel's final lines, bears little relation either to *eros* or *agape* as they are traditionally understood. Ultimately, it verges on euthanasia: "He took me in his arms and held me with a mighty force, so that the breath went out of me in a rush. From that embrace there was no warmth to be had" (198). The gift here is the gift of death.

Age of Iron traverses a great distance from Elizabeth's initial conception of charity as alms to the receptive mutuality of this deathly embrace within an ascetic marriage. Despite the chill of its final lines, the novel cannot help but offer a kind of optimism grounded in the conceit that the text's very existence fulfills Vercueil's promise. Though the relational structure of giving and receiving emerges in the "gift" of Vercueil's gaze in the novel's opening moments, the characters initially remain mired in their separateness, across which little reciprocity seems possible. *Age of Iron* depicts an evolving logic of charity that ultimately comes to rest in the figure of intimate *caritas* and receptive generosity. The nature of this change can be seen in Elizabeth's repeated invitations to Vercueil to come lie beside her: "'Mr. Vercueil!' I said. One eye opened. 'Come and lie down'"—an invitation he declines early in the novel (113). He accepts a later request, however, when "he lay down at my back, on top of the bedclothes" (185). Theirs is a textual embrace, expressed within the bonds of physical intimacy in a postreproductive mode slightly adjacent to erotic desire. Coetzee's theme is once again self-imposed abjection; tracing Elizabeth's path toward vagrant death, one she briefly walked alongside Vercueil, he charts a course beyond both church and state. While this sense of bleak resignation owes much to the stalled political process in South Africa during the period before Nelson Mandela's release from prison in 1990, underpinning this contextual reading lies a more pervasive commitment to ascetic antihumanism in Coetzee's fiction.

THE GIFT OF SEX

Since 1996, when she made her debut in a lecture he gave at Bennington College, Elizabeth Costello has been a fertile conceit for J. M. Coetzee. During his Bennington lecture, as he did in his more well-known contribution to the Tanner lecture series at Princeton University in 1997 and 1998, Coetzee declined to read the expected essay, or even to speak, as he puts it, in his own person. Instead, without preamble, Coetzee gave a reading of a story about a fictional novelist, Elizabeth Costello, who delivers rebarbative and controversial lectures on the subject of animal rights at a fictional college that invited her to participate in a prestigious lecture series not unlike the ones at Bennington and Princeton. With these "lectures" and their *mise en abyme* qualities, Coetzee stages a series of performance and textual experiments that reach their climax in his 2003 novel, *Elizabeth Costello*. From the mid-1990s until her posthumous departure from Paul Rayment's house at the end of *Slow Man* (2005), Elizabeth proves to be deeply useful to Coetzee in his long-standing attempts to rethink the vexed questions of canonization and authorial intent begun in earlier works like *Foe* and *The Master of Petersburg*.

In *Elizabeth Costello*, Coetzee's concern with self-mortification and abjection moves into explicitly sexual territory, such that the gift of sex constitutes the novel's signal ethical event. Elizabeth conceives of her erotic encounter with a dying man in terms of *caritas*. She describes having spent many days "at the old man's bedside," offering the care of companionship though there was "nothing pleasant in any of this" (152). The old man in question, Aidan, is an aged artist whom Elizabeth's mother met in their shared nursing home ("They were a couple, in a civilized kind of way," Elizabeth explains) and for whose paintings Elizabeth once posed (145). In one such session, with the painting apparently stagnant, Aidan, mute from a laryngectomy, passes her a note: "Wish I could paint you in the nude . . . would have loved that" (147). Aidan's tone is one of lament over lost strengths, but Elizabeth responds by removing her bra and wrap. At the time, Elizabeth understood herself to have acted out of a desire for self-assertion and an instinct for sexual autonomy, but nonetheless the scene evokes another scene from her sexual history, which she also keeps a secret:

> When she was nineteen, she remembers, she allowed herself to be picked up. . . . At the last minute she could not go through with it. . . . But Tim or Tom would not listen. When she resisted, he tried to force her. For a long time, in silence, panting, she fought him off. . . . [Eventually] he began to hit her seriously. He lifted her off the bed, punched her breasts, punched her in the belly, hit her a terrible blow with his elbow to her face. When he was bored with hitting her he tore up her clothes and tried to set fire to them in a waste-paper basket . . . it was her first brush with evil. (165)

In contrast to the return-of-the-repressed quality that colors her memories of physical and sexual abuse, the memory of her erotic charity percolates to the surface of her consciousness in response to a visit with her sister, Blanche. Blanche is a Catholic nun and medical missionary in rural Zululand whose keynote speech at a college graduation, "The Humanities in Africa," constitutes the occasion of the novel's fifth "lesson." While Blanche uses her oration to argue that the "Humanities," grounded in a vision of Hellenism, "lost [their] way long ago" and are now "on their deathbed," Elizabeth traces the motivating force of her argument to the contempt with which Blanche's version of Christianity treats the human body (122, 123). A month after their encounter, Elizabeth still does not, in her words, "want to give up on [their] dispute yet" and refuses to "vacate the field" (148). Seeing her strongest argument against Blanche condensed in her encounter with Aidan, she describes the episode in a letter to her sister that appears to the reader as an interpolated narrative. She insists that posing seminude for a dying man mirrors the embodied *caritas* of the Virgin Mary: "When Mary blessed among women . . . tips her sweet pink nipple up before our gaze, when I, imitating her, uncover my breasts for old Mr Phillips, we perform acts of humanity" (150).[29] Acts like these are crucial to our self-articulation as humans, she continues, because they "are not available to animals, who cannot uncover themselves. . . . Nothing compels us to do it, Mary or me. But out of the overflow, the outflow of our human hearts, we do it nevertheless: drop our robes, reveal ourselves, reveal the life and beauty we are blessed with" (150).

If Elizabeth's argument seems forced and rather trite in its conception of gender, the fault lies not in what it intends but rather in its choice of imagery, its capitulation to Blanche's terms of engagement, and its contextual slippage. For one thing, Elizabeth seems to be echoing the argument David Lurie makes to seduce Melanie Isaacs into bed with him the first time in *Disgrace*: "A woman's beauty does not belong to her alone," David flirts, "it is part of the bounty she brings into the world. She has a duty to share it" (16). The strategy and the words are not his, either; David borrows them from a Shakespearean sonnet, a quotation from which breaks the erotic thrill: "'From fairest creatures we desire increase,' he says, 'that thereby beauty's rose may never die'"—a witticism that Melanie takes as her cue to leave (16). Though Coetzee structures his text to make "argument" a vexed genre in the best of circumstances, "argument" is not, to use Elizabeth's words, a "field" Coetzee will vacate or a dispute on which he will "give up."[30]

Comparing her physical generosity with the pain of Christ upon the cross, Elizabeth frames her action in the overtly Christian terms of revelation and blessing. Elizabeth's embodied *caritas*, as she describes it in her "letter," may borrow the visual and descriptive lexicon of Christianity, but the novel's primary embodiment of Christian ethics remains Blanche's.[31] As "Sister Bridget" she publicly embodies Catholicism, but as "Blanche"—the role in which we encounter her through Elizabeth—she speaks for a vision of Christianity as colorless as her name implies, a Christianity symbolized by a "Gothic," suffering Christ (138). For Elizabeth, Blanche's Christianity can be captured most poignantly in the image of the man at Marianhill Station who carves nothing but crosses and, on them, "a Christ dying in contortions . . . a man in the extremes of agony, deformed, ugly" (138–39). But just as the modes of sociality and images of corporeal suffering offered by Blanche's Christianity seem inadequate to Elizabeth, so too are secularist conceptions of progress that have no room for the somatics of pain or an ethics of self-abasement, except as negative limits against which they frame concepts of the good. As an effort aimed to recuperate an alternate, embodied, and feminist reading of Christianity infused with a Greek appreciation for human beauty, Elizabeth's anecdote and her analysis of it remain limited by its simplistic and unexplained assertion of equivalence between breast and blessing. More importantly, Elizabeth's argument depends upon a stricter dimorphism of gender roles and a more essentialized notion of "the feminine" than Coetzee's novel will allow.[32]

In fact, Elizabeth Costello's breast-centered evocation of the giving woman echoes Elizabeth Curren's assertions, early in *Age of Iron*, about a putatively maternal economy of generosity. For Hélène Cixous and Carol Gilligan, among others, these "maternal" gifts resist the economic structure of commodity exchange while cementing subjectively valorized interpersonal relationships.[33] In the tradition established by Marcel Mauss, the gift is a magical object that sutures the social fabric through bonds of reciprocal exchange; gifts, in Mauss's estimation, are never free. As was the case in my discussion of alms giving in the previous section, the idea of the gift is bound up with exchange, a register more alien to the embodied practices of *caritas*. While "the gift" is constituted through the social process of exchange and is not derived from the attributes of a particular object, its material, economic semiotics persist. Elizabeth Costello, meanwhile, receives no "credit" for or "return" on her actions: they are gratuitous, unwitnessed, kept secret for over half a lifetime, and profoundly divorced from any realm of social circulation as a result of Aidan's death. Elizabeth, after all, builds no relationship of mutual care with Aidan, who will soon be "burned to a powder and scattered to the winds" (155).

The novel pushes beyond this impasse just as the relationship between Aidan and Elizabeth moves beyond the roles of model and artist (or even artist and muse); with Aidan confined to bed and his illness terminal, their relationship becomes far more proximately erotic. Initially justifying her act in the blasé terms of spontaneity, "*Let's give the old boy a treat, let's brighten up his Saturday*" she says to herself before she "removes her dress, [and] her brassiere. Then she crosses back to the bed, sits down side-on where he can get a good eyeful" (153; italics in original). But, as the narrator wryly notes, "The story proceeds"; here is the description of what I am tempted to call the "climax" of the encounter, a twist in the story that she decides not to share with her sister, and that appears in the novel's standard third-person prose:

> It goes on long enough for her, the woman, [already seated naked on his sickbed] to drop a hand casually on the bedcover and begin to stroke, ever so gently, the place where the penis, if the penis were alive and awake, ought to be; and

> then, when there is no response, to put the covers aside and loosen the cord of Mr Phillips's pyjamas, old-man's flannel pyjamas such as she has not seen in years . . . and open up the front and plant a kiss on the entirely flaccid little thing, and take it in her mouth and mumble until it stirs faintly with life . . . nor is the smell pleasant either, the smell of an old man's nether parts, cursorily washed. (153–54)

It would be difficult indeed to imagine this scene translated into propositional statements of belief or defended by any deontological ethical system. Could Elizabeth tell the jury that subsequently sits in judgment upon her in the afterlife—a possibility, it should be observed, neither she nor the narrator considers—that she believes in giving erotic pleasure to dying men? By Kantian standards, her action would be aberrant at best; neither she nor the text seems interested in deciding whether the maxim of her action could be posited as universal law. In a different way, Elizabeth has made a serious wager on her ability to know the desires or needs of a dying man (a man whose ravaged throat prohibits him from speaking), and her act, however described, violates his alterity. Levinas thus joins Kant among the frowning jury, while Coetzee's tender evocation of the scene signals his endorsement of Elizabeth's wager.

The narrative tone in the passage veers between the sensual (the stroking of a bedcover), the tragicomic (his impotence, the "old-man's flannel pyjamas"), and the humbly self-aware ("It will happen to her too, in due course") (154). Elizabeth's intensely proximate engagement and direct tactile contact with Aidan collapses the distance that characterized the visual structure of Elizabeth's description in the letter to her sister, and this contrast helps to clarify the significance of the scene. While the visual scene increases her silent consciousness of her body's role in a particularly gendered economy, voice returns in an attenuated form with the "mumble" of oral sex—but only for Elizabeth. Elizabeth's touch and its explicitly genital nature, meanwhile, complicate her earlier attempt to account for the event along the lines of maternal gift.[34]

The Greeks, on whose ideals the "lesson," as Coetzee calls the chapters, has been focused, would not have a word or concept for her actions, according to Elizabeth's musings: "What name would the Greeks give to such a spectacle? Not *eros*, certainly—too grotesque for that. *Agape*? Again, perhaps not. Does that mean the Greeks would have no word for it? Would one have to wait for the Christians to come along with the right word: *caritas*?" (154). Elizabeth's conclusion startles and unsettles her, but she is compelled by its appropriateness nonetheless: "For that [*caritas*], in the end, is what she is convinced it is. From the swelling of her heart she knows it, from the utter, illimitable difference between what is in her heart and what Nurse Naidoo would see, if by some mischance . . . [she] were to fling open the door and stride in" (154).[35] In common parlance, Elizabeth's act is just a "mercy fuck"—a phrase defined by the *Oxford English Dictionary* as a "coarse slang" term for "an act of sexual intercourse offered out of pity or compassion." In *Disgrace*, David's mercy fuck with Bev Shaw occupies the same ethical continuum as the care he devotes to the carcasses of dead birds and dogs. In forsaking his own pleasure and abandoning the "rights of desire," David's transformation involves a vision of ethical action predicated on self-abasement and deep suspicion of personal pleasure and consequentialist notions of utility.

Like Melanie, Mr. Phillips does not apparently resist, but the reader does not receive any indication of his fulfillment, nor, indeed, are we assured that he did not find the entire experience profoundly awkward or even undesired. To assume his unproblematic complicity (he did catalyze the events with a rushed note) by his silence would be to misread the parallels between *Elizabeth Costello* and *Disgrace*. When David Lurie forces himself on his student, Melanie, she too does not resist: "All she does is avert herself, avert her lips, avert her eyes . . . not rape, not quite that, but undesired nevertheless, undesired to the core" (25). While Coetzee has carefully managed narrative parameters so that, on the basis of the information provided by the novel, David would never be convicted of rape in a court of law—mitigating circumstances include the lack of clear verbal refusal at the time of the event (25) and their subsequent consensual sex (29), placing him "beyond the scope of the law" (55)—his actions are clearly wrong. Unlike Elizabeth, David explains (but does not attempt to defend) the actions that cost him his job and cast him into disgrace with an appeal to the Greeks: "I became a servant of *Eros*," he explains (52), resting his case on the "rights of desire" (89).

Early in *Disgrace*, when David Lurie is hauled before a disciplinary committee at the fictional Cape Technical University to answer the charge of having sexually harassed his student, he refuses to play his designated role in what he perceives as a tawdry drama of confession in exchange for amnesty. In proceedings that unambiguously evoke the

Truth and Reconciliation Commission that dominated the South African public sphere with weekly televised broadcasts from 1996 to 1998, David refuses the invitation to confess or express contrition: "Frankly, what you want from me is not a response, but a confession. Well, I make no confession. I put forward a plea, as is my right. Guilty as charged. That is my plea. That is as far as I am prepared to go" (51). But while Coetzee suggests that, like all of us, David may indeed have "rights of desire," he does not necessarily have the right to act on that desire. David comes to understand the severity of this ethical "mistake" through a belated attempt to imagine the event from Melanie's perspective and to inhabit the feeling of defilement it conjures: "At this moment, he has no doubt, she, Melanie, is trying to cleanse herself of it, of him. He sees her running a bath. . . . He would like to slide into a bath of his own" (25).

The comparison between David's sexual aggression and Elizabeth's erotic *caritas* is intended neither to point out an ethical problem to solve (like David's "problem of sex") nor to place the actions on the same ethical continuum (as Elizabeth when she compares eating meat to the Holocaust). Instead, like the imagined prying eyes of Nurse Naidoo, the comparison between Elizabeth Costello and David Lurie serves to accentuate the contrast between the damage caused by David's solipsistic desire and Elizabeth's embodied, confident knowledge that her act was just, a confidence linked to "the swelling of her heart" (154). Nonetheless, Coetzee's fiction has never been willing to trade desire for the good, and in his most recent novel, *The Childhood of Jesus* (2013), Coetzee reaffirms the dichotomy between the good and the human: "From goodwill come friendship and happiness, come companionable picnics in the parklands or companionable afternoons strolling in the forest. Whereas from love, or at least from longing in its more urgent manifestation, come frustration and doubt and heartsore. It is as simple as that" (57).

THE PROBLEM OF BELIEF

In the last of the "lessons" that constitute *Elizabeth Costello*, we find the protagonist before gates of what may or may not be heaven, where she faces an impasse: a bureaucrat explains that she must draft a statement of belief before she can be allowed to pass. As Coetzee imagines it, the afterlife is a mixture of Kafka's "Before the Law" and an episode of *This I Believe*, the iconic show hosted by CBS Radio's Edward R. Murrow in the early 1950s.[36] But Elizabeth balks, indicating that there appears to be something watered down in the request: "Belief. Is that all?" she asks. "Not a statement of faith?" (194). Being able to offer with conviction the phrases of the Nicene Creed, the *Shahadah*, or the *Shema*—broadly performed claims that might serve as basic measures of normative religiosity for Christians, Muslims, and Jews respectively—would satisfy the demands of the rhetorical frame, but for Elizabeth (as for Coetzee himself and for the other protagonists of his novels) traditional religions have more often been subjects of contestation than agents of consolation. "What if I do not believe," Elizabeth demands, "what if I am not a believer?"(194). The gatekeeper responds in a tone that veers between open hostility and doggedly tolerant multiculturalism: "We all believe. We are not cattle. For each of us there is something we believe. Write it down, what you believe. Put it in the statement" (194). If the responses on offer from the mainstream religions are anathema to her, so too are those of robust atheism, like a belief in material science or the value of exclusive humanism; as she says, "Unbelief is a belief. . . . Disbelief becomes a credo too" (201). Quoting Polish Nobel laureate Czeslaw Milosz (a prize that Coetzee would win the year after *Elizabeth Costello*'s publication), Elizabeth refuses the idea of belief on professional grounds and delivers the following testimony: "I am a writer, and what I write is what I hear. I am a secretary of the invisible. . . . A good secretary should have no beliefs" (199–200). After being pressed by a panel of elderly male judges, however ("the whole thing put together from clichés, with not a speck of originality" [197–98], she reflects of the "*excessively literary*" scenario [200; italics in original]), Elizabeth revises her testimony and tells a story instead about the life cycles of the frogs she saw in her childhood, frogs that survived the dry season by entombing themselves in mud until the rains returned: "I believe in those little frogs," she insists, "it is because of their indifference to me that I believe in them" (217).

The dilemma Elizabeth faces, as well as the stratagems and narrative gambits through which she attempts to extract herself from it, offers a parable of the oblique and vexed relationship with the legacy of religion that unfolds in the course of Coetzee's writing career. For Elizabeth Costello, the problem with belief as the primary category of ethical and religious engagement is much the same as the trouble with the "rights of desire" David Lurie claims in defense of his acts of sexual aggression in *Disgrace*: it places too much faith in a conception of the subject as a bearer of rights and in the idea of individual agency to accommodate Coetzee's world-renouncing theological investments. The "lesson" of Costello's frogs and her claim to "believe in what does not bother to believe in me" (218) mirrors her approach to the question of belief in God: "I suspect that God would not look kindly on such a presumption—presumption to intimacy. I prefer to let God be. As I hope He will let me be," she clarifies (205).[37] After she has given her testimony before the court and told the story of the frogs, Elizabeth reflects on her performance: "She gives the frogs a tap with her fingernail. The tone that comes back is clear, clear as a bell. She gives the word *belief* a tap. How does belief measure up? Will her test work with abstractions too?" (222; italics in original). In the final pages before the novel's postscript, Elizabeth asks the gatekeeper, "'What chance do I stand as a writer, with the special problems of a writer, the special fidelities?' *Fidelities*. Now that she has brought it out, she recognizes it as the word on which all hinges" (224; italics in original). The rather subtle shift from creedal questions of belief to the less self-centered registers of fidelity closes the circuit of erotic embodiment and ethical praxis evoked by the episode of erotic charity earlier in the novel. As I see it, the satisfaction Elizabeth finds in the plural, adjectival term for "the quality of being faithful; faithfulness, loyalty" (from the Latin *fidês* or faith; *OED*) has a great deal to do with the logic of self-abasement that determines the choices of Coetzee's other ascetic protagonists.

For Coetzee, attending to the dimensions of ascetic experience means grappling with a different set of questions: What are the standards for ethical encounters between sentient beings in a world characterized by unequal distributions of power? With naive faith in religious certainties or innate human goodness forever foreclosed by the experience of abandonment and a history of violence, as they are in Coetzee's prose, what registers can evoke our animal being on the one hand and, on the other, our lingering sense of and will to transcendence? And finally, if we set about to face the naked and specific realities of human injustice and violence, can we still summon a space of hope and prevent our empathy from becoming yet another mask for violence? In the preceding sections I have followed Coetzee's protagonists through various practices of self-abasement and self-mortification as they cultivate ascetic forms of selfhood, claiming a powerful relation between giving and abjection. Focusing on K as the nexus between the pain of the individual and the structures of exception at the level of the state and the text, I have shown how Coetzee presents his suffering protagonists not merely as victims but also as ascetic agents. One of the primary implications of my argument has been to challenge the notion that readers can derive a normative or deontological ethics from the tragic theology that subtends his fiction and with reference to which Coetzee's novels often answer questions of right action against the needs of human flourishing and find their most reliable measure of the good in sustained practices of self-abasement.

In *Disgrace*, Coetzee takes seriously the ascetic idea that penance and self-abasement may be a necessary corrective to the complicity of white South Africans in the injustices of apartheid. For Lucy, self-abasement and shame involve ceding legal title to her farm and becoming a tenant of and symbolic third wife to Petrus, her neighbor, but also the man who seems to have sanctioned her gang-rape. "It is humiliating," Lucy admits, "'but perhaps that is a good point to start from again. Perhaps that is what I must learn to accept. To start at ground level. With nothing. Not with nothing but. With nothing. No cards, no weapons, no property, no rights, no dignity.' 'Like a dog,' [David states]. 'Yes, like a dog'" (205). Ironically and tragically, of all the characters in Coetzee's dark novel, it is Lucy who speaks Xhosa, who "lives closer to the ground" than David and her other white neighbors, she whose affective affinities are least able to be rendered in propositional form, she who in her work and her social life most attempts to build and strengthen her human community. It is she who, in her determination "to be a good mother and a good person" (216), comes close to the ethos phrased most poignantly by Antjie Krog in *Country of My Skull*: "And some say it, most just live it. We are so utterly sorry. We are deeply ashamed and gripped with remorse. But hear us, we are from here. We will live it right—here—with you, for you" (99). But while the process of bearing witness to the TRC offers Krog a vocabulary and a platform for making this public claim not to her rights but to her being-in-common, Coetzee's Lucy offers readers no consolations of this sort, not even a claim to humanness.

In the novel's dénouement, the altered conditions and practices of David's daily life offer a vision of ascetic antihumanism: "The clinic, more than the boarding-house, becomes his home. In the bare compound behind the building he makes a nest of sorts, with a table and an old armchair . . . and a beach umbrella to keep off the worst of the sun. . . . Twice a day he feeds the animals; he cleans out their pens and occasionally talks to them; otherwise he reads or dozes or, when he has the premises to himself, picks out on Lucy's banjo the music he will give to Teresa Guiccioli" (211). In the aftermath of his public disgrace, David undergoes a pervasive transformation: from metropolitan professor in Cape Town to volunteer in a clinic euthanizing animals in the rural Eastern Cape; from cynical, rationalist, womanizer to an agent of his own sexual self-abasement. What makes Coetzee's fiction so grueling for his readers is the unsparingly ascetic visions of his protagonists, against which his readers will inevitably fall short. As is the case with David's illogical, noninstrumental, and fundamentally antihumanist pursuit of a kind of ascetic sainthood, Coetzee's novels leave us with "little enough, less than little: nothing," other than the hope—perhaps, the faith—that this *via negativa* will ultimately bear us toward a better life (202).

CHAPTER 3

Time and Terror

On February 24, 2007, 207 people froze in place at exactly 2:30 p.m. in the main concourse of New York City's Grand Central Station, holding their poses while bemused onlookers shot photos and moved around them until, after five minutes, the participants unfroze and went about their day as if nothing unusual had happened. The spectacle, staged and filmed by Charlie Todd's Improv Everywhere group, elicited cheers of amazement from dazzled onlookers. The subsequent video, a viral success on YouTube, artfully accelerates its footage to emphasize the juxtaposition between the streaming motion of commuters and the still figures of the participants, frozen in a variety of poses of their own invention (examining train timetables, tying a shoe, kissing) and has garnered more than thirty million hits.[1] As a flash mob stunt, "Frozen Grand Central" emphasizes the flow, pace, and free mobility of modern life with the roguish joy of dissonant humor against the backdrop of a homeland security apparatus within which Metro Transit Authority police and military personnel armed with assault rifles, body armor, and bomb-sniffing dogs are a ubiquitous presence in the nation's largest and busiest train station, a location recognized by many as a likely target for terrorist attack.[2]

"Without a story," Naomi Klein observes in *The Shock Doctrine*, "we are intensely vulnerable to those people who are ready to take advantage of the chaos for their own ends. As soon as we have a narrative that offers a perspective on the shocking events, we become reoriented, and the world begins to make sense" (580). The kind of story Klein has in mind, an orienting metafiction that exploits crisis to effect radical change, has certainly been part of the government's response to 9/11. As I argue here, the seminal speeches and policy documents of the post-9/11 era open new space for the exercise of sovereign power, in part by transforming the homogeneous empty time of modernity into the ruptured, multiple temporalities of the war on terror. For readers and writers of literary fiction, the subjective experience of temporality and nonlinear narrative have been the hallmark of avant-garde experimentalism since the innovations of Woolf, Proust, and Joyce. As such, the multiple temporalities of the war on terror pose something of a conundrum: If "destabilization" has long served the critical community as a synonym for subversion, what happens when rupture becomes the status quo?

The experience of temporal unsettlement has been of paramount importance to the narratives that have addressed the 9/11 attacks and contended with their unfolding legacy in the subsequent decade. For its victims and for the billions around the world who watched, paralyzed, as disaster unfolded on television, the coordinated 9/11 strikes came as a cataclysmic shock. Within hours on a beautiful but otherwise ordinary Tuesday morning, four commercial jetliners were hijacked, and the World Trade Center's signature towers and a large section of the Pentagon, symbols of America's economic and military might, were reduced to smoking rubble. Whatever the attacks signify—the end of a brief era of optimistic globalism, a bold retaliation against an ungodly global hegemon, a national catastrophe, or an apocalypse outside ordinary time—one of the most pervasive effects of 9/11 has been the rise of a phenomenon I call *chronomania*: an obsession with time and a concomitant disruption of temporal experience that characterizes representations of the attacks and their aftermath across a rapidly expanding archive.

9/11 has given rise to a wide range of formal experimentation in prose fiction, a literary mode characterized by an acute awareness of the way the narrative arrangement of events undergirds the experience of time as a chronological trajectory or inflects the subjective experience of asynchrony. French novelist Frédéric Beigbeder titles the chapters of *Windows on the World* (2003) with digital clock readouts that track the minutes between 8:30 a.m., just before American Airlines Flight 11 crashed into the North Tower, and the time of its collapse at 10:29 a.m. Ian McEwan condenses the uncertainties of life after 9/11 in the brief temporal exposure of *Saturday* (2005), which chronicles twenty-four hours in the life of Henry Perowne on a day interrupted by a plane in flames and a violent encounter with a stranger. In the final pages of *Extremely Loud and Incredibly Close* (2005), Jonathan Safran Foer transforms the novel into a fantasy of time reversal by performatively incorporating the protagonist's backwards flip-book into the novel to create the kinetographic impression that the bodies photographed falling from the World Trade Center are, in fact, rising into the safety of the towers. Jess Walter's *The Zero* (2006) focalizes an amnesiac whose narrative jumps like "smooth skipping stones . . . bounding across the surfaces of time" in an extended metaphor for the disjunctions of the post-9/11 cultural condition (163). In the dramatic monologue of Mohsin Hamid's *The Reluctant Fundamentalist* (2007), the narrator reflects on how 9/11 altered temporality: "I had always thought of America as a nation that looked forward," the narrator intones; "for the first time I was struck by its determination to look *back*" (115). Don DeLillo's *Falling Man* (2007) stages anachronic leaps forward and backward in time as well as between central characters, all of whom experience temporality in discrepant and ultimately irreconcilable ways. In these and other narratives, 9/11 fictions inscribe the attacks within the matrix of narrative temporality and stage violence as a form of temporal injury or wounding.

In this chapter, I explore how novels by McEwan, Walter, and DeLillo, as well as a range of official narratives—among them *The 9/11 Commission Report*, President George W. Bush's address on September 20, the Quadrennial Defense Review of 2001 conducted by Defense Secretary Donald Rumsfeld, and the National Security Strategy (NSS) of 2002—frame 9/11 as a temporal event and cast the problem of understanding and responding to the attacks in terms of a clash between multiple conceptions of time. A diverse lexicon of temporal rupture and asynchrony emerged in the days and months following the attacks, beginning with the spontaneous and enduring use of "September 11" or, rendered numerically in the American idiom I use here, "9/11" to name the catastrophe. This name-date, torn out of calendrical history with the elimination of its referent year, signals the ambivalence of a temporal wound whose naming inscribes both annual recurrence and singularity.[3] Many of the early responses to September 11 in the Anglophone media compensated for the sudden collapse of geographic distance that had long separated the United States from its enemies by emphasizing the temporal distance between the "medieval," "barbarous," and "fundamentalist" perpetrators of the attacks and the modernity of the victims. Terms like *ground zero*, *preemptive war*, and even the nostalgically inflected *homeland* in *homeland security* constitute a new lexicon freighted with temporal intensities that both camouflage and serve as justification for some of the most sweeping changes to military strategy and systematic expansions to state sovereignty effected since the Second World War. The dichotomies of the war on terror depend in large part on dualistic notions of cultural conflict between Western modernity and the archaic forces of a fundamentalist Islam, as cultural critics Edward Said, Judith Butler, Bruce Holsinger, and others have argued.[4]

Neomedievalist rhetoric dusts off old Orientalist tactics to police the boundaries between "us" and "them," in part by denying what anthropologist Johannes Fabian in *Time and the Other* describes as the "coevalness" of the two parties in question. The medievalization of Islam—or, for that matter, of American foreign policy, as with President Bush's telling use of the term *crusade* as a synonym for the war on terror—is not, however, my primary subject here. Indeed, the denial of coevalness between "Islam" and "the West" serves in part to obscure the more complex temporal logic of the war on terror. In even the most conspicuously secularist 9/11 narratives—like McEwan's novel and *The 9/11 Commission Report*—not only does 9/11 chronomania facilitate vast temporal compressions, giving rise to the rhetoric of neomedievalism, it is also inflected by the instability and repetitions of trauma, the messianic and redemptive *telos* of resurgent nationalism, and the proleptic temporality of preemption.

"TIME TO GO SHOPPING"

McEwan's website (www.ianmcewan.com) offers, among other things, the recipe for the fish stew Henry Perowne prepares for his family's evening dinner in *Saturday*, complete with suggested variations for chefs lacking either Perowne's proficiency in the kitchen or his well-provisioned fishmonger. The proviso with which the recipe begins is particularly salient: "Where quantities are not stated," McEwan/Perowne offers sagely, "trust your instincts or desires" ("Henry Perowne's Fish Stew"). This advice, redolent with autoerotic, self-gratifying sensuality, says much about Perowne's temperament, but it significantly complicates his assertive secularity. Being told to trust our instincts and follow our desires bespeaks an epicurean hedonism linked to neither the main line of secular rationality nor any of the Abrahamic theologies.[5] Neither the incremental progress of scientific inquiry nor the well-lived life in Western religious traditions can be achieved according to this recipe. However, the attitude toward creatural life encapsulated by this ad hoc aphorism constitutes an important part of what destabilizes Perowne's subjectivity as a secular hero and complicates *Saturday*'s use of temporal form.

McEwan's public identification as an atheist (a self-understanding he shares with his protagonist), the novel's normative valorization of material science as the highest human achievement, and its systematic exploration of terrorism in the post-9/11 world compose a surprisingly unstable secular matrix.[6] McEwan's novel catalogs complex entanglements and cross-pressures that undermine the dyad of personal atheism and political secularism to which both Perowne and McEwan are openly committed. Reading against the grain of the novel's critical reception and authorial intent, I suggest that the rationalist secularism with which McEwan is commonly aligned inadequately describes the nexus of temporal and somatic practices at work in his own novel.

McEwan has been writing about 9/11 systemically and boldly since September 12, 2001, when he published "Beyond Belief," an article that meditates on the immediate aftermath of the attacks. Of 9/11, McEwan writes, "We knew we were living through a time that we would never be able to forget. We also knew, though it was too soon to wonder how or why, that the world would never be the same. We knew only that it would be worse." As I suggest here, McEwan's novels and essays explore his sense that the difference between the way the world was and the way it is or will be has a lot to do with secular conceptions of time. In *Saturday*, Perowne awakens at 3:40 a.m. on February 15, 2003, firmly embedded in this post-9/11 world, primed to see a burning plane, which he glimpses out his London window, as the result of a terrorist attack. For eighteen months he, together with "half the planet," has "watched . . . and watched again . . . the unseen captives driven through the sky to the slaughter" (15). "Airliners," Perowne reflects, "look different in the sky these days, predatory or doomed" (15).

McEwan's novel chronicles twenty-four hours in the life of a successful neurosurgeon, Perowne, planning on that secular Sabbath to play a game of squash and make a fish stew for a family gathering. His plan is interrupted when a car accident leads to an altercation with a street tough named Baxter who later holds the Perowne family hostage at knifepoint. As McEwan intends, the novel's free indirect narration, urban peripatetic journey, and single-day time span evoke Woolf's *Mrs. Dalloway*, while Perowne (effortlessly capable, sexually satisfied, and ultimately triumphant) bears a greater resemblance to Homer's Odysseus than to Joyce's Leopold Bloom.[7] Over the course of his Saturday, readers learn much about Perowne's creedal secularism. On numerous occasions the novel's third-person narrative doubles back in diagetic flashbacks in order to clarify the nuances of his atheist worldview. After he sees a plane flying toward Heathrow in flames, he muses that those "inclined to religious feeling" might appeal to "supernatural explanations" in order to explain the coincidence of his having risen and walked to the window at just that moment. Perowne, however, sees this tendency as evidence of human ignorance and narcissism, "the primitive thinking of the supernaturally inclined" (16). For Perowne, religiosity "belongs on a spectrum at whose far end, rearing like an abandoned temple, lies psychosis" (17). Later in the novel, much of what he sees in the city—like the protest against the Iraq War in London on September 15, 2003—continues to steer his thoughts in the direction of religion. When Perowne sees "three figures in black burkhas emerge from the taxi . . . he can't help his distaste, it's visceral" (127). The narrator takes pains to explain that Perowne's reaction is inspired not by racism but by a universal humanism that rejects the burkha as a symbol of the oppression of women and scorns any attempt to valorize religious dress as a symptom of the political correctness retailed by "cheerful pessimists from [his daughter] Daisy's college," a form of piety he finds particularly offensive (124).

In place of religion, Perowne maintains a thoroughgoing atheism grounded in scientific, materialist positivism. In a fugue on Philip Larkin's "If I were called in / To construct a religion / I should make use of water," Perowne decides that "he'd make use of evolution" (54). Indeed, while in a semiconscious state between waking and sleeping he thinks he hears Darwin's famous line "There is grandeur in this view of life" in the sounds of his wife's morning rituals.[8] McEwan doesn't want the reference to be confused or overly opaque: Perowne was reading a biography of Darwin in the bath the night before. Perowne's material and professional success supports his implacable belief in progress, a belief that he juxtaposes with what he sees as the automatic liberalism of an academy whose "young lecturers . . . like to dramatize modern life as a sequence of calamities" (77). "This is an age of wondrous machines," Perowne maintains, and he quotes from Nobel Prize–winning scientist and noted atheist Peter Medawar that "to deride the hopes of progress is the ultimate fatuity, the last word in poverty of spirit and meanness of mind" (77). The only positive spin Perowne can give to the history of religion when he thinks about it is to suggest that the ability to conceive of the transcendent (i.e., to invent religion) confirms the genius of the human imagination. The practice of medicine, meanwhile, confirms his belief in the ultimate materiality of the universe: "A man who attempts to ease the miseries of ailing minds by repairing brains is bound to respect the material world, its limits, and what it can sustain. . . . The supernatural was the recourse of an insufficient imagination" (66). While he respects the longing for transcendence, Perowne (and, I believe, McEwan) values the impulse only to the extent that it serves as a catalyst for investigation of the material, immanent world. There is a kind of Nietzschean moral failure, to Perowne's mind, in religious worldviews, an attitude that places him securely in the camp of ideological secularists like Christopher Hitchens, Sam Harris, Daniel Dennett, and Richard Dawkins.

In recent years, McEwan has been among the writers most commonly aligned with the so-called new atheism of thinkers like Dawkins and Hitchens.[9] Elaborating on his views on the role of religion in the public sphere in an interview for PBS's "Faith and Doubt at Ground Zero," McEwan encourages this comparison, calling religion a "morally neutral force" but asserting a strong commitment to political secularism: "People must be free to worship all the gods they want, but it's only the secular spirit that will guarantee that freedom." Friends with McEwan since the 1980s, Hitchens sees *Saturday* as a vehicle for atheist evangelism, oddly praising the novel in the *Atlantic* as an encomium to reason despite its emphasis on instinct.

Neither a day of the formal workweek nor the day of rest in the Anglican afterlife of British society, Saturday, for Perowne, is a day consecrated to a consumerist culture. Celebrating his Saturday binds atheist rationalism to free market economics: "The secular authority, indifferent to the babble of various gods, will guarantee religious freedoms. They should flourish. It's time to go shopping" (126). The arrogantly indifferent tone of dismissal in the "babble of various gods" and the vaguely self-deprecating humor with which Perowne advocates consumerism as a viable alternative to religious culture develop into a more robust and pragmatic claim. "It isn't rationalism that will overcome the religious zealots," Perowne speculates, "but ordinary shopping and all that it entails—jobs for a start, and peace . . . the promises of appetites sated in this world, not the next. Rather shop than pray" (127).

Perowne's creedal and political secularity, conceptually buttressed by a view of religion as private belief, stands in uneasy tension with his somatic practices, however. Despite Perowne's professed philosophical commitments, in truth he values action over introspection and celebrates split-second certainty over rational reflection. In this way, the novel and its protagonist offer alternatives to the rationalist ontology and deliberative forms of public reason to which Perowne and McEwan pledge their allegiance. *Saturday*'s "timeless" present can be seen in a variety of intuitionist moments, where the novel represents and asserts the value of conditioned responses, careful training, and a cool head under pressure. Whether the circumstance in question is a squash game, a jazz riff, or a challenging neurosurgery, for Perowne, "Decisions are all" (21). Perowne is a man profoundly at home in his own body. McEwan establishes Perowne's somatic aptitudes and confidence systematically, beginning with the novel's first line, when Perowne "wakes to find himself already in motion. . . . The movement is easy, and pleasurable in his limbs, and his back and legs feel unusually strong" (1). Early morning sex with his wife comes with "effortless seduction. . . . His wish come true, not a finger lifted, the envy of gods and despots" (52). He moves with what the narrator describes as "almost comic facility" (2), accomplishing everything from repairing aneurysms to cooking fish stew with efficient technical mastery and an admittedly "egotistical joy in his own skills" (23). He even drives with "unconscious expertise" (81).

The novel's celebration of intuitionism reaches its zenith when a car accident ignites an altercation between Perowne and the three men he has just seen hurrying out of a lap-dancing club. His primary adversary turns out to be a "fidgety, small-faced young man . . . [with a] general simian air," who gives his name only as Baxter (88). When, following the predetermined codes of an "urban drama" scripted by "a century of movies and a half a century of television," Baxter explodes into violence, Perowne lets his physical intuitions guide his actions while another part of his mind engages in scientific diagnosis (86). In the time it takes Baxter to throw his first punch, the "droning, pedestrian diagnostician" in Perowne's mind "notes [Baxter's] poor self-control, emotional liability, explosive temper, suggestive of reduced levels of GABA among the appropriate binding sites on striatal neurons" (92). After he has been punched once and shoved against a door in preparation for a more thorough beating, there is a brief pause; Perowne concludes that "he has, he reckons, a few seconds left" to defend himself before Baxter assaults him again (94). In these moments, in the very instant that his assailant "is drawing back his arm to strike," Perowne connects an array of observations about his assailant—moody outbursts, spasmodic movements—into a snap diagnosis of Huntington's disease, knowledge that he then uses to shift the power dynamic in his favor (94). "Your father had it. Now you've got it too," he pronounces coldly in an act he later intellectualizes as a form of "shameless blackmail" (95). Perowne's ploy works, allowing him to shift the scene from one in which he is the intended victim of retributive violence to one in which his assailant becomes his patient. The scene simultaneously asserts the power of medical science, one of the secular achievements celebrated by both protagonist and narrator, and affirms and valorizes somatic confidence and intuitionist judgments over rational reflection.

Elsewhere in the novel, the anachrony of memory threatens to shatter the controlled temporality of both progressive history and the atemporal presentism evinced by Perowne's instinctual responses. When Perowne utters the word *crash*, a word "trailing memories of the night as well as the morning," during a conversation between points in his squash game, the word's associative connections trigger an involuntary eruption of memories: "Everything that's happened to him recently occurs to him at once. He's no longer in the present. . . . He occupies the wrong time coordinates, or he's in them all at once" (107). The blows to his grasp of the present prove symbolically fatal: now that his concentration is broken, his opponent springs in "for the kill shot" (107). As Perowne operates on Baxter later in the novel, time again becomes a blur of attention and action: "Well over an hour has passed," Perowne realizes, of which he has not been aware (261). "For the past two hours he's been in a dream of absorption that has dissolved all sense of time, and all awareness of the other parts of his life. Even his awareness of his own existence has vanished. He's been delivered into a pure present, free of the weight of the past or any anxieties about the future. . . . It's a little like sex," he reflects (266).

By valuing the sensuous present and sinking happily into semiconscious somatic habits, Perowne displays a strong preference for living life in what William James would call the "specious present" rather than the *tensed* world of past, present, and future, or any chronometric world, for that matter.[10] According to Perowne, James "had the knack of fixing on the surprising commonplace—and in Perowne's humble view, wrote a better-honed prose than the fussy brother" (56). Perowne is thinking about chapter 9, "The Stream of Thought," in James's 1890 opus *The Principles of Psychology*, when he delivers this erudite lecture on James. Following McEwan's lead, readers find that later in that work, in his chapter "The Perception of Time," James explores the philosophical concept of the specious present: "*The original paragon and prototype of all conceived times is the specious present, the short duration of which we are immediately and incessantly sensible*" (631; italics in original). James's hermeneutic is Perowne's highest and best achievement.

When Baxter enters Perowne's home and threatens to kill his wife and rape his daughter, Perowne plunges into James's "specious present," a sense of expanded awareness of the shortest durations and smallest movements, while the novel, in contrast, invites the reader to draw connections between this terrifying event and acts of international terrorism. Baxter's intrusion exposes the fragile aristocratic safety that undergirds the Perowne family's affluent lifestyle, with their Fitzroy Square home and its triple locks and digital alarms, just as the terrorist attacks on New York and London erased the boundary between zones of conflict abroad and domestic tranquillity. It is easy to see Baxter's invasion as a substitution for the violence that does not take place within the representational frame of the novel, namely the 9/11 attacks and the Second Gulf War. While the novel invites this analogy—indeed, Perowne himself is tempted to understand his suffering in terms of the sudden conjunction of home front and war front—such thinking exemplifies the kind of spurious readings of which the novel is systematically critical. There is simply no evidence on which to make any causal claims that would substantiate an analogy between Baxter's assault and Islamist extremism or the war on terror, though many strong readers have made this mistake.[11] McEwan's novel individualizes terror but also pathologizes it: Baxter's violent outbursts arise not out of dissatisfactions with the class divisions plaguing contemporary British society but out of an incurable disease. Thus, if we were to follow this false analogy to its necessary end, the causes of Islamist terrorism would rest, finally, in incurable genetic pathology. Instead, I suggest that we see the desire to read Baxter's intrusion as an allegory of global terrorism as precisely what Perowne's "psychiatric colleagues call a problem, or an idea, of reference," something he identifies as a weakness at the beginning of the novel (16). To subscribe to this interpretation would mean falling victim to one of the chief narcissisms of the post-9/11 world: the notion that we live in an unbounded, ever-present time of terror.[12] We are displaying, in Perowne's derisive terms, the weakness of a religious mode of thinking characterized by "an excess of the subjective, the ordering of the world in line with your needs" (16–17).

I have demonstrated how in *Saturday* identitarian secularism depends upon an understanding of historical time that works against the apparent time dilation experienced in moments of instinctual response. Before he returns to his bed after the long arc of his day, Perowne's sense of temporality enlarges in a second meditation by the window at which the day began. As he thinks of the future, he considers the perspective of a man one hundred years earlier, standing at the same window in February 1903, almost "envying this Edwardian gent all he didn't yet know" (286). Perowne's reflections on political violence conflate the secular despotisms of Hitler, Stalin, and Mao with the groundswell of Islamist radicalism of the late twentieth and early twenty-first centuries: "Here they are again," he muses, "utopianists, zealous men certain of the path to the ideal social order . . . totalitarians in different forms, still scattered and weak, but growing, and angry, and thirsty for another mass killing" (286). By the end of the novel, however, Perowne's atheist humanism loses its claim as a rational intellectual project and seems instead to be afloat on an island of atemporal corporeality.

PLOTTING TIME

For Don DeLillo, the challenge of responding to the events of 9/11 has less to do with making the continuum of history explode than with putting it back together again. In a short, incandescent essay published in *Harper's* and the *Guardian* in December 2001, "In the Ruins of the Future: Reflections on Terror and Loss in the Shadow of September," DeLillo confronts us with a twofold weaponization of plot that seems to infect and disable his subsequent attempts at storymaking. "Terror's response," DeLillo suggests, to "the power of American culture to penetrate every wall, home, life and mind" "is a narrative . . . that has been developing over years, only now becoming inescapable. . . . Our world, parts of our world, have crumbled into theirs, which means we are living in a place of danger and rage" (33). The power of the terrorist, "his edge, his strength," DeLillo adds, inheres in the logic of his narrative, which occludes the "defenseless human at the end of his gaze" behind the veil of his "vision of judgment and devastation" (34). "Plots reduce the world," DeLillo writes, and the aspiring terrorist living in Florida, attending flight schools in preparation for the plane attack, "builds a plot around his anger and our indifference" (34). Writing fictions has suddenly become implicated, for DeLillo, with the terrorist "plot" itself and with the Manichean fictions of vengeance and injury that spawn the war on terror.

As DeLillo seems to tell it in the opening paragraphs of "In the Ruins," secular narratives of economic progress and boundless futurity contrast with the anachronistic desires of "the terrorists of September 11 [who] want to bring back the past" (34). In a series of binary juxtapositions, "In the Ruins" contrasts Western culture, overtly coded as secular, scientific, and capitalist, against Islam as its premodern ideological antithesis: "The future has yielded, for now, to medieval expedience, to the old slow furies of cut-throat religion. Kill the enemy and pluck out his heart" (37). After the 9/11 attacks, DeLillo observes, "we have fallen back in time and space" (38)—a fall symbolized by the collapse of the North Tower's "huge antenna falling out of the sky, straight down, blunt end first, like an arrow moving backwards in time" (39). DeLillo's essay juxtaposes the retrograde temporality of "a global theocratic state . . . so obsolete it must depend on suicidal fervor to gain its aims" (40) with "our" future-oriented culture in which "the dramatic climb of the Dow and the speed of the internet summoned us all to live permanently in the future, in the utopian glow of cyber-capital" (33). Future and past, utopia and dystopia: in these assertions of temporal and ethical asymmetry, DeLillo performs only to sabotage some of the most prevalent tropes circulating in the American cultural imaginary in, as he puts it, "the shadow of September." DeLillo and McEwan are doing similar things here—crafting narratives that appear to fulfill prevalent post-9/11 stereotypes and fantasies and then undermining and disproving them. Chief among the dichotomies DeLillo marshals is the notion of Islam's fundamental anachronism. As Judith Butler notes in her discussion of developmental narratives of secularization, "Islam is conceived as not of *this* time or *our* time, but *another* time, one that only anachronistically emerged in this time" (6; italics in original). DeLillo acknowledges that "the sense of disarticulation we hear in the term 'Us and Them' has never been so striking" (34). As Edward Said put it only days after the tragedy, "'Islam' and 'The West' are simply inadequate banners" in a time when "rational understanding of the situation is what is needed . . . not more drum-beating" ("Islam"). But precisely because such firm bifurcations and their reductions end "in the rubble," DeLillo argues that "it is left to us to create the counter-narrative" (34).

For DeLillo, these counternarratives are epitomized by "the smaller objects and more marginal stories in the sifted ruins of the day," such as ephemeral 9/11 memorials, fragmentary images, and literary fictions in which "the writer tries to give memory, tenderness, and meaning to all that howling space" (39). "In the Ruins," an early rehearsal of material that he would develop into his novel *Falling Man* by 2008, serves as one such counternarrative; in a story fragment embedded amid his attempts to historicize the conditions leading up to 9/11, DeLillo's microfiction splices vivid descriptions of one couple's story into the fabric of his argument. The detailed particulars of Lower Manhattan in the aftermath of 9/11 as seen through their eyes complicate and destabilize the teleological energy of the essay's binary juxtapositions, forcing readers to the uncomfortable realization that the desire to "kill the enemy and pluck out his heart" rests equally with the perpetrators of mass-murder suicide as with those for whom thoughts of vengeance preceded those of mourning or self-critical analysis (34). DeLillo "contrasts al Qaeda with America," as Linda Kauffman argues, "but he deconstructs the very dichotomies others reinforce" ("Wake of Terror" 356). In a final analeptic vignette, the narrator describes how "one month earlier" he saw a Muslim woman, "young and slender, in a bright silk headscarf," praying on the sidewalk of Canal Street, "partly concealed by a couple of vendors' carts" (DeLillo "In the Ruins" 40). In the aftermath of 9/11, belatedly, as it were, the image comes to signify for the speaker a profound unity that restores the coevalness of religious experience and techno-capitalism:

> I looked at her in prayer and it was clearer to me than ever, the daily sweeping taken-for-granted greatness of New York. The city will accommodate every language, ritual, belief and opinion. In the rolls of the dead of September 11, all these vital differences were surrendered to the impact and flash. During the hadj, the annual pilgrimage to Mecca, the faithful must eliminate every sign of status, income and nationality, the men wearing identical strips of seamless white cloth, the women with covered heads, all recalling in prayer their fellowship with the dead. Allahu akbar. God is great. (40)

Hadj and metropolis, death and prayer, Arabic and English—in the plurality that characterizes DeLillo's New York, religiosity renders legible the palimpsestic subjectivity of a world in which layered identities evince multiple forms of temporal and spatial meaning. As such, religious practices can foster the productive dissonance emergent in the multiple narratives and disparate geographies of 9/11 that might slow the inexorable drumbeat of war.

"The writer wants to understand what this day has done to us," DeLillo reflects, but is plagued by uncertainty: "Is it too soon? We seem pressed for time, all of us. Time is scarcer now. There is a sense of compression, plans made hurriedly, time forced and distorted" (39). The essential precondition for attaining such an understanding, DeLillo imagines, would be a suspension of plot that dilated the time between event and narrative resolution, opening a space in which to perform the work of mourning and reflect upon the complex history beneath the media spectacle. In his analysis of DeLillo's essay, Marco Abel explains this process as a valorization of deferral through which "literature and film can respond to the contemporary moment . . . [by] pausing in the space in which images are made to circulate, thus provoking a suspension of judgment" (248). It is this moment of suspension, I argue, that we see literalized in the performance art of the Falling Man.

Two images constitute the imaginative poles of Don DeLillo's temporal iconography in *Falling Man*. First, and most obviously, the public spectacle of those who chose to jump from the Twin Towers on 9/11—indelible images of men and women frozen in mid-fall by photographs and explored in the performance art of DeLillo's eponymous Falling Man.[13] DeLillo's second spatialization of temporal form, one more cryptic in meaning and unexamined by critics, is the scene of the evacuation through the stairwells, a long, winding descent shared by those who survived the attacks. The descent of the stairs connects protagonist Keith Neudecker and a black woman named Florence Givens.[14] Keith, a thirty-nine-year-old lawyer working for a real estate firm with offices high in the North Tower, staggers out of the building and down the streets of Lower Manhattan on the first page of DeLillo's novel, accompanied by the sound of the South Tower's collapse. He is carrying a briefcase not his own, one that he subsequently discovers belongs to a woman named Florence Givens As she describes it at the beginning of her affair with Keith, on the stairs "she was dazed and had no sense of time. . . . Times they had to walk blind, smoke so thick, hand on the shoulder of the person in front" (55). Memories of the descent evoke Florence's dislocation and the uncompleted process of her grief, but they lack the spectacular quality of the mass-mediated images of planes hitting the towers, men and women jumping, and towers coming down: "I feel like I'm still on the stairs," she confesses to Keith, "If I live to be a hundred I'll still be on the stairs. It took so long it was almost normal in a way" (57). The experience of the hypnotic descent (more an orderly march than a chaos of smoke and confusion) of seventy-nine stories below the impact zone is a recurrent subject in the narratives recounted by survivors. In DeLillo's novel, the stairs signify a temporal abyss, a flow outside the normal flow of time, another version of the frozen eternity that structures the Falling Man's performance art with its suspended moment of arrested time.

So important was the experience of the stairs to survivors that the National September 11 Memorial at the World Trade Center site has made a memorial of them. Museum visitors will encounter stairs and enact their passage in the final exhibit of the memorial, where they will walk up a long and irregular staircase alongside the archaeologically excavated remains of the "Survivor's Stairs," the staircase that led from the North Tower ("That was him coming down, the north tower," Keith reflects in *Falling Man*) and Austin Tobin Plaza down to Vesey Street. Had he been a real person, Keith might well have, like many hundreds of others, descended these stairs on his instinctual flight north, toward the home he once shared with his estranged wife, Lianne. According to the memorial's website, the "stairway served as a vital route to safety for many people," and the designers hope that reinstalling the stairs in the National September 11 Memorial will convey a "powerful reference to the survivors' story" (National September 11 Memorial). Long after construction had commenced on the new World Trade Center towers, the "Survivors' Stairs" stood, a spectral but quite cherished remnant of the former buildings. In the memorial, according to director Alice Greenwald, passing the stairs will be a "cer emony" that "reinforces a fundamental cultural message: We all live in a post-9/11 world and, in that sense, every one of us is a 9/11 survivor" (Dunlap).

Describing the evacuation of the towers, in which tens of thousands descended the emergency stairwells, the *9/11 Commission Report* focuses on the firefighters, men who climbed, "passing a steady and heavy stream of descending civilians. Firemen were impressed with the composure and total lack of panic shown by almost all civilians. Many civilians were in awe of the firefighters" (299). For DeLillo's Keith and Florence, their separate but simultaneous experience of the descent of the stairs "was their pitch of delirium, the dazed reality they'd shared in the stairwells, the deep shafts of spiraling men and women" (91). When Florence dances for Keith during one of their trysts, she echoes this structure as she, dervishlike, "danced in slow motion for a time . . . nearly trancelike, and began to whirl in place, ever slower, facing him now, mouth open, eyes coming open" (93). Reflecting on his encounters with Florence, Keith emphasizes the temporal similarity of their shared moments and the descent of the stairs; both are "another kind of eternity, the stillness in her face and body, outside time" (157). "The timeless drift of the long spiral down" experienced by Keith and Florence symbolizes the mode of suspension prior to ethical judgment or agential action that the novel attempts to reclaim as a site of resistance to the teleological war on terror.

The novel's form echoes this spiraling pattern, beginning with the collapse of the South Tower (at approximately 10:00 a.m.) and ending with the moment of the first plane's impact seventy-five minutes before. With reference to the fixed point of the unnumbered "day of the planes," the episodes in DeLillo's novel extend analeptically and proleptically backwards and forwards in time. The episodes themselves divulge the identities of their focal characters and their temporal locations with reference to the chronological order of events only haltingly; to read the novel one must work to reconstitute a cogent sense of character and action from inconclusive pronouns, a form of textual difficulty that rewards rereading. In fact, "plot"—the pattern of events across time—becomes the problem the novel attempts to overcome.

Against the central role performed by chronological form and forensic accuracy in stabilizing official responses to events, *Falling Man* attempts to tell the story of 9/11 in a way that short-circuits the process of reorientation, refusing to make a single message or plot cohere from a complex world.[15] DeLillo has left enough markers for careful readers to construct a temporal sequence out of the novel's nonlinear narrative, but only vague patterns cohere from the mise-en-scène of characters and events that connect through the invisible transfer point of 9/11.[16] A similar logic informs DeLillo's scrupulous avoidance of the name "September 11," which never appears in the text, freeing the disaster to float in an empty, timeless state of repetition. In its rejection of plot, in its resistance not just to linear sequencing but also to the novelistic narrative mode, the novel works against the forms of temporal cohesion DeLillo associates, problematically, with terrorism itself.

Though they constitute a relatively small percentage of *Falling Man*'s overall word count, several members of the hijacking team serve as counterfocalizers to Keith's narrative trajectory. DeLillo's contrapuntal narrative strategy juxtaposes Hammad and Amir's narratives with those of Keith and Lianne in a structure similar to that of the *9/11 Commission Report*, in which the perpetrators vie with victims and emergency workers for narrative time. For Hammad, the planes plot offers a directionality to time, a telos: "The time is coming" (82). DeLillo combats the commonplace portrayal of terrorists as medieval, substituting the backward-looking temporality of "fundamentalism" for a vision of professionalized, modern hijackers who see themselves in terms of a "progressive" historical narrative. Plot drew them together more tightly than ever. Plot closed the world to the slenderest line of sight, where everything converges to a point" (174).

The idea that there is an ethical value in understanding the stories of others has long been integral to justifying the social function of literature within the academy and literary culture more broadly. In his reflections on the relationship between narrative and ethics in *Tests of Time*, novelist and literary critic William Gass argues that the restorative power of stories inheres in a structural homology between storytelling and cognition: "Stories break up the natural continuum of life into events," he writes; they "arrange these segments in a temporal sequence, in order to suggest that whatever happens earlier is responsible for what happens later" (5). In "Terror: A Speech after 9/11," Gayatri Spivak brings her long-standing project of an ethics of alterity to bear upon the specifics of mass murder suicide attacks. She writes, "I believe that we must be able to imagine our opponent as a human being, and to understand the significance of his or her action. It is in this belief . . . that I have tried to imagine what message it [mass murder suicide attacks] might contain" (93). It is precisely this empathic transposition that DeLillo attempts to achieve through his narrative focalization on Hammid and Amir in *Falling Man*. Speculating on empathy in "In the Ruins," DeLillo asks, "Does the sight of a woman pushing her stroller soften the man to her humanity and vulnerability, and her child's as well, and all the people he is here to kill?" The answer, he asserts, is a resounding no: "He does not see her" (2).

By asserting the radical asymmetry between plotting and seeing, DeLillo revises Spivak's thesis, reminding readers that neither literature nor the empathic imagination performed in literary reading will prevent terrorist acts. Literature will not make terrorists "feel" the plight of victims, which is almost exactly the role played by literature in McEwan's *Saturday* when the power of poetry—or, more specifically, of Matthew Arnold's *Dover Beach* recited by a pregnant, naked young woman—interrupts Baxter's violent trajectory.[17] In *Falling Man* and "In the Ruins," the problem with plot is temporal both in nature and in its symptoms. These cross-pressures are enacted most vividly in the narrative traversal or exchange of focalization between Hammad on American Airlines Flight 11 and Keith in the North Tower, which occurs in a subordinate clause of the novel's final section. Two worlds—victim and perpetrator, terrorist and citizen—kept rigorously separated come together and traverse one another in DeLillo's description of impact: "A bottle fell off the counter in the galley. . . . He watched it spin more quickly and then skitter across the floor an instant before the aircraft struck the tower, heat, then fuel, then fire, and a blast wave passed through the structure that sent Keith Neudecker out of his chair and into a wall" (239).

The frozen temporality of the Falling Man, meanwhile, evinces a desire to freeze or escape time and plot; his performance art literalizes the temporal disruption and unexpected return of traumatic experience. Against and through these ruptures, DeLillo's novel experiments with religiously coded rituals as characters in the novel engage in various acts of ritualistic self-binding as self-preservation with discrepant experiences of 9/11. Keith and Lianne's son, Justin, for instance, is in a state of protracted denial: he watches the skies for "Bill Lawton" (bin Laden) and keeps collections of pencils. Lianne interprets the collection socioeconomically: "It was awful in a way, all these fragments of status washing up in some little kid's room" (38). More importantly, however, the pencils signify interrupted writing and the rituals that infuse every aspect of life for the Neudecker family: Justin sharpening the pencils would "crank and blow, crank and blow, a ritual more thorough and righteous than the formal signing of some document of state by eleven men with medals" (39). Justin's language rituals include his attempt, beginning with a school game, to speak only in monosyllables. Keith thinks of his son's linguistic self-binding as evolving from "an instructive form of play" into a "solemn obstinacy, nearly ritualistic" (160). Justin's verbal asceticism contrasts sharply with Florence's logorrhea: "She talked about the tower, going over it again . . . in minute and dullest detail" (90). Lianne takes up churchgoing, attending Catholic masses with regularity; she also runs, thinking of "long-distance running as spiritual effort" (233).

Rituals of self-binding unite the characters in obsessive, repetitive behavior. Keith Neudecker's gambling is thus an attempt to escape time in every "new deck" of cards. The Las Vegas hotels he frequents day and night are interchangeable, with oxygen-enriched air and curtained windows: "Days fade, nights drag on, check-and-raise, wake-and-sleep" (226). Similarly, the spectacle-spaces of the Las Vegas Strip and the large poker tournaments he attends there provide a "crucial anonymity," divested of narrative and imbued with only a "mingling of countless lives that had no stories attached" (204). In forsaking his career as an attorney in New York for that of a poker player in Las Vegas, Keith flees global capitalism's symbolic epicenter for its fantasy simulacrum; in a similar way, Keith plays poker for the chips themselves, rather than for the money they supposedly represent. The iterative nature of poker, particularly the games of five-card stud and five-card draw, with their restricted range of game play, highlights the importance of form over content.[18] These rituals, like the spiraling motion of descending the stairs and the novel's circular form, point to a curative suspension beyond secular time. The novel spirals back to its point of origin in its final pages, but the repetition encodes difference. In his memory, Keith makes the descent of the stairs into an image of pilgrimage, evoking the hadj from "In the Ruins": "They walked down," Keith reflects in the novel's final vignette, "thousands, and he was in there with them. He walked in a long sleep, one step and then the next" (243).

KAIROTIC GOVERNMENTALITY

Under its congressional mandate to "examine and report upon the facts and causes relating to the terrorist attacks . . . [and] make a full and complete accounting of the[ir] circumstances," the *Final Report of the National Commission on Terrorist Attacks upon the United States*, better known as the *9/11 Commission Report*, begins with a narrative time line. Using the simple past tense, in a voice devoid of interiority but rich in temporal data, the *Report* tracks movement in time and space. The story begins at dawn with an ironically pastoral envoi: "Tuesday, September 11, 2001, dawned temperate and nearly cloudless in the eastern United States. . . . For those headed to an airport, weather conditions could not have been better for a safe and pleasant journey" (1). The document then tightens its aperture to the 6:00 a.m. flight from Portland to Boston taken by two of its central characters, Mohamed Atta and Abdul Aziz al Omari. Readers learn, for example, that "Atta and Omari arrived in Boston at 6:45. Seven minutes later, Atta apparently took a call from Marwan al Shehhi. . . . They spoke for three minutes." A steady barrage of ticking clocks marks the intersecting plots of the four teams of hijackers: "Shehhi and his team . . . boarded United 175 between 7:23 and 7:28" (1–2); "At 7:18, Mihdhar and Moqed [hijackers of American Airlines Flight 77] entered the security checkpoint" (3); American Airlines Flight 11 "took off at 7:57" (4); "At 8:19" flight attendant Betty Ong used an airphone to report the hijacking and "At 8: 23, the dispatcher tried unsuccessfully to contact the aircraft" (5). The stopwatch-driven succession culminates in the instant when, "at 8:46:40, American 11 crashed into the North Tower of the World Trade Center. All on board, along with an unknown number of people in the tower, were killed instantly" (7). In the *Report*, the aesthetic and epistemological importance of precise, objective temporal measurement reaches its zenith at the very moment—the impact of American 11 with the North Tower—when surprise and devastation most eclipsed intelligibility.[19] This conspicuous precision to within the hundredth of a second invites us to investigate what this forensic paradigm has to say about the profound wounding that occurred in the attacks of 9/11.

In the case of the *9/11 Commission Report*, by refashioning disaster as chronology, the narrative aims to replace victims with knowers. It does so, first, by establishing an authorial subject in command of its perceptual, technological, and temporal fields, and second, by attempting to shape personal and collective understandings of 9/11 through securing its events—which unfolded in multiple locations and were witnessed in myriad ways—on a single, immanent time line. The goals of such a narrative are clear: the chronometric novella that begins the *9/11 Commission Report* is in part a hook designed to catch a national audience primed by thrillers like the television series 24, but it is also an attempt to incrementalize and disaggregate horrific events. They are placed along an easily understood linear plot with a subject whose history, that of the American people, functions as a seamless stream, connecting events that come before and after on its time line. While such a narrative trajectory might seem inherently aligned with state power and the homogeneous empty time of modernity, my analysis of the *Report*'s temporality aims to recover the transgressive agency implicit in chronometric narrative and to clarify the role played by secular time in attempts to suture the wounds of national trauma.

Especially since the official recognition of post-traumatic stress disorder, or PTSD, in the 1980 *Diagnostic and Statistical Manual of Mental Disorders III* (*DSM-III*), for which the American Psychiatric Association established diagnostic criteria, the phenomenon of temporal belatedness associated with trauma has been extensively studied.[20] Clinicians and theorists investigating time-sequencing disorders have argued that temporal disruption is both a symptom of psychic wounding and a constitutive feature of that injury. After 9/11, a culture fluent in the vernaculars of post-traumatic stress disorder has ensured that the methods and concerns of trauma studies, with its emphasis on belatedness and recurrence, have played a pervasive role in critical and creative writing about the events of 9/11.[21] In another vein, philosophers and cultural theorists have investigated the political and phenomenological implications of 9/11's putative singularity as an event of rupture, either asking how the disaster operates outside the flow of historical time or attempting to formulate more historicist accounts.

Beginning with the authors of the *Report*, a group threatened by potential discord, the time line as a genre seeks to stabilize uneven subjective experiences and organize discrepant narratives from a quantifiable, external perspective.[22] On the heels of a tumultuous genesis, the National Commission on Terrorist Attacks upon the United States—initially opposed by the White House, subject to intense opposition and stonewalling by various government agencies, and marred by the resignation of Henry Kissinger, its first chair—released its final report in late July 2004 to widespread acclaim.[23] Published in book form by the independent literary press W.W. Norton with an initial print run of over half a million copies, which sold out in less than a month, and widely viewed on the Web, the *Report* reads more like a political thriller than the bureaucratic white paper a bipartisan committee with a $15 million budget and a staff of over eighty might be expected to produce.[24] The *Report* reorganizes findings culled from over two million pages of documentary evidence gathered from dozens of government agencies, testimonial material from twelve public hearings held between March 2003 and June 2004, and the results of over a thousand interviews into a contiguous narrative with a coherent sense of character and action that can be read linearly and with ease, relegating references and notes to appendices at the end of the volume.[25] Against the heightened partisanship of the upcoming 2004 elections, the commission's five Republicans and five Democrats claimed to speak "without dissent" in a document that, they asserted, represents a total "unity of purpose."

Far from being disabled by the pressures of audience expectations and collaborative authorship, its authors, led by commission chair Thomas Kean, vice-chair Lee Hamilton, and executive director Philip Zelikow, produced a narrative whose self-conscious status as an object of aesthetic consumption foregrounds urgent, plot-driven prose.

Even critical reviews tended to celebrate the document's literary merits. The report is, as jurist Richard Posner called it in his critical review for the *New York Times*, "an uncommonly lucid, even riveting, narrative" and "an improbable literary triumph." This sense of literariness derives in large part, I want to suggest, from the *Report*'s treatment of narrative time, objective time, and their relationship to the wounds inflicted on 9/11.[26] The *Report*'s chronological narrative and declarative, unembellished voice produces a strong sense of urgency. During the reading experience one feels a rapid "flow" of temporal events related in the third person, such that in only a few minutes of reading, the *Report* covers an experienced time stretching from 6:00 a.m. to noon on 9/11, creating an effect of temporal compression.[27]

When I asked Philip Zelikow, the executive director of the 9/11 Commission and the person most responsible for the *Report*'s form and tone, about this chronometric approach to history, he described it as the cultivation of the *Report*'s "House Style"—a voice free of polemic and, to whatever extent possible, of interpretation. This was one of the primary goals he established during his first meeting with commission chair Kean and vice-chair Hamilton. The goal of the commission was to create a document written in a "dry, unadorned style designed around a rigorous substructure of time and narrative." Zelikow aimed to focalize what people knew at particular moments in history and clarify how individuals understood their choices in the moment, rather than succumb to what he termed "the blinding force of hindsight."

Rendering the events as a series of successive, punctual instances fosters a sense of simultaneity that unites a national audience, a marshalling of collectivity integral to Benedict Anderson's account of print capitalism and the hegemony of the modern nation-state. At the same time, however, the *Report* reinforces temporal boundaries between politically secular Western nations and a "Muslim world [that] has *fallen behind* the West politically, economically, and militarily for the past three centuries" (362; italics added). Such temporal distancing recruits what anthropologist Johannes Fabian called the denial of coevalness to enforce hierarchy; the report, to borrow from Fabian, uses a "discourse that consistently places those who are talked about in a time other than that of the one who talks" ("Other Revisited" 143). Moreover, the shared public time of the *Report* offers an implicit reproach both to what its authors see as the flawed historiographic practices characteristic of an "extreme Islamist version of history"—one that enflames hatred through selective interpretation—and to the secularized religious rhythms of nationalist sentimentalism (50). In this light, the combination of chronological form and scientifically precise temporal measurement can be seen as part of an attempt to inculcate and buttress secular national values in opposition to religious experience. Marking time serves as a cipher for the *Report*'s systemic bid for "objectivity," a position it juxtaposes with the religious and ideological commitments of radical Islamism.

Because of its very literariness, however, the *Report* cannot sustain the denial of coevalness it attempts to assert. As its authors keenly understand, the precise measurements and operational complexity of al Qaeda's attack depend on the distinctly "modern" temporal logic modeled in the *Report*'s narrative. In other words, the authors of the *Report* and the agents of the attack share the chronometric imperatives of global trade claimed as the exclusive province of secular capitalism. Nowhere are these characteristics more visible than in the planning of the planes operation by Khalid Sheikh Mohammed (KSM). As the *Report* suggests, "KSM presents himself as an entrepreneur seeking venture capital and people. He simply wanted al Qaeda to supply the money and operatives needed for the attack while retaining his independence" (154). Consistent with his self-proclaimed role as independent contractor in an economy of global terror, KSM emphasizes the bureaucratic, corporate dimensions of al Qaeda's structure: "Upon arriving in Afghanistan, a recruit would fill out an application, with standard questions, such as, What brought you to Afghanistan?" (234). Ironically, the *Report* makes it clear that terrorism operates in, through, and against secular culture. The phenomenon Randy Martin calls the "financialization of daily life" describes al Qaeda at least as well as Wall Street. The "precise time allocations, clear-minded calculations, [and] uninterrupted self-control" that Martin sees as characteristic of twenty-first-century American capitalism are, in the eyes of the 9/11 Commission, the seminal attribute of al Qaeda's approach to terrorism (2). Operational sophistication and advanced technology are constituent parts of terrorism's paradoxical modernity; "In a sense," the *Report* suggests, the members of terrorist organizations "were more globalized than we were" (340).

At a basic evidentiary level, the question of what was known and done on the morning of 9/11 is a matter of no small importance for understanding various government agencies' responses to the terrorist attacks. Among other things, the meticulous chronological scaffolding constructed by the 9/11 Commission casts serious doubt on the adequacy of the military's preparedness, as well as on the accuracy of their accounts of their response on 9/11. In particular, the commission's chronology of events contradicts the repeated insistence by the Federal Aviation Administration (FAA) and the North American Aerospace Defense Command (NORAD) that United 93, which crashed in Pennsylvania, would have been intercepted before reaching its target in Washington, D.C. Nevertheless, there is a high degree of empty formalism in the 9/11 Commission's approach: after all, there is little utility in the knowledge that the first plane struck at 8:46:40 a.m. On a pragmatic level, however, identifying the temporally disruptive power of 9/11 reflects an astute recognition within the Bush administration that the terrorist attacks afforded a unique opportunity for political action—not only in its immediate aftermath but in any of its citational presents.

In his September 20 address to a joint session of Congress, the national public, and, beyond it, a global audience, President Bush set out to reassure a stricken nation, name its antagonists, and outline the parameters and goals of a militarized response. The narcissistic evasion of the rhetorical question at the heart of the speech ("Why do they hate us? . . . They hate our freedoms") and the portrayal of a broader Manichean drama between good and evil tell a simplistic, already-weaponized story. But despite sustained attempts to gloss the events of 9/11 within the familiar nationalist topoi of freedom, heroism, and justice, the official narratives of the Bush era constitute less of an orienting metafiction than a tangled web of analeptic and proleptic leaps that provoke and maintain a state of crisis instead of preparing the ground for its resolution.

Beginning with his brief statement on 9/11 ("Statement"), Bush-era speeches and policy documents enmesh the terrorist attacks in a discourse of temporal rupture. As the president intoned on September 20, "All of this was brought upon us in a single day, and night fell on a different world" ("Address"). The binary metaphor of day and night, established here with a keen emphasis on the "fall" that defines their separation, pervades Bush's lexicon in the aftermath of the attacks. The elegant and formally complex September 20 speech, arguably the most important rhetorical moment in what would become the war on terror, deploys a series of catachrestic claims that underscore the way the attacks both constitute and trigger temporal dislocations: "*Tonight* we are a country *awakened* to danger and called to defend freedom" (italics added) because, he argues, "we face new and sudden national challenges" presaged by unprecedented acts of terrorism. Lending rhetorical force to these claims with a chiasmus that echoes the earlier crossing of day and night, the speech reaches its climax when Bush declares, "Whether we bring our enemies to justice or bring justice to our enemies, justice will be done."

It is difficult to think critically about the rhetoric of surprise without seeming to lend support to the ranks of 9/11 conspiracy theorists. However, for national security experts and administration officials, the idiom of the unexpected must be weighed against the repeated warnings and public pronouncements of impending terrorist attacks in order to understand its ideological value. In the rambling fatwa issued in August 1996, Bin Laden outlined the goals of a global war against the United States (IslamToday); a second fatwa published in February 1998 gave the stark injunction that "to kill the Americans and their allies—civilians and military—is an individual duty for every Muslim who can do it in any country in which it is possible" (Bin Laden et al.). With this rhetoric corroborated by the open secret of al Qaeda training camps in Afghanistan, the two embassy bombings in 1998, and the bombing of the USS *Cole* in 2000, systematic terrorism against the United States and its interests was, by 2001, known to constitute a significant threat. In the spring and summer of 2001, National Security Council counterterrorism coordinator Richard Clark and others issued increasingly dire warnings about terrorist activities.[28] Neither the strategy of simultaneous hijackings—successfully implemented in the quadruple hijacking of planes bound for New York by the Popular Front for the Liberation of Palestine on September 6, 1970—nor the targeting of the World Trade Center, bombed in 1993, was unique to 9/11. Significant attacks on the United States and its interests "were a question not of 'if' but rather of 'when' and 'where,'" as Samuel Berger, national security adviser to the Clinton administration, told the president in early 2000 briefings (*9/11 Commission Report* 182). More pressingly, the CIA contributed an article to a security brief delivered to President Bush in Crawford, Texas, on August 6, 2001, entitled "Bin Ladin [*sic*] Determined To Strike in US," that outlined efforts by al Qaeda operatives, including those with US citizenship, to "follow the example of World

Trade Center bomber Ramzi Yousef."[29] Indeed, the NORAD military exercises under way on 9/11 ironically contained a simulated hijacking, leading the Boston control center to inquire whether the request to "scramble some F-16s" was "real-world or exercise" on the morning of the attacks (*9/11 Commission Report* 20).

Beyond their obvious utility in denying culpability for failing to disrupt terrorist networks prior to the attacks of 2001, claims regarding the epochal nature of 9/11, particularly those emphasizing suddenness and rupture, translate the experience of surprise and shock into a politically mobile idea: the attacks become an atemporal event whose force severs the causal and epistemological relationship between the past and the future. In a carefully argued analysis of the president's September 20 address, literary critic Donald Pease claims that the speech was "designed to lessen the events' traumatizing power through the provision of an imaginary response to a disaster that could not otherwise be assimilated to the preexisting order of things" (2). It seems to me, however, that something of the opposite is the case. While this and other speeches attempt to channel the affective response of a wounded nation, they do so precisely by maximizing rupture to shatter any preexisting historical order. A better trope than assimilation would be peripeteia, a device we see at work in Bush's September 20 address when a series of quick crystalize the temporal compression subsequently seen in the workings of the war on terror: "Our grief has turned to anger, our anger to resolution" ("Address").

The Quadrennial Defense Review (QDR), the primary public document that outlines national military strategy, published on September 30, 2001, is unsurprisingly devoted to the "new era" of national security inducted after 9/11, and it is here that the emergent Bush Doctrine fully articulates the ontology of temporal rupture. By tradition a highly narrative genre, the QDR of 2001 attempts to tell the story of 9/11 and its implications for national security in such a way as to forge consensus, if not to blunt the edge of defense policy. One of the most striking aspects of the 2001 QDR, conducted by Defense Secretary Donald Rumsfeld, is the surprise attacks' precipitation of broad uncertainty: "A fundamental condition of our circumstances," Rumsfeld maintains, is that "the United States cannot predict with a high degree of confidence the identity of the countries or the actors that may threaten its interests and security." If the past can no longer be used to predict the future, the military must "establish a new strategy for America's defense that would embrace uncertainty and contend with surprise."

In other words, the disappearance of history at the heart of chrono-mania denies any narrative that considers the role played by American policies in creating the material conditions out of which 9/11 arose. In its place, Rumsfeld substitutes the dystopian imaginings of greater violence yet to come. Uncertainty about the future is used to discredit analysis of the past, specifically of the connection between American foreign policy and anger in the Muslim world.

At the same time as the logic of preemption and the temporality of trauma were deployed to sever the continuity of cause and effect, the president continued to forge opportunistic contiguities between America's two great twentieth-century foes, communism and fascism, and its new enemies in the twenty-first. He described al Qaeda on September 20 as "the heirs of all the murderous ideologies of the twentieth century," insisting that "they follow in the path of fascism, Nazism, and totalitarianism" ("Address"). In his prayer service remarks at the National Cathedral on September 14, a day consecrated to prayer and remembrance, President Bush used crisis to connect the present with a cyclical pattern of heroism: "In every generation, the world has produced enemies of human freedom. They have attacked America because we are freedom's home and defender, and the commitment of our fathers is now the calling of our time" ("National Day"). In the Bush administration's telling of history, one strikingly similar to Francis Fukuyama's, "The great struggles of the twentieth century ended with a decisive victory for the forces of freedom—and a single sustainable model for national success: freedom, democracy, and free enterprise" (George Bush, "National Security Strategy"). With time itself torn asunder by the attacks, temporal instability facilitates analeptic leaps into the nation's mythic past, conjoining 9/11 with an unlikely array of historical moments in public and political discourse.

If the Cold War policies of deterrence and containment operated with a fundamentally reactive logic, the war on terror instead claims the necessity of preemption. The National Security Strategy (NSS) of 2002, the first such document prepared by the White House after 9/11 and a radical departure from its predecessors, aggressively consolidates the imperatives of preventative war. The seminal characteristic of the "new thinking" advocated by the White House and Department of Defense in the NSS and elsewhere is its proleptic temporality. In the months and years after 9/11, the evolving contours of the Bush Doctrine systematically consolidated its claim on the future by simultaneously evoking the future perfect—imagining what will have happened—and a fabled history, trading on the currency of trauma to underwrite an interminable war on terror.

President Bush chose the unique setting of his June 1, 2002, West Point commencement address, where he spoke as commander in chief at the nation's oldest military academy on the occasion of its bicentennial, to deliver what was arguably the most important articulation of the preemptive strategy that would be the hallmark of his administration. President Bush first evokes the institution's history—"the long gray line that stretches two centuries behind you"—that foregrounds connections between the graduates he addresses and those of the legendary 1940s, before going on to identify what he calls the "gravest danger to freedom" at the "perilous crossroads of radicalism and technology." In the West Point address, the president argues that these "new threats . . . require new thinking. Deterrence . . . means nothing against shadowy terrorist networks with no nation or citizens to defend. Containment is not possible." Instead, he asserts, "All Americans must be forward-looking and resolute, to be ready for preemptive action" designed to confront threats "before they emerge" ("President Bush Delivers Graduation Speech").

In written testimony to the 9/11 Commission in 2004, in support of the Afghan campaign begun on October 7, 2001, Rumsfeld observes that "in light of September 11th, no one questions those actions" ("Testimony"). But in extending his conclusions, Rumsfeld departs from the tradition of just war theory that legitimizes aggressive retaliatory action and moves into the uncertain terrain of prophecy, here in the guise of a double hypothetical: "Today, I *suspect* most would support a *pre-emptive* action to deal with such a threat" (my italics). As he explains, the lack of credible evidence of an immediate threat proves, not the injustice of action, but a failure of imagination and a flawed epistemology:

> Imagine for a moment that we were back before September 11, 2001. Imagine that a U.S. President had looked at the information then available, and gone before the Congress and the world, and said: "We need to invade Afghanistan, overthrow the Taliban, and destroy the al-Qaeda terrorist network," based on what little was known before September 11th. How many countries would have joined in a coalition? Many? Any? Not likely. We likely would have heard objections to "pre-emption" similar to those voiced before the Coalition launched Operation Iraqi Freedom.

In an ironic twist, though the links between al Qaeda and Saddam Hussein's regime that were used to justify preemptive war against Iraq were never substantiated, Iraq became central to al Qaeda only ex post facto. Quoting Bin Laden in his 2006 address to the Military Officers Association ("Iran and the War on Terror"), President Bush emphasizes that for al Qaeda, "The most . . . serious issue today for the whole world is this Third World War . . . [that] is raging in [Iraq]." Proleptically repositioning the war's effect as a cause, the president marshals this evidence to buttress eroding support for the war: "And that is why we must not, and we will not, give the enemy victory in Iraq."

The doctrine of preemption—or, in its more anodyne formulation, anticipatory self-defense—both echoes and extends the temporal (il)logic of the war on terror. It does so by recruiting narrative plausibility and the evidence of 9/11 to circumvent the thresholds initially used to justify preemptive aggression by Secretary of State Daniel Webster in 1842. In a letter to British diplomat Henry Stephen Fox, Webster argues that such threats must be "instant, overwhelming, leaving no choice of means, and no moment of deliberation. . . . [Any] act justified by the necessity of self-defense, must be limited by that necessity, and kept clearly within it" (qtd. in Bzostek 67). As Annie McClanahan argues, "The doctrine of preemption develops its narrative logic from the corporate practice of 'scenario thinking' . . . as a way to capitalize on (if not produce) the perception of 9/11 as a constitutively 'unpredictable' event" (42–43). Tracing scenario thinking to Herman Kahn, whose scenarios about nuclear war for the Rand Corporation in the 1950s replaced quantitative probability with narrative plausibility, McClanahan observes that "the doctrine of preemption not only adopts scenario thinking's conflation of imaginability and likelihood, it imports it into law: preemption transforms the grounds for what counts as evidence and for what justifics military intervention" (49). But because the goal of anticipatory action is to prevent the very terrorist strikes whose execution would have substantiated the need to strike in the first place, the proleptic futurity of the war on terror depends, paradoxically, on the public's ability to maintain the violence of 9/11 in memory as a continuous present.

The erasure of historicity enabled by assertions of 9/11's singularity can thus be seen to parallel and produce the boundless temporality of the war on terror, a conflict that, as President Bush asserted on September 20, 2001, "begins with Al Qaeda, but . . . will not end until every terrorist group of global reach has been found, stopped and defeated"

("Address"). Speaking even more hyperbolically on September 14 in his National Cathedral address, the president maintained that, "just three days removed from these events, Americans do not yet have the distance of history. But our responsibility to history is already clear: to answer these attacks and rid the world of evil" ("National Day"). It comes as little surprise then, that Rumsfeld would grimly observe in the QDR of 2006 that "the United States is a nation engaged in what will be a long war."

In his analysis of realism, Fredric Jameson argues that "narrative forms construct their new world by *programming* their readers; by training them in new habits and practices, which amount to whole new subject-positions . . . [by producing] new categories of the event and of experience, of temporality and of causality, which also preside over what will now come to be thought of as reality" (*Signatures* 166). Far from being disabled by the shattered temporality of 9/11, state power has integrated rupture and nonlinear time into the very fabric of the national imaginary and the seminal legislation of the post-9/11 period. This transformation should summon us to reexamine one of the most widely held convictions of historiography and cultural theory: that modernity, and particularly the modern nation-state, are governed by a particular form of secular time consciousness. In the dominant account, modernity conceives of history as unfolding in what Walter Benjamin called "homogeneous, empty time" ("Theses" 261). Indeed, the idea of modernity is constitutively rooted, as Matei Calinescu puts it, "within the framework of a specific time awareness, namely, that of *historical time*, linear and irreversible, flowing irresistibly onwards" (13). In Benedict Anderson's influential account, "The idea of a sociological organism moving calendrically through homogeneous, empty time is a precise analogue of the idea of the nation, which is also conceived as a solid community moving steadily down (or up) history" (26). As Anderson argues, national communities depend upon the concept of simultaneity produced by the novel and the newspaper, discursive spaces that connect the actions of millions of disparate individuals within externally measurable and uniform time—a temporality denoted by the deceptively simple concept of simultaneity (25–26). In this way, modern states can be understood as fundamentally chronopolitical entities. For Benjamin, as for thinkers of the contemporary Left like Judith Butler and Talal Asad, to contend effectively with state power and its dominant ideologies one must begin with a critique of its chronopolitical underpinnings: namely, its hegemonic secular temporality.

In "Sexual Politics, Torture, and Secular Time," an essay that interrogates the instrumentalization of 'progressive' sexual politics by a political culture that conceives of Islam as its premodern Other, Judith Butler invokes Walter Benjamin's critique of progress as an antidote to the coercive effects of state power. As Butler sees it, "The point . . . is to establish a politics that opposes state coercion and violence, and to build a framework that can see how the violence done in the name of preserving a certain modernity . . . is the most serious threat to freedom"—a task made possible by Benjaminian dialectics (19). By rejecting narratives of progress in favor of an understanding of the way the past flashes up in the continuous present, Butler hopes to deactivate a political dispensation that legitimizes the war on terror as a civilizing mission. She explains: "The 'constellation' which is one's own era is precisely the difficult and interruptive scene of multiple temporalities, ones that cannot be reduced to cultural pluralism or a liberal discourse of rights" (20). Benjamin's meditations on temporality coalesce around the idea of progress, a concept harnessed variously by social movements from National Socialism to Hegelian Marxism. Rejecting the idea that the causal connections between events unfolding in a continuous temporality of past, present, and future manifest in Enlightenment concepts of progress, Benjamin placed his hope in an *interruptive* philosophy of history. In convolute N of the *Arcades Project* and "Theses on the Philosophy of History," Benjamin sets out to forge this relationship between past and present in a montage. As he suggests in a well-known passage, "It's not that what is past casts its light on what is present, or what is present its light on the past; rather, image is that wherein what has been comes together in a flash with the now to form a constellation. In other words, image is dialectics at a standstill. For while the relation of the present to the past is a purely temporal, continuous one, the relation of what-has-been to the now is dialectical: is not progression but image, suddenly emergent" (*Arcades Project* 463 N2a, 3).

Butler is, I believe, mistaken in her claim that a homogeneous concept of historical time in fact subtends state power. As I have been arguing, multiple and disjointed temporal frameworks inform government responses to 9/11. I have shown how, far from depending upon a secular conception of progressive developmental history, the temporality of the war on terror borrows much from the deliberate rupturing of homogeneous time and the provocation of those flashes that, in Benjamin's terms, "make the continuum of history explode" ("Theses"). In the post-9/11 era, it seems that those who most want to cause such disruptions are likely to do so to justify new forms of domination—like the proleptic and messianic temporalities of the Bush Doctrine—or to articulate an ideological gloss for acts of mass murder suicide (al Qaeda) rather than to empower cultural critique.

As I have argued, in speech after speech, beginning with his address on the evening of September 11, President Bush and other apologists for the war on terror enmeshed the event in a discourse of rupture that produced new constellations of historical meaning. 9/11 halted calendrical flow and, in the resultant temporal rift, opened new connections between past, present, and future. This systematic cultivation of 9/11 chronomania in the Bush administration's war on terror suggests that modern time consciousness is neither as homogeneous, as secular, nor as hegemonic as has previously been maintained. By examining narratives of state power, we can begin to see how the war on terror, far from being disabled by chronomania, integrates nonlinear time into the very fabric of the national imaginary and the seminal legislation of the post-9/11 period. In this way, modern states can be understood as fundamentally chronopolitical entities. But, as I have been arguing here, after 9/11 we no longer inhabit a "secular" time, if "we" ever did. After 9/11, the time-signature instead has become fundamentally kairotic: temporality is experienced and narrated not as homogeneous but rather as uneven, saturated, multiple, and marked by decisive turning points. *Kairos*, the ancient Greek term for the propitious moment, denotes, in the theological sense that I deliberately invoke here in the context of the Bush administration, an epochal moment in history. It expresses a qualitative impression of temporal fullness produced by the intersection of the eternal with historical time.

On a pragmatic level, identifying the kairotic power of 9/11 reflects the astute recognition within the Bush administration that the terrorist attacks afforded a unique opportunity for political action—not only in its immediate aftermath but in any of its citational presents. In the new, multidimensional temporality of the war on terror it is not, as Benjamin feared, time deployed as *chronos* that presages oppression or the messianic cessation that constitutes the hallmark of revolutionary praxis. Instead, in the proleptic and analeptic constellations of 9/11, technocapital and state power have subsumed kairotic time. In other words, the official narratives of 9/11 are trying to have it both ways: to emphasize their rational, technoscientific approach to clock time and also to draw upon the force of the sacred and a religious notion of "higher" time. The *Report* asserts temporal mastery over unpredicted events by constructing a time line, a chronometric form that attempts to move readers away from affective responses surrounding victimhood toward those of agency. At a very basic level, such a process deactivates the kairotic rupture triggered by the war on terror by drawing readers through the time of catastrophe and, figuratively, out the other side. While such a narrative form might seem inherently aligned with state power and the homogeneous empty time of modernity—and thus easily summoned to the service of militarized patriotism—in the context of kairotic governmentality, the stopwatch-driven narrative of the *Report* can be seen in a different light as both restoring and denying the coevalness of terrorism's victims and perpetrators.

GROUND ZERO

Homeland Security's instrumentalization of trauma and the integration of temporal rupture into the logic of the war on terror impel the plot and narrative form of Jess Walter's novel *The Zero*, a dark and comic meditation on the psychosocial aftermath of the September 11 attacks. Despite a few favorable reviews and a National Book Award nomination, the novel failed to gain the attention it deserves on what has become a rapidly growing shelf of 9/11 novels. *The Zero* depicts the recovery effort, nascent counterterrorism and homeland security initiatives, and the altered polity of New York through the eyes of Brian Remy, a police officer present at the World Trade Center at the time of its collapse who later works a nebulous counterterrorism beat amid the wreckage of "The Zero," the novel's disaster-worker patois for the acres of wreckage in Lower Manhattan. At the opening of the novel, readers encounter Remy as he awakes disoriented on September 12, 2001, nursing a head wound of unknown provenance. Walter's protagonist appears to suffer from dissociative disorder or pathological memory loss, a condition that leaves him with few memories of the day before; he must use available evidence to reconstruct his own failed suicide attempt.[30]

Disjointed temporality serves as the novel's central formal conceit: *The Zero* constitutes a series of narrative "flashes" or fragments whose jagged edges—often breaking off and commencing midsentence—mirror Remy's dissociative experience of time as he moves in and out of lucid windows in his own life. The story, like Remy's conscious experience, jumps from moment to moment "forward" in time, entirely coincident, we are to believe, with the succession of events in Remy's brief periods of self-consciousness. Neither Remy nor the reader knows what happens to him between narrative fragments. But while the novel experiments with disruptions relative to a continuous flow of public time, its temporal orientation remains relentlessly linear, like an arrow shot forward from the evental "zero" of the terrorist attacks. In formalist terms, the novel's *fabula*, or the structure of events, and *sujet*, the prose order, coincide; the only "infidelities to the chronological order of events," as Girard Genette would call them in *Narrative Discourse* (29), consist in the "gaps" in Remy's consciousness and the text. The plot of the story that Remy and the reader piece together is relatively straightforward: after the terrorist attacks, Remy is hired by a secret counterterrorism agency to trace the whereabouts of March Selios, a woman with Saudi connections who the government suspects was tipped off about the attacks in time to escape the buildings; as he pursues clues about Selios, Remy plunges deeper and deeper into the paranoid and spectral worlds of intelligence, law enforcement, and counterterrorism.[31] In a style reminiscent of Paul Auster's postmodern crime novels, *The Zero* parodies the generic conventions of the political thriller and detective fiction to explore broader questions of identity, meaning, and temporal experience in the war on terror. Despite their devastating effects on Remy's personal life, sharp dissociations and proleptic temporal rifts are, Walter suggests, endemic to the post–September 11 cultural experience and, more specifically, serve as positive attributes for soldiers in the war on terror, in which the loss of memory ironically makes Remy more effective as a counterterrorism operative.

Walter invites readers of *The Zero* to interpret both his narrative style and Remy's experience of temporal distortion as symptoms of psychic trauma, a "diagnosis" Walter self-consciously performs by including Remy's periodic encounters with his psychotherapist in the text. In one of the narrative flashes, readers find Remy lying on the Freudian couch during a lucid spell; the passage begins midsentence: "'HALLUCINATORY IMAGES,' Remy's psychiatrist, Dr. Rieux, was saying" (194; all caps in original). Dr. Rieux speculates that witnessing the collapse of the Towers has left Remy traumatized: "What you're describing is textbook PTSD. Visions. Stress-induced delusions. Dissociative episodes. Maybe even Briquet's syndrome" (194). An extensive body of clinical testing, theoretical analysis, and anecdotal narratives testifies to the way traumatic events involving death and injury can disrupt a healthy subject's sense of time and the workings of memory. During traumatic experiences—genocide, war, natural disaster, rape—external stimuli overwhelm our cognitive processes in the moment of experience and return in flashbacks, dreams, and other panicked relivings that disrupt the flow of daily life. For Freud, the temporal disruptions symptomatic and constitutive of trauma relate to the mechanics of *Nachträglichkeit*, which James Strachey translates as "deferred action." Lacan and Laplanche, who reinvigorated the concept in subsequent work, used the French term *après-coup*, denoting the mechanism by which traumatic traces are recoded at later times with new meanings. For Cathy Caruth the term becomes *belatedness*; as she argues in her influential work from the mid-1990s, "A traumatic event cannot be 'assimilated' or experienced fully at the time, but only *belatedly*, in its repeated *possession* of the one who experiences it" (4–5). It is to the deferred action of trauma that Remy's psychiatrist attributes his implausible narrative about covert counterterrorism efforts: "It's all right there in the literature. Survivors can expect to experience delusions, persecution, paranoia. Delirium. Hell, after what some of you guys went through that day . . . I'm surprised you don't have flying monkeys drive you to work" (195).

But while trauma studies has generated extensive analysis of the aesthetic challenges and ethical implications of literary representations of trauma, there are several reasons to be skeptical of applying these methods and their attendant questions to Walter's *The Zero*. First, Walter systematically discredits psychoanalytic approaches by satirizing Dr. Rieux, who ignores empirical evidence and misdiagnoses Remy's symptoms. As Remy patiently explains, quoting ophthalmological rhetoric, "My eyes are flaking apart. Macular degeneration and vitreous detachment. I see flashers and floaters" (65). When Remy informs Dr. Rieux that he has a medical condition disturbing his eyesight, the psychiatrist denies Remy's claim: "No. I don't think so," he declares, pointing as evidence to a medical report based on information Remy has intentionally falsified, "*Disability due to chronic back pain*" (196; italics in original). Dr. Rieux also ignores the "gaps" of which Remy complains, the novel's foundational narrative conceit. "'Gaps?' he asks, 'What gaps?' 'The *gaps*,' Remy said" (196; italics in original). Moreover, as the careful reader knows, Remy's problems with temporality precede September 11, though they get faster and more frequent subsequent to the attack (77). During an earlier psychoanalytic session, Dr. Rieux interprets his physical symptoms symbolically, fastening onto Remy's description that "strings" impair his visual field: "And do these strings tie you to the world. . . . Are these ropes binding you, or holding you down. . . . Aren't these the tethers that keep you from floating away?" he asks (147–48). Rejecting psychoanalytic readings for physiological ones Remy explains, "No," Remy replies, "they're little pieces of tissue floating in my eyes. My ophthalmologist says they're floating in the gel inside there" (148).

Dr. Rieux's thin diagnosis suggests instead the inadequacy of existing categories of analysis by underscoring the power of September 11 to distort reference retroactively. The temporal disturbances and lapses in memory that constitute *The Zero* hardly constitute a textbook example of post-traumatic stress: for one thing, Remy's temporal skipping obeys an obsessively linear trajectory, distinguishing his experience of temporal compression, rupture, and prolepsis from the recurrent or cyclical temporality at the core of trauma. Despite the futural orientation of Remy's temporal trajectory, with his consciousness like a "skipping stone . . . bounding across the surfaces of time," we might usefully see Walter's protagonist as a version of Walter Benjamin's angel of history, who is propelled "into the future to which his back is turned, while the pile of debris before him grows skyward" ("Theses" 258). The evidentiary paradigms and quick narrative construction that made Remy effective as a detective serve him well coming out of the gaps between dissociative episodes. Finding himself in new situations, he quickly interprets his setting and his clothes and observes his somatic instincts at a slight distance from the execution of his movements. Meeting a government mole in a suspected terrorist cell for a money drop, Remy, who remembers nothing about how he came to the meeting in the first place, can readily promise to forget about their encounter. Despite his best intentions, Remy cannot fight the trajectory of the war on terror toward torture or the media commodification of trauma. His attempt to free a suspect brought into international waters for what the Bush administration would describe as "enhanced interrogation" turns out to be a prescripted ploy to gain the suspect's trust. In *The Zero*, the continuum of history has been replaced by the media's "cycle of opportunity: first inspirational stories . . . then the backdrop stories . . . then the big money—thrillers" (151). Remy's memory loss finds its inverted mirror in the commodification of memory; as Remy's former partner on the police force puts it, quoting the talent agent who approached him for material about September 11, "A story like mine is like owning a good stock. . . . Guy asks, do I wanna sell my stock? Do I wanna sell him my experiences. . . . Bet your ass I'll sell my experiences. I sure as hell don't want 'em anymore" (150).

Like the damage to his eyes—the "flashers and floaters that danced like scraps of paper blown into the world"—Remy's woundedness cites September 11 but without reference to the dominant discourse of either trauma or heroism. Instead, Walter imbeds the novel in an intertextual network of twentieth-century experimental prose including Kafka's *The Castle*, Alain Robbe-Grillet's *In the Labyrinth*, and Camus's *The Plague*, a narrative temporality that operates unbeknownst to Remy but that connects narrator and reader to earlier texts. Most importantly, Walter's Dr. Rieux evokes the narrator of Albert Camus's *The Plague*, a doctor of the same name who bears witness to the epidemic that decimates the Algerian city of Oran. Temporal disruptions are integral to both Camus's novel and his narrator, who suggests that the plague triggers disorders that are temporal in nature: "The first thing that plague brought to our town was exile," but this exile is more temporal than spatial; it is "undoubtedly the feeling of exile—that sensation of a void within . . . that irrational longing to hark back to the past or else to speed up the march of time, and whose keen shafts of memory stung like fire" (71). Like the covert reading of *The Castle* by a hospital orderly and the book report on *In the Labyrinth* mistakenly identified as a terrorist manifesto, the reference to Camus in Walter's character of Dr. Rieux opens new connections between past and present that interrupt the proleptic leaps of Remy's dissociative episodes.

Trauma has become not an affect but an industry and a new currency in the market of cultural cachet. The return of the repressed associated with trauma underwrites another form of "return" in the era of the trauma industry, where it justifies psychoanalytic sessions and become a billable expense on a lawyer's invoice for preparing April Selios's application for the federal September 11 Victim's Assistance Fund: "The lawyer pointed to two columns on the bottom of the page, deductions for 'Vicarious Trauma' and 'Compassion Fatigue.' . . . As you might imagine," the attorney informs Remy, "these are difficult cases . . . emotionally" (174; ellipsis in original). Remy's son Edgar cashes in on the cultural addiction to trauma by allowing the rumors that his father was killed in the September 11 attacks to underwrite a public mourning that gives him popularity and direction. Ironically, Edgar too indicts the phenomenon of vicarious trauma: "What are people in Wyoming really grieving? A loss of safety?" he asks, "the emptiness of their Palm Pilots and SUVS . . . ? Generalized grief is a fleeting emotion" (34). Instead, mourning as real his father's fictional death gives pitch and moment to a grief that otherwise lacks reference; as he tries to explain, "Don't tell me I shouldn't be devastated by the death of *my* father just because he isn't dead!" (35). It would be easy to attribute Edgar's grief over the death of his living father simply to the savage humor that inflects *The Zero* more generally, but for the structural homology between Edgar's compelling but counterfactual cultural performance and the masquerades performed in the novel in the name of national security.

After receiving medical leave from the police force on the pretext of chronic back pain, Remy enters the murky world of domestic counterterrorism intelligence. In Walter's fiction, as in the actual response, the race to locate culpable parties and prevent further acts of terror blurs the line between conspiracy theory and sound evidence, between law enforcement and extrajudicial action. In the semantic universe of Walter's text, as in Camus's, meaning proves an elusive quarry, and *The Zero* takes great pleasure in satirizing obsessive hunts for meaning based on thin causal connections. Walter depicts a burgeoning hermeneutic industry devoted to analyzing the textual remnants of the "The Zero": agencies have collected whole hangars full of paper from the Towers that lie in piles under "billboard-sized sign[s] that quoted . . . 'Imagine the look on our enemies' faces when they realize that we have gathered up every piece of paper and put it back!'" (100). Walter satirizes nearly everything about the national response to 9/11, from the obsessive gathering of material from the disaster site, to the commercialization of patriotism, to the corruption and incompetence of the intelligence apparatus. Walter adopts a tone of withering scorn in his excoriation of "The Boss,"—a thinly veiled portrayal of ex-New York City police commissioner Bernard Kerik, for whom Walter briefly worked as a ghostwriter—who is satirized in the novel as a psychotic archivist: "'By god, we will gather every receipt, every purchase order, every goddamned piece of paper . . . otherwise . . . well, I think you know.' 'Sir?' 'They win,' The Boss whispered" (54–55).

Confusion reins, Walter suggests, in a paranoid world where "The Boss" maintains that "every question we ask is a love letter to our enemies" (54). As Remy confides to a supposed informant, "I find myself in these situations. I don't know how I got there, or what I'm doing. I don't know what's going to happen until after it happens. I do things I don't understand and I wish I hadn't done them" (128). Each time he returns to consciousness, Remy tries to reassert a linear temporality, attempting "once again to find the loose string between cause and effect" that would reconnect fragmented moments into a conscious continuum (4). In the narrator's words, "This was the problem. These gaps in his memory, or perhaps his life, [were] a series of skips—long shredded tears, empty spaces where the explanations for the most basic things used to be" (5). Though not prone to philosophizing, Remy speculates: "This is a life, he thought, smooth skipping stones bounding across the surfaces of time, with brief moments of deepened consciousness as you hit the water before going airborne again, flying across the carpool lane, over weeks at a desk" (163).

In *On the Phenomenology of Internal Time* Edmund Husserl asserts that "memory flows continuously, since the life of consciousness flows continuously and does not merely piece itself together link by link into a chain. Rather, everything new reacts to the old" (56). In this influential passage, Husserl means to mark the continuous nature of time as well as two-way causality in which memory inflects and is reshaped by the present.[32] In *The Zero*, Walter shatters this relationship between new and old to metaphorize the sense of rupture triggered by the government's response to September 11. "How had April described her grief—as a fever dream? A dream—that would help explain the gaps, and the general incongruity of life now—the cyclic repletion of events on cable news, waves of natural disaster . . . snippets of songs sampled before their original release, movies remade before they came out the first time, victories claimed before wars were fought, drastic fluxuations in the security markets . . . all of it narrated by fragments of speeches over staged photo ops accompanied by color-coded warnings" (263). For the satirist, the recovery effort and the war on terror offer a rich bounty of targets, one largely untapped by a national media that obeyed a strong self-censorship bias in the wake of the atrocities. Walter's more pervasive social commentary—that we are all like Remy, living dissociatively in order to escape the cognitive dissonance of the profoundly illogical national responses to September 11—uncovers the "gaps" in the public discourse of the war on terror covered over by the commodification of trauma.

CHAPTER 4

Messianic Narrative

Fugitive Pieces, a 1996 novel of the Shoah and its intergenerational aftermath by Canadian novelist and poet Anne Michaels, crystallizes the problems of representation and interpretation endemic to fictions of encountered loss in vivid, poetic prose that carries readers across decades, speakers, and continents. In its gathering of fragments, *Fugitive Pieces* opens itself again and again toward ethical encounters with an unwitnessed past. One notable passage, narrated by Jakob, a child survivor of a Nazi raid whose memoirs constitute Part One of Michaels's novel, serves as my entry point. Though he never witnesses these events, Jakob imaginatively reconstructs the experiences of concentration camp detainees forced to exhume the mass graves of Jews executed during the Nazi attempt to eliminate not only the Jewish people but also the very evidence of that destruction. Michaels is not herself a Holocaust survivor. In fact, she was born in Canada to émigré parents in 1958. Nor were her parents direct witnesses to or victims of the Nazi genocide. This very distance clarifies the creative project of Michaels's novel, which devotes itself not only to articulating the lasting devastation the Shoah inflicts on survivors but, more interestingly, to performing the inheritance of the losses of the past by those in later generations and by humanity writ large. Imagining Jakob imagining concentration camp detainees as they imagine the dead, Michaels stages what I call a messianic encounter with the past:

> When prisoners were forced to dig up the mass graves, the dead entered them through their pores and were carried through their bloodstreams to their brains and hearts. And through their blood into another generation. Their arms were into death up to the elbows, but not only into death—into music, into a memory of the way a husband or son leaned over his dinner, a wife's expression as she watched her child in the bath; into beliefs, mathematical formulas, dreams. As they felt another man's and another's blood-soaked hair through their fingers, the diggers begged forgiveness. And those lost lives made molecular passage into their hands.
>
> How can one man take on the memories of even one other man, let alone five or ten or a thousand or ten thousand; how can they be sanctified each to each? (Michaels 52)

As I see it, Jakob's question (How can we take on the memories of the Other?) poses the central aesthetic problem of *Fugitive Pieces*, perhaps of reading as such, and, in doing so, presupposes an unspoken, a priori, ethical obligation to perform this potentially impossible task. This presupposition of obligation, without which the call would be hollow—namely, that one must struggle toward the Other of history—*is* itself messianic. In this passage, the encounter with the past is apocalyptic for the imagined Jewish victims, for Jakob, and for readers of the novel. I am reminded of Benjamin's prophetic phrase "*Even the dead* will not be safe from the enemy," as well as of the quasi-eschatological violence of the past as we "seize hold of a memory as it flashes up at a moment of danger" (Benjamin, "Theses," thesis 6; italics added). Jakob's narrative lurches between embodiment and abstraction: he offers at once a profoundly physical description of the encounter and one that shatters the body into disconnected pores, blood, and molecules—material in turn bound to the immaterial registers of dreams, beliefs, and theorems. The biological and "molecular" account of intergenerational inheritance as something of the blood, while ironically close to both Nazi ideology and the Jewish notion of election, on closer inspection privileges the proximity of encounter inscribed within a linear temporality. These uncomfortable proximities, like the tension between Michaels's sensuous prose and the violence of genocide, reflect a crisis of agency staged by juxtaposing the compulsory exhumation by camp detainees of their murdered coreligionists with the willed encounter staged by Michaels (in the writing of the text) through Jakob himself.

Thinking about Michaels's novel in these terms makes clear that a messianic imagination empowers not only Jakob's access to the past but Michaels's composition and the readerly experience as well. By presenting the catastrophe of the Shoah to its readers, *Fugitive Pieces* participates in the chain of witness, educating its readers about the events of the past. As the dominant trends in Holocaust studies insist, this testimony—however many levels removed it may be—fulfills an essential mission to bring readers within the fold of conscience. While this pedagogical function is doubtless present, Michaels's work asserts the fundamentally *creative*—not testimonial—event of narration. Jakob's imaginative exhumation obeys the logic of a messianic event, bringing the advent of the new in the guise of the past. *Fugitive Pieces* insists upon relating to the past not only through acts of speech or memory but through assumption, cataclysm, and transformation. As a result, the injunction to "take on the memories of even one other man," posed in the form of a rhetorical question, takes on two meanings. Memories are a burden to be borne by subsequent generations (this is axiomatic to any testimonial theory of Shoah literature), but in Michaels's text they must be "taken on" in a second sense as well: they must be confronted, seized, and in a very real sense violated to bring about the new.[1]

World literature is in the midst of an epochal shift: the violent history of the first half of the twentieth century is fading from living memory, but the events of the First and Second World Wars continue to dominate the imagination of writers—and readers—of subsequent generations. This chapter considers historical fiction by novelists born, like Michaels, after the defining world-historical cataclysms of the midcentury but whose fictions stage problematic encounters with and inheritance of an unwitnessed and catastrophic past. I suggest we think of these works as an important subgenre of historical fiction I call messianic narrative, a category that includes novels like Michaels's *Fugitive Pieces*, Orhan Pamuk's *Snow*, and Haruki Murakami's *The Wind-Up Bird Chronicle* (in which we encounter the Shoah, the Armenian Genocide, and the Japanese experience of the Second World War, respectively), as well as a host of other works of global Anglophone fiction, like Nicole Krauss's *The History of Love*, Jonathan Safran Foer's *Everything is Illuminated*, Toni Morrison's *Beloved*, W. G. Sebald's *Austerlitz*, Ahdaf Soueif's *Map of Love*, and Ian McEwan's *Atonement.*

The history of trauma in the twentieth century—and the conflation of much of that history to trauma—has focused most critical debate on novels like the ones I discuss here through the lenses of witness, testimony, and psychoanalytical accounts of traumatic experience. The psychoanalytic heritage of trauma theory generates a persistent bias toward versions of postmemory and the scriptotherapy thesis, which, hewing to the teleology of the Freudian mourning process, emphasizes the curative function of narrative: "writing about trauma can lead toward individual and collective healing and alleviation of symptoms" (Vickroy 8).[2] Postcolonial and ethnic studies have sensitized readers to the way narratives salvage disavowed pasts in order to reclaim the voices of the disenfranchised, but much of the work by today's global writers falls beyond the pale of this redemptive vision. Such readings risk demoting the literary to a mere gloss on the "authentic" experience of trauma while positing a curative trajectory often resisted by the novels themselves. Suggesting a distinction between narratives of encounter with loss and those with a therapeutic trajectory, I call attention to the way these writers stage the encounter with unwitnessed traumas of the past as a form of messianic event.

In this chapter I try to think through the temporal implications of Walter Benjamin and Jacques Derrida's theories of weak messianism in order to develop new ways of approaching questions of time, trauma, and agency in texts that aim to bear witness to the unwitnessed past. The kinds of questions a messianic critique encourages in thinking about the past include the following: If we conceive of the past (with its determinant content) as Other to us, what orientations toward it can we take? What obligations, what hospitality, what justice do we owe to this other? What places, sensibilities, and practices can hasten the encounter with the past? How do we describe and theorize the nonrelation across the abyss marked by this otherness? And finally, how can we hold on to hope while resisting curative platitudes? Thinking messianically thus complicates and challenges the secular commitments that inform the notions of witness, testimony, and trauma that dominate critical discourse on violence and literature. In this way, the messianic points beyond the judicial model that authorizes testimonial accounts and decenters the role of psychoanalysis.

A history of Judaic, Christian, and Shi'ite messianic thought—as well as the secularized legacy of the messianic within both the revolutionary Marxist traditions on the left and the democratic-capitalist messianism that infuses neoliberal ideology on the right—is beyond the scope of this chapter.[3] Instead, I want to use a few key points in the philosophy of messianism to illustrate the way novels of encountered loss adopt a messianic relation to the past, suggesting that what unites seemingly disparate novels like *Fugitive Pieces*, *Snow*, and *The Wind-Up Bird Chronicle* is how they figure encounters with the past-as-other in messianic terms.[4] In particular, my argument tracks a tradition of messianic thought from its emergence in the Frankfurt School, where cultural critique explicitly conjoins utopian Marxism with the inheritance of Judaic theological messianism, through Hannah Arendt's concepts of natality and forgiveness, to Derrida's late work on faith, the messianic, and undeconstructable justice in order to stress the resources that the messianic offers as an alternate theory of trauma and as an orientation toward the past.

In the most common sense, shared by the three Abrahamic faiths, "messianism" expresses a belief in a redemptive future signaled by an individual savior. Though the etymology of *messiah* leads us back to the Aramaic/Hebrew word for an agent of God anointed with oil, the term emerges in the Anglophone tradition as an invention by the translators of the Geneva Bible, "intended," according to the *Oxford English Dictionary*, "to give it [the anointing ceremony] a more Hebraic aspect." Even here the temporal axis of messianism refuses to point unproblematically toward the future, signaling instead to the Hebraic past, just as Judaic messianism is torn between restorative and utopian trajectories.

As I will briefly show, messianic thought is a conflicted field of tensions not easily reified into simple belief in redemption or in a redeemer. Indeed, scholars recognize the difficulty of speaking of "Christian" or "Jewish" messianism in the singular, recognizing instead the splintered and irreducibly plural and historical messianisms even within Judaism alone in the centuries immediately surrounding the birth of Jesus and within the early Christian community. Critical theory, engaging with messianism in the early twentieth century, was among the first modes of thought to approach the messianic as a subject of more than theological interest. In particular, members of the Frankfurt School used a secularized redeployment of the tropes of Jewish messianism to express their disenchantment with modernity and to endorse a revolutionary, apocalyptic model of political change. For Weimar intellectuals like Benjamin, Adorno, Horkheimer, and others, convinced as they were of the failure of progressive models of reason and liberal politics, Jewish messianism offered a vision of violent apocalypse followed by the advent of an unknowable utopian future.[5] Theodor Adorno's messianic Marxism is subtly manifest in *Negative Dialectics* and more strikingly present in

Minima Moralia, where he echoes Walter Benjamin's redemptive vision of criticism. In the concluding section of *Minima Moralia* (a moving passage worth quoting from at length) he writes: "The only philosophy which can be responsibly practiced in face of despair [*sic*] is the attempt to contemplate all things as they would present themselves from the standpoint of redemption. . . . Perspectives must be fashioned that displace and estrange the world, reveal it to be, with its rifts and crevices, as indigent and distorted as it will appear one day in the messianic light. To gain such perspectives without velleity or violence, entirely from felt contact with its objects—this alone is the task of thought" (247). Adorno's emphasis on messianic criticism as a *necessarily* nonviolent project contrasts sharply with Benjamin's rhetoric of violent rupture and jocular masculine force: "The historical materialist leaves it to others to be drained by the whore called 'Once upon a time' in historicism's bordello. He remains in control of his powers, man enough to blast open the continuum of history" (262). Adorno, tying this practice to the negative dialectics of his earlier work, continues: "But it is also the simplest of all things, because the situation calls imperatively for such knowledge, indeed because consummate negativity, once squarely faced, delineates the mirror-image of its opposite" (247). We can see a similar movement of thought in Horkheimer, whose early optimistic utopianism, like Adorno's, is deeply invested in a secularized idea of Jewish messianism as a trope for political rupture and the emergence of new political orders.

One of the original traveling theories, the messianic idea arises out of the long, diasporic history of Judaism; as Gershom Scholem and others repeatedly stress, Jewish messianism develops within and in response to the condition of exile, and thus it speaks to the endemic modern experience of homelessness. Perhaps of equal importance, Jewish messianism not only enacts but also demands critique: the fear of embracing false messiahs bequeaths a legacy of disputing the emergence of any determinate messiah as an individual (from Jesus to Sabbatai Zevi and later to Hitler). It was not until Scholem, the philosopher and historian of German-Jewish extraction most widely known as the founder of academic studies of Kabbalah, that continental philosophy first engaged the messianic on its own terms. Scholem, Benjamin's lifelong friend who, along with Franz Rosenzweig, had profound influences on the more well-recognized thinkers of the Frankfurt School, is unequivocal in his assessment of messianism's focus on trauma. "Jewish Messianism," as he writes in *The Messianic Idea in Judaism*, "is in its origins and by its nature—this cannot be sufficiently emphasized—a theory of catastrophe. [It is a] theory [that] stresses the revolutionary, cataclysmic element in the transition from every historical present to the messianic future" (7). From Scholem, who writes his authoritative treatise on the messianic after the Second World War, we hear the echo of "Shoah" and destruction in the rhetoric of cataclysm.

We would do well to keep in mind the injunction with which Scholem begins his seminal work on the messianic. "Any discussion of the problems relating to Messianism is a delicate matter," he writes, "for it is here that the essential conflict between Judaism and Christianity has developed. . . . A totally different concept of redemption determines the attitudes to Messianism in Judaism and in Christianity" (1). Although we should be skeptical of Scholem's stark oppositions, his dialectic charts an important field of tensions at work in the messianic idea: first, he distinguishes the public, historical character common to Judaic messianism from the Christian concept of a private, spiritual redemption. Second, within the "common ground of messianic hope," Scholem bifurcates Jewish messianism into restorative and utopian trajectories (4). Messianic time either restores a lost Davidic kingdom or opens toward the arrival of a totally unknowable future; it is this latter anarchic-utopian messianism that has infused the entire discourse of radical otherness. To reiterate, we, like Benjamin and Derrida, inherit from Scholem a vision of the messianic that is not reified in the figure of a savior but is a map of catastrophe and redemption, public and private, and a trope for temporal rupture.

Scholem observes that the messianic idea in Judaism is, historically, at once adaptive to the contexts and pressures of particular eras and yet irreducible to particular contexts, resulting in pendulum-like swings between historical moments when the apocalyptic/utopian messianic mode is in ascendancy and others dominated by the conservative/restorative pole. Likewise, circumstance conditions the relative emphasis placed on nationalism and Jewish statehood. Scholem discusses the restorative and conservative messianism that Moses Maimonides attempts to raise to the level of authoritative principle in his codification of Jewish law in light of the very real threats of rampant apocalypticism (26). In contrast, the relatively distant memory of the apocalypticism of the Middle Ages and the successful rabbinic expurgation of the Sabbatian legacy made possible, in Scholem's view, the willing embrace of utopian strains of messianism aligned with a linear concept of rational progress in the late nineteenth century, and ultimately the Frankfurt School's nihilism. If we extend the spirit of Scholem's insight to Derrida's recuperation of a "structural messianism," an idea of the messianic wholly prior to any determinant content, it seems clear that his intervention, like my own, is conditioned by and responsive to a critical distance from religion that marks a secular age.

As an alternate theory of trauma, messianic thought highlights what we might call the paradox of agency: If the messianic signifies the promise of radical change, what, if anything, can be done to usher in that change, to draw closer the messianic future? It is in terms of the anxiety of agency that Benjamin's—and later, Hannah Arendt's—activist, interventionist ethos departs from that of Derridian/Levinasian expectation. For Benjamin, as for the Apostle Paul and the early Christian community, redemption might be just around the corner. As Benjamin conceived of it, "Every second of time was the strait gate through which the Messiah might enter" ("Theses" 264), while for Derrida the messianic names the openness to an Other who will never arrive. If for Derrida the messianic marks the infinite horizon of a future yet to come and a boundless alterity, Benjamin yearns for the messianic salvage of a past threatened by fascist concepts of progress and homogeneous, teleological time. As Benjamin argues, the critic must "recognize . . . the sign of a messianic cessation of happening, or, put differently, a revolutionary chance in the fight for the oppressed past." They must grasp "the constellation which his own era has formed with a definite earlier one" (263). Thus he establishes a conception of the present as the "'time of the now,' which is shot through with chips of Messianic time" (263). Benjamin describes the activity of the critic and the nature of history with a strikingly physical and material vocabulary that employs terms of seizure, gathering, and fragments. Following the trace of this diction, we find the vestige of Isaac Luria's (1534–72) Kabbalistic mysticism. In the Lurianic cosmology, as described by Scholem and consequently introduced to Benjamin, God formed "vessels" within which to manifest God's being, "but the vessels could not contain the light and thus were broken. This is the phase which the Kabbalists call the 'breaking of the vessels' . . . the light was dispersed" (45). "Healing the world" or *tiqqun* is thus conceived as a gathering of fragments, which are for Benjamin, in Harry Zohn's translation, the aforementioned chips of messianic time. In this way, Benjamin offers a vision of the messianic in which achieving a new relationship with a past lost to historiography is one and the same as the longing for the arrival of the unknown, the wholly Other, which is more traditionally associated with messianism. The crucial point is that messianic time is a cataclysmic hinge, a violent threshold between any determinant moment in the present or past and the advent of an undetermined order.

Of the thinkers who have wrestled most explicitly with the problematics of agency within an explicitly messianic framework, Hannah Arendt stands out as deserving of special consideration. Unlike either the philosophers of the Frankfurt School or Derrida and his contemporary interlocutors, Arendt does not dwell in a self-reflexive fashion on the messianic elements of her work. Arendt's contribution to the messianic comes not in her critiques of totalitarianism but rather in her concept of the *vita activa*. In the tripartite division of labor, work, and action, only in the third sphere does the human animal actualize its capacity for freedom by forging new beginnings within the condition of human plurality. Arendt describes action in *The Human Condition* as "the actualization of the human condition of natality"; she explains that "the new . . . always appears in the guise of a miracle. The fact that man is capable of action means that the unexpected can be expected from him, that he is able to perform what is infinitely improbable" (178). Action is "boundless" and "inherently unpredictable" but continually moves beyond the intentions and control of the actor. In a sense, Arendt's category of "action" falls victim to its own power: without a way to redeem or salvage the possible implications of one's actions, Arendt suggests, the weight of absolute responsibility would condemn those who aspire to the *vita activa* to perpetual indecision. The solution, overtly theological, lies not only in our capacity to make and keep promises but also in our power to forgive. I suggest that we take seriously the religiosity of Arendt's language: "It is like a miracle, like the revelation of divinity, that meaning should have a place in this world," and perhaps more poignantly, "The miracle that saves the world, the realm of human affairs, from its normal, 'natural' ruin is ultimately the fact of natality. . . . Only the full experience of this capacity can bestow upon human affairs faith and hope, those two essential characteristics of human existence" (213).

"FUGITIVE" PIECES OF MESSIANIC TIME

In this context, we must reexamine the plea for absolution uttered by the Jewish slave laborers during the forced exhumation of the mass graves in Michaels's *Fugitive Pieces*. "As they felt another man's and another's blood-soaked hair through their fingers, the diggers begged forgiveness" (52). The very grammar of the enunciation disintegrates: What wrong has been committed? Against whom? Who—or what—could answer their plea? On the one hand, Michaels evokes the debilitating guilt attested to by survivors whose existence was subject to mere chance, the psychic effect of being reduced to bare life. But the passage is not a simple mimetic representation of survivor psychology: if we insist that where no wrong has been committed no forgiveness is possible, and no moral agent exists to respond, the call for forgiveness becomes a call across the abyss, marking the absolute rift between present and past and calling for a purification utterly impossible in the unredeemed world. This is an impossible forgiveness, much in the way that the inheritance of the Shoah is an impossible task, but necessary nonetheless.

Seeking absolution emerges in this specific context as part of a messianic orientation. Pleading for forgiveness enables the weak messianic encounter, as we can see in Michaels's insistent linking of forgiveness and encounter: "The diggers begged forgiveness. *And* those lost lives made molecular passage into their hands" (italics added). This emphasis on forgiveness as facilitating a relationship with the past aligns Michaels with Arendt's messianic conclusion that forgiveness "may be the necessary corrective for the inevitable damages resulting from action" (*Human Condition* 239) and thus a part of the "miracle that saves the world" (247). In Michaels's text we see a similar messianic constellation of catastrophe, forgiveness, and redemption as they collapse into one another in the unstable space of the imagined encounter with the past.

The novel begins with a scene of resurrection and the exhuming of a grave (not, in this case, that of Holocaust victims, but of the narrator): Jakob Beer, a seven-year-old Polish Jew, digs out of the peat in which he has buried himself and approaches a stunned archaeologist excavating an Iron Age village preserved in the bog that was Jakob's erstwhile crypt. He screams "the only phrase I knew in more than one language . . . in Polish and in German and Yiddish, thumping my fists on my own chest: dirty Jew, dirty Jew, dirty Jew" (Michaels 13). During the Nazi raid in which his sister and parents were murdered, Jakob hid behind a wall and thus "did not witness the most important events of my life" (17). With these coordinates—traumatic loss, archaeological reconstruction, burial, the radical implosion of language, and the failure to witness—firmly in place, the novel continues, charting Jakob's course from traumatized survivor, through his rehabilitation by Athos, a Greek archaeologist, into his adulthood as a Holocaust poet writing in English, to his discovery of romantic love shortly before an untimely death in 1993.

If the entirety of the novel were contained in the trajectory I just described, then *Fugitive Pieces* would be a moving, if rather predictable, work of trauma fiction that staged the work of remembering, repeating, and working through suffering. But Jakob's narration—and with it the curative trajectory—accounts for less than two-thirds of the text; a second narrator, Ben, himself a child of survivors who encounters his own lost past through reading Jakob's poems and memoirs, takes up the story after Jakob's death and passes his narrative *and* Jakob's on to the novel's readers. In the light of this second, mirrored narrative encounter with the past, the properly messianic qualities of *Fugitive Pieces* come into sharper focus. Indeed, encounters with an unwitnessed past proliferate throughout the novel: Michaela, Jakob's wife, who "mourns the burning of the library at Alexandria as if it happened yesterday," becomes an empathetic witness to Jakob's loss (176); Jakob himself "cross[es] over the boundary of skin into Michaela's memories, into her childhood" (185). Ben, born after the war, inherits both his parents' unspoken histories and Jakob's narrative; and, finally, we as readers, if we are attentive and open, encounter the entire series through Michaels's fiction.

Indeed, Jakob begins within the melancholic circuit, possessed by the loss of a sister he cannot mourn, but matures into the creative project of opening himself to losses he did not experience. For example, before Jakob adopts a messianic orientation toward the past, memory appears in the guise of violence: Jakob describes "images rising in . . . [him] like bruises" (19), "memory cracking open. The bitter residue flying up into . . . [his] face like ash" (105); he is "scalded" (23) and "ambushed" by time for which he is a "lightning rod" (105). Jakob lacks an orientation to the events of the past capable of channeling its force or asserting agency. Historical research, the "avalanche of facts" (93), similarly fails to transmute his possession by the past into a mode of being capable of taking on the memories of the Other. In one of the novel's most troubling passages, Jakob, and by extension Michaels, "blaspheme[s] by imagining" his sister Bella in a concentration camp and ultimately attempts to picture her death in a gas chamber. While he begins with a determinate goal—"I want to remain close to Bella" (167)—the resulting encounter is not with his lost sister but with a most profound alterity. Jakob writes, "Some gave birth while dying in the chamber. Mothers were dragged from the chamber with new life half-emerged from their bodies. Forgive me, you who were born and died without being given names. Forgive this blasphemy" (168).

Fugitive Pieces suggests that the most inconceivable alterity may be joy. We are told in an initial page of frame narrative that Jakob, Michaela, and their unborn child die in a car accident. Jakob's narrative ends with a prayer to the child he never knows he and his wife have conceived, enacting the messianic logic of intergenerational memory that I have been describing:

> Child I long for: if we conceive you, if you are born, if you reach the age I am now, sixty, I say this to you: Light the lamps but do not look for us. Think of us sometimes, your mother and me. . . . Light the lamp, cut a long wick. One day when you've almost forgotten, I pray you'll let us return. That through an open window . . . the sea air of our marriage will find you. I pray you will suddenly know how miraculous is your parents' love for each other. . . . Once I was lost in a forest. I was so afraid. My blood pounded in my chest and I knew my heart's strength would soon be exhausted. I saved myself without thinking. I grasped the two syllables closest to me, and replaced my heartbeat with your name. (195)

It is worth lingering over Jakob's rhetoric: the cramped space of prayer, the insistent pleading for forgiveness. From the dead Jakob begs forgiveness, calling to an Other who can never answer the call; to the not-yet-born, a prayer for openness. The most striking thing about Jakob's narrative—in addition to its heart-wrenching anguish and beauty—is its treatment of agency and power. My point becomes clearer when we compare the willed abjection of prayer and pleading—the core of Michaels's weak messianic agency—with the messianic agency Benjamin sought in the historical materialist project to "seize hold" "of the genuine historical image as it flares up briefly" and "blast[s] open the continuum of history" with the "constellation which . . . our era has formed with a definite earlier one" (255). For Benjamin, the messianic not only offers an apocalyptic model for political change but also formulates an assertive individualism of empowered action. It expresses the yearning for an event that enables a particular kind of access to the past: "Only a redeemed mankind receives the fullness of its past—which is to say, only for a redeemed mankind has its past become citable in all its moments" (254). The weak messianic task illuminated by Michaels's fiction eschews precisely this kind of sovereign violence while echoing its orientation and instead embraces Arendt's equally messianic understanding of originality ("The new . . . always appears in the guise of a miracle"). Michaels closes off the trajectory of biological inheritance—Jakob's child dies unborn—as if to cast the reader into the address of the prayer. If, as Arendt suggests, "The miracle that saves the world . . . from its normal, 'natural' ruin is ultimately the fact of natality" (*Human Condition* 213), Michaels's novel seems to add that the reading event as natality "can bestow upon human affairs faith and hope, those two essential characteristics of human existence" (213).

If we bring the resources of a critical messianism to bear on fictions of inheritance, we can begin to see them, and the act of reading, as a performative solicitation to the past as Other that transmutes an isolated and devastating inheritance into a communal act that holds something like an emancipatory promise. In contradistinction to strong messianisms of political rupture or apocalypse and redemption, the weak power of a literary messianism voices the faith that we can bear even the most devastating of inheritances and that the rift between present and past can be bridged. Thinking messianically casts light on the events of encounter, anxieties of agency, and meanings of disaster that attend those who, in Michaels's terms, attempt to "take on the memories of even one other man." Literature cannot redeem the past, but we might say instead that messianic narratives unfold as if toward just such an impossible event.

VARIATIONS

That Michaels, a Jewish novelist writing about the defining event of modern Jewish history, should, whether consciously or not, summon messianic registers to engage disaster and redemption does not in itself suggest an emergent global trend. That Haruki Murakami and Orhan Pamuk's work can productively be engaged in these terms—indeed, that their work models a messianic reading practice—suggests that we need a more robustly comparative theological perspective in literary studies. Murakami's work follows the damaged lives of ordinary people in a surreal world—from the Kobe earthquake, to the sarin gas attack in the Tokyo subways, to the legacy of Japan's imperial past and the scars of the Second World War. Like Michaels's, Murakami's work is hard to classify within the limits of any generic or national frame. To Anglo-American and Japanese readers alike, his novels, translated with significant authorial oversight, present startling fusions: seemingly realist narratives flaunt ubiquitous metaphysical hijinks, American jazz music and popular culture saturate a landscape of Shinto shrines and Tokyo love hotels, and stories from the Second World War erupt as seeming non sequiturs within contemporary plots. Murakami's positive reception in the Anglophone world has typically championed this postmodern texture. However, it is often at the expense of adequately coming to terms with the way his work deploys a rhetoric of mysticism or enchantment in order to reckon with Japan's traumatic past and its paradoxical vestiges in the era of neoliberal capitalist globalization.

This "enchantment" manifests itself stylistically in the strangeness particular to Murakami's prose, a bending and stretching of "the real" that is evocative of paintings by Salvador Dalí. In this style, Murakami generates a phenomenology of encounter that resonates productively with a field of messianic tensions. In *The Wind-Up Bird Chronicle* Murakami blends relationships to the past based on empathy and archive, which on their own fail to sustain the task of inheritance, with a mystical, apocalyptic encounter with the past as Other. *The Wind-Up Bird Chronicle*, Murakami's most historically ambitious work of fiction to date, is something of a spoof on the detective novel *qua* mystical bildungsroman. The novel tells the story of Toru Okada and his search for his lost cat and his lost wife, reckoning along the way with Japan's legacy of violence and the threat of political totalitarianism. Responding to the seeming disconnect between the novel's ambitions in the realm of history and its centripetal episodic structure, a reviewer for the *New York Times* remarked that "the juxtaposition of the harrowing, all-too-real war stories with the marvelous, supernatural events in Toru's quest feels contrived. The war narratives were almost certainly composed separately and then inserted into the novel to support its grand aspirations" (Jamie James 1). Regardless of the circumstances of their composition, my argument insists on the opposite conclusion: that the war narratives and their relation to the present lie at the heart of Murakami's messianic creative project.

In one scene, the omniscient narrator—whose perspective is focalized through Toru—describes the protagonist, reflecting on the occasion when his now-disappeared wife informed him of her decision to abort their pregnancy without his consent, knowledge, or presence, a moment he believes was the turning point in their relationship.[6] Toru goes out to a bar where a musician finishes his set, asks for the lights to be dimmed, and then addresses the audience with a speech uncannily suited to Toru's state of mind:

> As you are well aware . . . in the course of life we experience many kinds of pain. Pains of the body and pains of the heart. . . . In most cases, though, I'm sure you've found it very difficult to convey the truth of that pain to another person: to explain it in words. People say that only they themselves can understand the pain they are feeling. But is this true? I for one do not believe that it is. If, before our eyes, we see someone who is truly suffering, we do sometimes feel his suffering and pain as our own. This is the power of empathy. Am I making myself clear? . . . The reason people sing songs for other people is because they want to have the power to arouse empathy, to break free of the narrow shell of the self and share their pain and joy with others . . . and so tonight, as a kind of experiment, I want you to experience a simpler, more physical kind of empathy. (239)

After this extraordinary speech, the man takes a candle and slowly lowers his palm over the flame. "You could see the tip of the flame burning the man's palm. You could almost hear the sizzle of the flesh. A woman released a hard little scream. Everyone else just watched in frozen horror. The man endured the pain, his face distorted in agony. What the hell was this? . . . After five or six seconds of this, he slowly removed his hand from the flame" (239). As it turns out, the performance was a kind of magic trick, and the man presents his uninjured hand to the audience for their inspection.

To readers of ethical theory, this is Levinas or Edith Stein played up for Sartrean effect. But note Toru's reaction of confusion and revulsion, which reflects the reader's similarly stunned reaction, even though by this point in the text we are somewhat habituated to vexing accounts of violence. Does this failure to summon empathy challenge Levinasian ethics? Even bracketing the issue of authenticity temporarily, if we take the performer seriously, he seems to declare that radical alterity is bogus—no Other is wholly Other. Bearing direct visual witness to the pain of another creates an involuntary "physical" response and interpersonal connection. Elsewhere in the novel, sexual intimacy and touch serve as vectors for empathic connection. When Toru touches another character's scarred face, he observes, "Waves of her consciousness pulsed through my fingertips and into me" (Murakami 326). This experience of emotive transfer upon physical contact bears a striking resemblance to the performer's assertion that the witness can share the physical sensation of another. All the same, we may very well be mistaken in our empathic ascriptions. The structural relationship between the performer and Toru mirrors that of Murakami and his readership, creating the unsettling experience that the fiction in which we are bound is something of a trick or ruse, yet one similarly effective and equally enchanting—especially since Toru later assaults this man (the reader is suspicious he may be one of the "metaphysical entities" that populate Murakami's novels) with a baseball bat.

How then do we make sense of the scene earlier in the novel, in which Toru listens to a story of suffering narrated by Lieutenant Mamiya, a survivor of Japan's Manchurian front in the Second World War and a long detention in Soviet gulags? He describes to Toru the experience, kept hidden since the war, of a secret mission across the Mongolian border during which he was captured by a group of Mongol warriors led by a Russian intelligence officer. The Russian officer proceeds to torture Mamiya's superior, Yamamoto, with graphic perfection. After an eloquent description of the history of Mongolian brutality and their skill as skinners of sheep, he pauses to present the skinning knife to the man about to be tortured for his inspection: "I want you to look at this knife. Closely. It is a very special knife, designed for skinning, and it is extraordinarily well made. . . . They can take a man's skin off the way you'd peel a peach" (159). The officer describes the process in detail, and then orders the Mongol to skin Mamiya's superior alive, forcing Mamiya to watch until "all that remained lying on the ground was Yamamoto's corpse, a bloody red lump of meat from which every trace of skin had been removed" (160). They then throw Mamiya down the shaft of a dry well and leave him for dead. After these events, Mamiya is an entirely broken man; as he says, "Real life may have ended for me deep in that well in the desert of Outer Mongolia. I feel as if, in the intense light that shone for a mere ten or fifteen seconds a day in the bottom of the well, I burned up the very core of my life, until there was nothing left" (170). In the novel's present, Toru sits at the bottom of a metaphorical dry well of his own, mirroring Mamiya's experience, and reflects on the strange performative demand for empathy he witnessed at the bar.

For Mamiya, trauma exceeds the power of empathy (witnessing the torturing of Yamamoto, Mamiya "did nothing but vomit. Over and over again"); for Toru, empathy across trauma seems impossible (160). Toru seemingly makes no response at all in the event of his bearing witness to Mamiya's tale. Instead, he is the ideal confessor but remains separated from any powerful experience, until, that is, the narrative accesses other modes of representing alterity when the novel breaks the rules of testimonial and evidence and becomes surreal. The gap separating self from other does at least "seem" to be bridged in the out-of-body experiences that make up much of the novel, in which Toru passes between one world and the next (the description is Murakami's). "The real" of the novel is more porous in certain sacral and ritual spaces—in this case a dry well into which Toru descends and which mirrors the Siberian well in which Mamiya suffered. In these mystical moments, Murakami offers an alternate phenomenology of the encounter with loss grounded in a set of spiritual practices that center on ritual spaces; the existence of marginally coextensive "worlds," "energy," or "flow" immanent to our world but beyond the pale of positive science; and a rejection or overturning of the law.

Understood as a form of apostasy from the laws of realism, the novel's rejection of mimesis can be seen as the stylistic analogue of the apostasy and renunciation required of any messiah, as was indeed the case within a Pauline conception of Christianity. The apostate messiah is a familiar trope too among followers of a less well-known factional leader, Sabbatai Zevi, the seventeenth-century Jewish mystical leader whose conversion to Islam and transgressions against Mosaic law were seen among followers as evidence of his status as messiah. As Scholem stresses in his writings on the messianic, messiahs overturn existing orders; messianic thought in all its forms is nonevolutionary and posits rupture, disjunction, and nonidentity. It is also a name given to hope, to faith itself, such that Derrida speaks of a structural messianism implied by the I-Thou relationship and any idea of justice. In the example of Sabbatai Zevi, the necessary apostasy of the messiah implies a new form of double coding and double reading, already familiar to many Diaspora Jews who, like the Marranos of Spain, were forced to live dichotomous public and private religious lives. Murakami's book demands a similar double reading, in this case of a narrative space that is a space of enchantment threatened by false messiahs.

In the case of Orhan Pamuk's *Snow*, while many critics in the Anglophone world have focused on the political themes that make the novel such a compelling read, such critiques tend to exclude what the narrator, Orhan, claims is "the heart of our story," namely the question "How much can we ever know about the love and pain in another's heart?" (259). By placing *Snow* in dialogue with *Fugitive Pieces* and *The Wind-Up Bird Chronicle*, I want to trace the effect of the unacknowledged trauma of the Armenian Genocide in the novel on its own terms and, on a larger level, to construct a comparative framework within which the echoes of Jewish, Shinto, Islamic, and Marxist messsianisms can be seen working across Anglophone fiction. In *Snow*, though the narrator can retrace the steps of his murdered friend and plunder the archives of his letters and journals, Ka's lost poems underscore the abyss that ultimately separates self and other, present and past. To understand the messianic sorrow implicit in this paradox, we must learn to be attentive to the way the spectral presence of the Armenian Genocide illuminates the abyssal nature of history, which, for Pamuk, finds its analogue in both the otherness of those we know best and in the creative process itself.

During interviews, Pamuk's relatively strident tone when speaking on the subject of the Armenian Genocide ("Thirty thousand Kurds and a million Armenians were killed in these lands [Turkey]. Almost no one dares to speak out about this but me"), which led to his indictment on charges of insulting Turkishness, offers a vivid contrast to the oblique references to the tragedy in his fiction.[7] In *Snow*, the Armenians are present only in their absence: "There had been a large Armenian community [in Kars]," the narrator notes, eliding the facts of genocide and human agency. "It no longer existed, but its thousand-year-old churches still stood in all their splendor" (20). Most explicitly, during a political meeting Ka overhears "a defeatist in the crowd [who] slyly asked, 'And whatever happened to the millions of Armenians who once lived all across Anatolia, including Kars?'" (296). Indeed, Pamuk seems to have chosen Kars as the novel's setting for its status as a uniquely palimpsestic border town, bearing traces of Armenian, Ottoman, Russian, and finally Turkish rule. Often, during Ka's peripatetic ruminations, "he tarried before an empty old Armenian house," though the reader is not privy to his thoughts during these delays (166). The narrator makes no attempt to imagine himself into the world inhabited by the Armenians, no attempt to heal the wounds of the past with words. Instead, the narrator tries to understand Ka, and specifically to recover the nineteen inspired poems that came to Ka "from outside, from far away" during his stay in Kars (122).

Orhan makes expansive claims of omniscience ("I begin this story knowing everything that will happen to him [Ka] during his time in Kars"), but he is unable to recover the poems themselves (5). In this way, the absent presence of Ka's poems in Pamuk's novel is structurally analogous to the absent presence of the Armenians in Kars. Ka "did not believe himself to be the true author of any of the poems that came to him in Kars. . . . He believed himself to be but the medium, the amanuensis, in a manner well exampled by the predecessors of his modernist bête noires" (377). So close is the experience of poetry to prophecy for Ka—"I can't be sure, but I think it is God who is sending me the poems," he tells a young Islamist in a confessional moment—that Ka finds himself starting to believe in God (124). Ka never fully understands his poems, however, and never writes again after he leaves Kars; likewise, though the narrator tracks every trace of Ka's life, even going so far as to "pretend . . . [he] was Ka," the other remains lost amid archives, just like the empty shells of the Armenian houses and churches of Kars.

On the novel's final page, the narrator relates an emphatic rejection of empathy, and a warning to the reader, spoken by Necip, a devout young writer from Kars: "I'd like to tell your readers not to believe anything you say about me, anything you say about any of us. No one could understand us from so far away" (426). Though Necip implies that the distance between a reader in the West and his life in Kars can be bridged with sufficient local knowledge, the novel itself arrives at a more radical distinction. In answer to the narrator's question "How much can a man hear another's voice inside him?"—an echo of Michaels's "How can one man take on the memories of even one other man?" (52)—*Snow* suggests that we can hear it only faintly but that we must open ourselves to it nonetheless, knowing full well that it may never come.

By bringing the resources of a critical messianism to bear on fictions of encounter, I have argued that we can see them, and the act of reading, as a performative solicitation to the past as other. This transmutes an isolated and devastating inheritance into a communal act that holds something like an emancipatory promise. I would like conclude by parsing a distinction between the logic of penitence and that of the messianic. Ian McEwan's *Atonement* (2001) begins as a work of realist fiction told by a seemingly omniscient narrator, Briony Tallis, offering something of a portrait of the artist as a young girl. The novel is set in the late 1930s, during which the precipitous events of Germany's rearmament sift out into the Home Counties where the Tallis family resides in a country estate. The crux of the story revolves around a series of misrecognitions, Briony's "authorly" attempt to forge a coherent narrative out of events even as she employs them within a Gothic trajectory,[8] and false testimony: thirteen-year-old Briony watches a silent tableau unfold between her older sister Cecilia and Robbie Turner, a servant's son who is also Cecilia's schoolmate at university, in which the two struggle over a vase they are both trying to fill; when it breaks and falls into the fountain, Cecilia strips down to her underwear and climbs into the fountain to retrieve the pieces. When Briony later reads a note Robbie has her carry to Cecilia (he gives her the "wrong" version, the private one, in which he adds the line "In my dreams I kiss your cunt, your sweet wet cunt. In my thoughts I make love to you all day long"), her naïveté prevents her from understanding the note and therefore she misinterprets the complex mutuality of desire to be coercion when she interrupts Cecilia and Robbie having sex in a dark corner of the library (80). When, later that night, Briony's cousin Lola is raped by an assailant she cannot identify, Briony (who does not see the man clearly either) "knows" it was Robbie: "She could describe him. There was nothing she could not describe" (155). On the basis of her testimony, Robbie is imprisoned, released only to serve in the infantry, and Cecilia never forgives her sister.

During the course of the war, Briony realizes the magnitude of the crime she has committed and attempts to atone for it, trying in meaningful ways to make amends with Cecilia and Robbie by redacting her statements and confessing her lie to her family. Only in the final section of the novel, set in the present day, do we learn that the novel we have been reading is actually a work by Briony herself, that Cecilia and Robbie both died in the war, and that the novel Briony has written is an attempt to offer them an alternate ending.[9] Briony uses fiction in the attempt to set things right, not "in the service of the bleakest realism," but rather in the hope that "as long as there is a single copy, a solitary typescript of my final draft, then my spontaneous, fortuitous sister and her medical prince survive to love" (350). But the fiction is merely that, as Briony explains: "How can a novelist achieve atonement when, with her absolute power of deciding outcomes, she is also God? There is no one, no entity or higher form that she can appeal to, or be reconciled with. . . . There is nothing outside her . . . no atonement for God, or novelists, even if they are atheists" (350–51).

The principle of atonement articulated by Briony and McEwan implies a fuzzy ontology that can be brought into tighter focus through the lens of weak messianism. Atonement, "the condition of being *at one* with others; unity of feeling, harmony, concord, agreement; the means or agent of appeasement; the restoration of friendly relations," arises, as the *Oxford English Dictionary* reveals, from the phrase that the word condenses (at-*one*-ment), as in the sixteenth-century examples, "to reconcile hymselfe and make an onement with god," and "the redempcion, reconciliacion, and at onement of mankinde with God the father." Atonement is thus both an act undertaken by a specific agent and, more importantly, the description of an intersubjective state. Of course, Briony's equation of equivalence between the novelist and God is an intentionally cynical one. The entire novel has been "about" the plurality of perspectival grounds within which particular events achieve meaning and the importance of justice and reconciliation in the realm of human others and our personal, familial, and historical lives (rather than any transcendent appeal to divine grace, for instance).

The idea of atonement maps a series of tensions between its concrete denotation (atonement as a model of a retributive debt and reconciliation) and its more abstract connotation (atonement as a modality of being). The messianic, however, arises out of an entirely contradictory sense of ontology, namely that relation, oneness, retribution, and forgiveness are all a priori impossible in the radical sense within the world of immanence. As Benjamin might put it, "Only a redeemed mankind receives the fullness of its past" ("Theses" 254), or, in Adorno's words from the closing lines of *Minima Moralia*, the atonement Briony seeks is possible only from "the standpoint of redemption" (254). The messianic offers an account of an orientation toward the very other(s) Briony denies when she claims that "there is nothing outside her" (350). We might say, finally, that the conclusion Briony and McEwan reach in the final lines of *Atonement* ("It was always an impossible task, and that was precisely the point. The attempt was all") is the beginning of a messianic orientation toward the past (350).

CHAPTER 5

Reading Islam

In 2002, the University of North Carolina at Chapel Hill was engulfed by a firestorm of controversy for selecting Michael Sells's *Approaching the Qur'an: The Early Revelations* as the summer reading text for incoming first-year students. On its "Carolina Summer Reading Program 2002" webpage, specifically citing the tragic events of the previous fall as inspiring its choice, the university explained:

> Westerners for centuries have been alternately puzzled, attracted, concerned, and curious about the great religious traditions of Islam. These feelings have been especially intense since the tragic events of September 11. *Approaching the Qur'an* is not a political document in any sense, and its evocation of moral "reckoning" raises questions that will be timely for college students and reflective adults under any circumstances. The Carolina Summer Reading program is especially happy to offer a book of enduring interest this year that also offers the Carolina community an appropriate introduction to the literature and culture of a profound moral and spiritual tradition that many of us now wish to learn more about.[1]

Students were asked to read Sells's book, compose a one-page response prior to their arrival on campus, and participate in a two-hour seminar led by faculty and staff during orientation. For a growing number of first-year college students, a discussion of a novel or work of literary nonfiction in a small-group seminar constitutes the first academic experience of their college career; at UNC in 2002, it was an object lesson in academic freedom and the rise of anti-Islamic sentiment.[2] Outrage over the assignment was immediate and systematic, catapulting UNC's summer reading program into national headlines and ultimately the courtroom. While highlighting the surge of interest in Islam after 9/11, the controversy also underscores the incendiary nature of debates about the role of religion in the public sphere and, more specifically, raises questions with far-reaching epistemological and pedagogical implications about what kind of knowledge reading "about the great tradition of Islam," as UNC put it, might be expected to produce.

James Yacovelli, of the Family Policy Network, claimed in a Fox News interview on July 8, 2002, that reading *Approaching the Qur'an*, which includes annotated translations of thirty-five of the Qur'an's 114 suras and a compact disc recording of Qur'anic recitation in Arabic, could lead to conversion. Whether in good or bad faith, Yacovelli attributed transformative power to the reading experience: teaching the book, he asserted, was "really a veiled coercion to get students to accept Islam."[3] Alleging infringements on the First Amendment's protection of free religious exercise and violations of the establishment clause, several incoming freshmen backed by Yacovelli's socially conservative Christian advocacy group filed a lawsuit to bar the assignment on constitutional grounds. For its part, the university stood by its choice of text and made a principled defense of academic freedom; it also noted that concessions in the assignment specifically allowed students "opposed to reading parts of the Qur'an because to do so is offensive to their own faith" the option of composing a statement on why they elected not to read the book. On August 19, three hours before the orientation sessions were scheduled to begin, the Virginia Fourth Circuit Court of Appeals issued a unanimous decision denying the requested injunction, and students in 160 discussion sections, attended by reporters from the *New York Times*, CNN, FOX News, and the *Chronicle of Higher Education*, began their university educations by briefly discussing the thirty-five suras translated and analyzed in Sells's book.

From the standpoint of constitutional law, the legality of UNC's assignment was hardly in doubt. Since the origin of the field in the late nineteenth century, religious studies programs of various sorts have become ubiquitous in university education and have avoided serious legal challenges based on First Amendment grounds. The landmark 1963 Supreme Court case *Abington v. Schempp* drew sharp distinctions between unconstitutional school prayer and desirable academic study of religion; the UNC assignment hews carefully toward the latter. Writing for the majority in *Abington*, Justice Tom Clark asserts that "one's education is not complete without a study of comparative religion," adding furthermore that "nothing we have said here indicates that . . . study of the Bible or of religion, when presented objectively as part of a secular program of education, may not be effected consistently with the First Amendment" (274). In short, though specifically concerned with the issue of mandatory school prayer and Christian holy texts, the decision explicitly affirms nondevotional uses of religious materials more broadly—what Clark calls "teaching *about* the Holy Scriptures or *about* the differences between religious sects," without which "it would be impossible to teach meaningfully many subjects in the social sciences or the humanities" (374; italics added).

As a community-building exercise, the UNC assignment attempts to distinguish the knowledge-seeking ethos of the university from the muscular, Islamophobic patriotism circulating at that time in the American public sphere. But though the assignment praises Islam as the source of "great religious traditions"—a phrase that both gestures to the diversity of Islamic life and echoes the repeated assertions made by the Bush administration and others in the wake of 9/11 that Islam is a "religion of peace"—the robust statement of difference between "us" and "them" embedded in the assignment maintains the premise of Islam's alterity.[4] The cultural sensitivity and assertions of political neutrality evident in the assignment are indeed problematic, though for reasons different from those raised by conservatives, who faulted the university for its culture of political correctness as a part of a more general campaign to delegitimize academia through allegations of liberal bias. In a double-edged gesture of exclusion and openness, the assignment conceives Islam as an object of study that is both the (non-Western) Other and, unmoored from its political or religious modalities, a subject of universal "moral" significance. Though the assignment deliberately echoes the semantics enshrined in *Abington v. Schempp* regarding the study of religion in public education, in this case reading "about" Islam seems less to imply a secular approach to sacred materials and more to articulate a framework of identity and difference. While it extends the open hand of a putatively inclusive pluralism, the assignment nonetheless foregrounds the cultural rift between an explicitly non-Muslim Western reading audience and the object of study. This assumption is both factually incorrect (many college students are, of course, Muslim) and methodologically suspect.[5] On the one hand, the assignment echoes a "clash of civilizations" rhetoric that erroneously assumes the coherence of the subjects it purports to investigate and on behalf of whom it speaks, while on the other hand it amplifies a dangerous tendency to tokenize religious minorities, a situation all too common in the experience of Muslim Americans.

While it would be hard to imagine that UNC or any other public university would assume that Jewish Americans, who constitute a minority roughly equivalent in size to that of the American Muslim population, would not be part of an incoming class, Muslim students seem conspicuously overlooked as potential participants in the assignment, or, indeed, as "Westerners."[6] Those who would cite the history of "Judeo-Christian" culture to excuse this bias would do well to remember the relative novelty of "Judeo-Christian" as a concept: the now-familiar term was disseminated only during and after the Second World War.[7] Though estimates regarding Muslim populations in the United States vary widely, between five and seven million Americans currently identify as Muslim (Esposito 220–23).[8] According to Gallup's *Muslim Americans: A National Portrait*, a report based on a 2009 poll, American Muslims are a growing, young, and well-educated minority with high levels of employment. American Muslims are "one of the most diverse religious groups in the United States," with 35 percent identifying as African American (an explicit reminder of Islam's long tenure in the "West"), 28 percent as white, 18 percent as Asian, and 18 percent as "other" (10). Not only do a greater percentage of American Muslims achieve college degrees than the general US population (29 percent vs. 25 percent), Muslim Americans also are strongly represented in high-income brackets and technical fields (11–12). While South Asian Muslims, including those from India and parts of the Indonesian archipelago, have long lived as minority communities within larger political formations, the globalization of Islam means that more Muslims than ever are living as minority communities rather than in areas Islamized through conquest, which historically created more homogeneous Muslim societies. These statistics and the diasporic trajectories they represent are significant reminders of existing pluralism and long global histories of interconnection.[9] Large, significant, and diverse Muslim populations are a fact, and diverse Anglophone

Muslim reading publics constitute a trend of growing statistical and cultural significance.[10]

The desire on the part of the European and American reading publics to learn more about Islam in the aftermath of 9/11, a phenomenon of which UNC's summer reading assignment offers a particularly lucid example, spurred the publication of numerous books aiming, in one way or another, to satisfy an Anglophone, non-Muslim audience eager for information. In the month after 9/11, Penguin Classics printed an additional twenty thousand copies of N. J. Dawood's paperback English translation, *The Koran*, a version originally published in 1956 and widely regarded as an inadequate edition that propagates sexist and violent images of Islam.[11] This fivefold increase in sales, though small in absolute terms, reflects both a general groundswell of interest in Islamic studies and the ingrained patterns of prejudice within which notions about Islam have circulated in Anglophone culture, trends with enduring impacts on patterns of cultural production and consumption.[12]

In part, this failure can be traced to the fact that literary portrayals of Islam, like those in visual media—and the networks of circulation, debate, and cultural consumption of which they are a part—trend more toward the pleasures of projective fantasy and xenophobic fear-mongering than toward the difficult work of exchange, engagement, and translation.[13] More often than not, images of Muslims in Anglophone fiction and memoir conform to familiar, mass-mediated stereotypes that cast characters in limited, gendered ways. The most common role for Muslim men is that of the bearded fundamentalist or suicide bomber.[14] The Muslim man as playboy hydrocarbon billionaire, another commonly circulated image, puts a contemporary spin on what was once the dominant image of Islam in narratives of the 1500s through the collapse of the Ottoman Empire: the Muslim man as decadent, sexualized, effeminate Turk.[15] Muslim women, meanwhile, are ubiquitous as the covered objects of Islamic oppression. Books by and about such women have emerged as among the most conspicuously successful publishing phenomena of the past decade: "The veiled, oppressed Muslim woman," notes *New York Times* columnist Lorraine Adams, "has become overexposed. American book clubs consume her memoirs. Novels about her, so long as they are bleak, appear in the windows of our bookstores. Intellectuals argue over how she should be described and who can save her."[16]

READING PIETY

The first chapter of Khaled Hosseini's *The Kite Runner*, a brief frame only three paragraphs in length, establishes the voice of its confessional first-person narrator, Amir, and maps the novel's ethical, temporal, and geographic coordinates. Its dated heading, December 2001, anchors the novel to the newly begun Afghan war; "unatoned sins" introduce theological and retrospective preoccupations connecting California to Kabul; and a hymnic phrase, "*There is a way to be good again*," establishes its prominent redemptive teleology (2; italics in original). The novel, which spent more than four years on the *New York Times* best-seller list after being passed over by major publishers, elicited a resoundingly sympathetic reception from an American and later an international audience. Their hunger for nuanced accounts of an enigmatic nation suddenly central to global politics found satisfaction in the universal ethical themes discussed in book clubs, chat rooms, and classrooms—regret, redemption, love, friendship—and the particularity of its setting, which depicts Afghanistan under Zahir Shah, the Soviet invasion, and the Taliban in mimetic prose lush with ethnographic detail. But what is the relation between the novel's redemptive ethical trajectory and its religious one? To put it another way, how does the novel construe the relationship between being good (again) and being Muslim?

Through several close readings of the novel's depictions of piety, I want to parse out why Amir's nascent religiosity in no way threatens the novel's comforting message to its overwhelmingly Christian audience. While the novel does not model rigorous theological inquiry, and neither Hosseini nor I write as an *alim*, a scholar recognized as an arbiter on religious matters, Hosseini's depictions of specific forms of Muslim religious revival in his spiritual bildungsroman nonetheless reward close examination. The plot begins in a vibrant Kabul of secular universities and Sufi poetry under the modernizing rule of Zahir Shah. Early in the novel, Islamic piety is simply and negatively correlated with social class: Amir's father, Baba, an affluent Pashtun businessman, embodies a fierce pro-Western Kemalist secularism; his servant Ali, a poor, illiterate Shi'a and a member of the oppressed Hazara minority, is the novel's figure of piety and has earned the status of *hafiz*—one who has memorized the Qur'an. The novel culminates, however, with a personal crisis in which Amir undergoes a conversion experience that leads him from the identitarian secularity of his childhood to the life of a devout and practicing Muslim. Between these two poles unfolds the novel's well-known plot trajectory, which begins, we are told in the novel's first line, "on a frigid overcast day in the winter of 1975" (1). Amir, then thirteen years old, has ventured out to a kite-fighting competition with his childhood companion Hassan, the cleft-lipped son of his family's servant with whom he was raised. Despite the strong bond between them and his friend's unyielding loyalty, Amir fails to come to his aid when Hassan falls victim to the novel's arch-villain, Assef, a half-German Nazi sympathizer, who rapes Hassan while Amir looks on. After fleeing to America with his father in the aftermath of the Soviet invasion and leaving his past behind, Amir returns to Afghanistan in the summer of 2001 at the behest of his family friend Rahim Kahn, who reveals that Hassan (who is actually Amir's half-brother) and his wife have been murdered by the Taliban, leaving their son, Sohrab, in an orphanage. Traveling with a false beard to Kabul, Amir finds Sohrab in a military compound where he has been forced into sexual slavery by Amir's childhood nemesis, Assef, who joined the Taliban to indulge his sadistic fantasies. In a scene that replays the trajectory of their earlier conflict, down to Assef's brass knuckles, Amir stands his ground against his enemy at a harrowing physical cost—until Sohrab steps to Amir's aid and ends the David and Goliath conflict with his slingshot, unknowingly making good on his father's threat a generation earlier to put a stone through the eye of Amir's oppressor.

The melodramatic plot, which Meghan O'Rourke accurately faults in her review of the novel as "an allegory of redemption and healing . . . too neatly reflected in the novel's tidy mirror," affirms the justness of the US cause in Afghanistan and valorizes the inevitable wounding that wars incur. But while Hosseini's text clearly leverages its ideological compatibility with a newly ascendant interventionist foreign policy, the stakes of religious revival in the novel are more ambivalent.[17] For the Anglophone audience of *The Kite Runner*, religious resurgence among young Muslim men is a subject coded primarily in terms of security threats. In policy debates and editorials, discussions of Islamist revivalism are commonly tied to calls for Islamic "reform," "liberalization," or "secularization."[18] In the North Atlantic world, as Saba Mahmood argues, "Against the backdrop of two decades of the ascendance of global religious politics, urgent calls for the reinstatement of secularism have reached a crescendo that cannot be ignored. The most obvious target of these strident calls is Islam" ("Secularization" 323).[19] In *The Kite Runner*, however, Amir's religious resurgence operates in parallel with political secularization.

Once-commonplace understandings of secularization as a universal process and of the secular as the absence of religion have been replaced, in recent years, with more complex accounts that have overturned the secularization thesis dominant in the social sciences. Within much of the global Muslim community, however, secularism is often perceived as antithetical to Islam's basic tenets. In 2011, IslamOnline, the multilingual Doha-based portal, reported that a broad consensus among Muslim scholars holds that "Islam is fundamentally opposed to secularism" and that the majority of Muslims view secularism as a doctrine of "unbelief" ("Islam and Secularism"). Though paradoxical from a perspective that sees religion as the opposite of the secular, critical secularity studies have renewed the relevance of religious knowledge and helped restore its importance within comparative study. Through these methodologies and the new interdisciplinary networks of knowledge they produce, we can see how in Hosseini's novel Amir hybridizes the somatic practices of Islam and the conceptual armature of Protestant Christian "secularity" to form a translation zone between Islam and Christianity and, in doing so, polices boundaries around non-normative forms of religious subjectivity.[20]

School provides Amir's first formal encounter with Islamic theology and religious instruction: in the fifth grade, Amir reports, "we had a mullah who taught us about Islam" (15). Amir's religious education consists largely of memorization of verses from the Qur'an in an Arabic he cannot understand, followed by indoctrination in ethical precepts at odds with his father's capitalist, atheist beliefs. The encounter Hosseini stages between atheism and traditional Islam is not meant to be an equal one, as a comparison of their respective avatars makes clear: "Mullah Fatiullah Kahn, a short, stubby man with a face full of acne scars and a gruff voice," represents the latter, while the physically impressive Baba, Amir's father, champions secularism (15). The novel represents religious education as somatically and intellectually unpleasant: after the mullah "lectured" the students on the importance of charity, performing the hadj, and prayer, he "told us one day that Islam considered drinking a terrible sin; those who drank would answer for their sin on the day of *Qiyamat*, Judgment Day" (16). The Qur'an is, for Amir, a closed text relegated to uncomprehending recitation: Mullah Kahn "made us memorize verses from the Koran—and though he never translated the words for us, he did stress, sometimes with the help of a stripped willow branch, that we had to pronounce the Arabic words correctly so God would hear us better" (15–16). In the novel's terms, the young men of the Taliban—an Arabic term for student—are not only intolerant, murderous warlords but precisely those students who would have been sympathetic to the vision of mullahs like Kahn.

Atheist secularism and laissez-faire capitalism constitute the central tenets of the world system of which Amir's father, Baba, imagines himself a part, and they form the domestic frame for Amir's religious resurgence. Baba's black Ford Mustang and the stories of his bear-wrestling past evoke a potent combination of muscular individualism and fiscal success, in which tradition and modernity are the warp and the weft of a single cloth. Against the example of piety represented by the diminutive mullah in Amir's school, Baba uses his towering figure and commanding social authority to inveigh against the tyrannies of religion: "Do you want to know what your father thinks about sin?" Baba asks, theatrically pouring himself a whiskey after Amir has asked him about the sins of alcohol. "You'll never learn anything of value from those bearded idiots. . . . There is only one sin, only one. And that is theft. Every other sin is a variation of theft" (17). In another tirade, Baba curses the mullahs who "do nothing but thumb their rosaries and recite a book written in a tongue they don't even understand. God help us all if Afghanistan ever falls into their hands" (270).

Baba offers readers a neoconservative fantasy in which "American" values and traditional cultural heritage serve as a formula for success in the developing world. To underline this compatibility, Hosseini aligns Baba's foreign policy positions with those of the American Right, particularly on the subject of Israel: "There are only three real men in this world, Amir," Baba tells his son, personifying nations much in the way Hosseini's narrative invites its readers to do more generally, "'America the brash savior, Britain, and Israel. The rest of them'—he used to wave his hand and make a phht sound—'they're like gossiping old women'" (125). When accused of allying with distant nations against his coreligionists, Baba rejects the relevance of Islam to what he identifies as questions of work ethic and a culture of dependency: "'Religion has nothing to do with it.' In Baba's view, Israel was an island of 'real men' in a sea of Arabs too busy getting fat off their oil to care for their own. 'Israel does this, Israel does that,' Baba would say in a mock-Arabic accent. 'Then do something about it! Take action. You're Arabs, help the Palestinians, then'" (125).[21] As Amir puts it after his father's death from cancer, Baba was "an unusual Afghan father, a liberal who had lived by his own rules, a maverick who had disregarded or embraced societal customs as he had seen fit" (180). More accurately, Baba lives by what José Casanova classes as the most radical form of "being secular," a "secularist secularity" characterized by "the phenomenological experience not only of being passively free but also actually of having been liberated from 'religion' as a condition for human autonomy and human flourishing" (60). If political secularism requires that the state ensure basic freedom of belief and (as opposed to laic and establishment models) act neutrally toward religions, Baba's *polemical* secularism actively seeks the extinction of religion. At the same time, the novel reveals how this ideology has become entangled with economic neoliberalism and a militarily interventionist foreign policy in the first decade of the twenty-first century.

Although Baba's self-construction relies on Charles Taylor's "subtraction stories" of secularization, the social and material forms of his actions closely follow the central ethical dictates of the Qur'an, particularly those of the early Meccan suras. The achievement in which he takes greatest pride, and one of the most memorable events in Amir's childhood, was his building of a modern orphanage in central Kabul, a project he designed, funded, and implemented without state support. Though Baba claims to be militantly "secular," his charitable deeds fulfill the duty of *zakat*, one of the five pillars of Islam, and are emblematic of the Qur'an's most distinctive and repeatedly invoked ethical precepts—generosity toward the orphan.[22] Baba is thus both an opponent of the welfare state and, behind this neoconservative screen, the epitome of the generous hero, the *karim*, willing to give up his fortune—spending "the balance of his life savings" on his son's wedding party—or his life in the service of others. Baba's self-sacrifice thus represents an ideal that is integral to the mythology of pre-Islamic Arabia adapted and transformed by the Qur'an's injunctions toward social justice.[23]

On the occasion of Eid Al-Adha, Muslims around the world mark the prophet Ibrahim's willingness to sacrifice his son and God's subsequent intervention with a festival. As Hosseini describes it, though "*Baba mocks the story behind this* Eid, *like he mocks everything religious,*" he sacrifices a sheep every year (76). With the same slightly pedantic tone that characterizes his use of Pashtun terms and Afghan place-names, Hosseini explains that, despite the fact that "*the custom is to divide the meat in thirds, one for family, one for friends, and one for the poor . . . every year, Baba gives it all to the poor*" (76; italics in original). By preserving—indeed, by exceeding—the intentions of religious law, Baba's specific mode of secularism, while closed to transcendence, nonetheless incorporates the values and ritual forms of normative Islam.[24] At other times, Baba's secular ethics take the vernacular forms of *Pashtunwali*, the unwritten code of the Pashtun tribes governing bravery and justice, *tureh* and *badal* in Pashto.[25] Despite his avowed secularity, Baba's construction of orphanages conforms more clearly to Islamic concepts of repentance or atonement through acts of charity than does Amir's more radical existential suffering, though *The Kite Runner* claims Amir as the observant Muslim. In these examples, it becomes clear that despite the vehemence of Baba's secularist ideology, the practiced forms of his secularity are not culturally unmarked products of universal reason, as many proponents of the secularization thesis have claimed; instead, they unfold along culturally specific trajectories that preserve and incorporate contingent Islamic norms.

Against the background of Baba's militant atheism on the one hand and the Taliban's violent, antimodern interpretation of Islam on the other, Amir's religious revival constitutes an attractive middle path. Amir's conversion occurs late in the novel, once he and Sohrab are recovering in the relative safety of Pakistan. Having discovered that the bureaucratic machinery of global governance has blocked Amir's attempted adoption, Sohrab slices his wrists in the bathtub; as he teeters between life and death, religious energies long dormant within Amir inspire a private revelation of divine transcendence that culminates in a public profession of faith. In the hallway of the hospital Amir recites the *shahada*, the normative Muslim declaration of belief that serves as a necessary condition of Islamic identity, and commits himself to what he sees as the straight path of Islam. After the final *sparagmos* of Sohrab's suicide attempt and the catharsis of conversion, the remainder of the novel offers little more than denouement: plot contrivances ensure Sohrab's adoption by Amir, though his emotional rehabilitation will take time. Finally, "One Tuesday morning last September, the Twin Towers came crumbling down and, overnight, the world changed" (362); two paragraphs later the Taliban have "scurried like rats into caves" (363). Between these world-historical changes, Amir "prayed morning *namaz*" while his wife slept; only now, after practice, he "didn't have to consult the prayer pamphlet [he] had obtained from the mosque anymore. . . . The verses came naturally . . . effortlessly" (364).

Beginning with sin and redemption, the novel renders key moments in Amir's spiritual awakening through the tropes and rhetoric of notable interfaith resonance. As an adult, Amir turns to forms of Islamic piety wholly new to his self-experience. In evangelical Christian parlance, Amir is born again. As a child "caught between Baba and the mullahs at school," he "hadn't made up [his] mind about God" (62), but as an adult he turns back to the "half-forgotten verses from the Koran" in times of emotional need (154). When his father is diagnosed with cancer, Amir incorporates the formal elements of Islamic prayer into the rhythms of his life, but, importantly, his return to Islam takes him not to a mosque but to the inner registers of an independent spirituality. As a religious man, Amir is quite literally home-schooled, removing him from potentially subversive Islamic collectives like the madrasa model of Islam critiqued earlier in the novel. Even in the United States, the institutional structures of religion remain anathema to Amir's nascent spirituality: at the funeral service held for his father in a Fremont, California, mosque, Hosseini describes the presiding mullah as arguing with an attendee "over the correct *ayat* of the Koran to recite at the gravesite" (175). At best, the mullahs are irrelevant to the religious community and detract from the point of an event designed to evoke respect and admiration for the atheist Baba's many acts of generosity.

After Sohrab's attempted suicide, Amir again turns to prayer in the hospital waiting area:

> I grab a white bedsheet from the pile of folded linens and carry it back to the corridor. I see a nurse talking to a policeman near the restroom. I take the nurse's elbow and pull, I want to know which way is west. . . . I beg. The policeman is the one who points. I throw my makeshift *jai-namaz*, my prayer rug, on the floor and I get on my knees, lower my forehead to the ground, my tears soaking through the sheet. I bow to the west. Then I remember I haven't prayed for over fifteen years. I have long forgotten the words. (346)

Interestingly, Amir's actions break the expected pattern of worship that he has initiated. Instead of reciting the *Sura Al-Fatiha*, "The Opening" that Muslims recite during all obligatory prayers, Hosseini chooses the *Shahadah*, the confession of faith: "*La illaha il Allah, Muhammad u rasul ullah.* There is no God but Allah and Muhammed is His messenger," Amir recites (346).[26] In what is more an act of conversion than a prayer, Amir sees the *Shahadah* as a rejection of his father's atheism: "I see now that Baba was wrong, there is a God, there always had been" (346). But it is also a rejection of Islam as an organized religion:

rejecting mosque and *ummah*, Amir sees "Him [God] here, in the eyes of the people in this corridor of desperation. This is the real house of God . . . not the white *masjid* with its bright diamond lights and towering minarets" (346).

Hosseini's conversion scene also seems carefully crafted to avoid the elements of Islamic practice most common for observant Muslims and most incendiary for his non-Muslim audience, beginning with the *takhbir*, the ritual chanting of *Allahu-akbar* with which the *salat*, the primary ritual prayer, would commence. The God Amir discovers as a source of respite at the nadir of his physical and emotional suffering is, Hosseini emphasizes, a far cry from the one the Taliban mullah invokes when he incites a crowd to cheer as accused adulterers are stoned to death. In this reading, Amir's God is not really a "generalized spirituality reflecting his moral development over the course of the novel," as O'Rourke has argued, but rather a specific form of Islamic praxis that has been accommodated to a secular frame. Bodily practice, rather than dogmatic theology, focalizes his religious experience: Amir turns to the comforting rhythms of Arabic prayer and the postures of *salat*, declaring "I will do *zakat*, I will do *namaz*, I will fast during Ramadan. . . . I will commit to memory every last word of His holy book, and I will set on a pilgrimage to that sweltering city in the desert and bow before the Ka'bah too" (346).

The Kite Runner makes the terms and affects of Amir's religious revival legible to the reformist history that Charles Taylor identifies within Latin Christendom's Protestant tradition. Protestant reforms, Taylor argues, shaped the category of religion through privatization, spiritualization, and a deep investment in the concept of autonomy as manifested in continued "pressure to adopt a more personal, committed, and inward form of religion" (37). Indeed, in Hosseini's hands, Amir's religious revival takes the form, not of an intellectually, theologically, or historically complex religious praxis, but of an immediate, private, and personal connection to spirituality and a notion of the oneness of God—precisely the kind of religious subject produced and regulated by the secular political formations of liberal pluralism. Above all, Amir conducts his religious practice in an intense privacy, hidden even from his wife: the novel specifies that Soraya, herself the victim of religiously motivated oppression, is asleep during Amir's prayers.

Despite the relatively little textual space they occupy, the somatic, liturgical, and theological terms of Amir's religious revival require careful parsing. The first major theological concept the novel introduces is that of sin, particularly the "past of unatoned sins" that haunts Amir for twenty-six years and catalyzes the novel's redemptive trajectory (1). To shape a pious, diasporic Muslim, Hosseini recruits the rhetorical forms of his reconstructed religious identity from a mixture of sources, leaning conspicuously on concepts that preoccupy Christian, rather than Islamic, theology. Broadly speaking, sin in Islam (*dhanb or thanb* in Arabic) is conceived not as an existential state as it is in Christianity, but rather as an act or deed that violates God's commandments. What exactly was Amir's sin? Amir believes he sacrificed his friend for his own happiness: he could "stand up for Hassan," or, he says, "I could run. In the end, I ran," he confesses to the reader, "I ran because I was a coward" (77). Thereafter, Amir lives in a state of guilt and culpability that transforms his very being. His existential alteration is easily recognizable within a Christian theological matrix, but this relationship to sin is not prominently modeled by any of Islam's denominations.

As in the similarly juridical traditions of rabbinic Judaism, the procedures used to interpret scripture and render authoritative interpretations within Islamic communities are governed by rigorous traditions. Writing in 1910, Ignác Goldziher, an eminent Hungarian-Jewish Islamicist whose *Introduction to Islamic Theology* remains a seminal volume in German and English, observes that "it would be an arduous task to derive from the Qur'an itself a system of beliefs that is coherent, self-sufficient, and free of self-contradiction" (155). As a result, determining the forms of life proper to Islam has always required consulting not only the *Qur'an* but also the sayings of the Prophet (hadith), supplemented by the evidence of tradition (sunna). While there are considerable differences among schools of Islamic jurisprudence in hermeneutical terms, most Muslims, Sunni and Shi'a alike, agree that sinful acts fall into several gradations: from great sins (*al-Kaba'ir*), beginning with an unforgivable act of polytheism or idolatry, to minor transgressions.[27] In the inevitable disputes that arise over what constitutes a Muslim way of life on the straight path (*sharia*) of Islam, or in questions about proper codes of conduct (*fiqh*), scholars and jurists seek out examples among the Companions of the Prophet Muhammad, whose testimony serves as the basis for authoritative interpretation. Abandoning Hassan to Assef's violence, running when he should have stood his ground, and profiting from Hassan's sacrifice—Amir returns home to bask in his father's praise—constitute clear and significant failures by Amir to follow Islamic standards for ethical action. Specific teachings in the Qur'an or hadith can be used analogically to address

Amir's actions; for instance, in an oft-quoted hadith, Abu Huraira narrates that the Prophet Mohamed commanded his followers to avoid seven great sins, among them fleeing from the field of battle (Hadith Bukhari 8:840).[28] But given that Amir is an indirect participant and a child, his actions are not, from a theological perspective, grounds for soul-wrenching judgment.

On the basis of evidence gathered anecdotally from Muslim students and online from chat rooms, reviews, and message boards, for most Muslims the significant sins committed in the novel are not those of Amir's cowardice but instead surround Soraya's premarital affair, the sexual abuse of children, and Assef's rape of Hassan. With regard to the former, Soraya confesses that "when [they] lived in Virginia, [she] ran away with an Afghan man"—a fact that she fears will jeopardize her engagement to Amir as it jeopardized her life and social standing (164).[29] Amir, mentally citing the guilty secret of his betrayal of Hassan, rejects talk of honor killings or the idea that her sexual history would affect his love for her, but in this Soraya claims he is "different from every Afghan guy [she's] met" (180). The father of the boy playing Hassan in the film version of *The Kite Runner* (2007) said the rape scene made him "afraid for the security of [his] son, and for the security of [his] family" and drove him to seek guarantees for relocation (Tang). Perhaps more importantly, "sin" is not a major concern as a conceptual category to the global English-speaking Muslim community, or even, in those terms, to the history of Islamic theology. Instead, the liveliest categories on portals serving the global Muslim community, like IslamOnline and the Fatwa Center of America, relate to issues like Islamophobia, family law, religious reform, and Islamic finance.[30]

Amir's confessional paradigm, moreover, which plays an integral formal and thematic role in the novel, has no direct analogue in Islam, where, as in Judaism, access to the divine unmediated by a clerical establishment is the norm. Thus, while Amir's confessions strike a chord within Hosseini's Anglophone readership, they do so among groups doubly primed to place an ethical value on confession by Christianity's unique emphasis on the relationship between speech and absolution and the secularized paradigm of psychoanalysis.[31] In contrast, the Arabic term for repentance, *taubah*, meaning "return," semiotically enacts the process through which Amir attempts to right the wrongs he has committed. As prominent Islamic scholar Ghulam Ahmad Parwez argues, "*Taubah* is derived from the root *T'aba,* which means to return. *Taubah* therefore does not mean vain regret or futile remorse. It means that when man realizes that he has been following the wrong path, he should have the courage to stop and retrace his steps" (97). According to Islamic consensus, seeking forgiveness (*istighfar*) for sinful acts requires a direct appeal to God, corroborated by righteous acts like works of charity. While the novel's secular frame obscures this genealogy, Amir's trip to Afghanistan can be seen as enacting a return that gives material form to the dictates of *taubah* as a literal retracing of steps. By framing Hosseini's depiction of religious resurgence within recent developments in the study of secularism and a comparative approach to Islamic theology, my intention is not to establish whether Amir is really a "good Muslim" or a heterodox one. Instead, such an analysis helps disentangle a cluster of religious and secular forces in the novel and clarifies the way the political and historical configurations of the novel's consumption make Amir's acts and beliefs meaningful.

THE LIMITS OF READING

Two methodological concerns are commonly brought to bear on overly textual approaches to religion. The first is that even among the three "bookish" faiths, religions are not just texts. Religions are complex social and historical systems with deep-rooted practices and mores that have evolved differently in specific locations around the globe. The second objection is more properly a critique of reading as a mode of knowledge production, based on the assumption that encounters with difference mediated by texts are inferior to those made through lived experience. In Christian Europe, translations of the Bible into vernacular languages and the evolution of the study of the Bible as literature, rather than as the word of God, were central developments in the deep history of secularization.[32] Textualist approaches to religion structured and often justified violent European encounters with other peoples during four centuries of colonialism; in the postcolonial twentieth and twenty-first centuries, as Masuzawa has argued, they have helped shape the "pluralist doctrine" that has, with the notable exception of Islam, "become the ruling ethos of our discourse on religion."[33] Critics of multiculturalism accurately observe that a cafeteria-style approach to world religions has produced a culture that views difference as a commodity and has reduced robust religious identities to bumper-sticker theologies. If Hosseini's novel helps us understand the ways that narratives of religious resurgence evolve dialogically with those of secularization, an almost equally popular, but more problematic, novel, Yann Martel's *Life of Pi,* calls attention to weak models of secular pluralism that promise literary pleasure while reducing the compass of religious experience to a constrained circle of text and private forms of mystical faith.[34]

Life of Pi offers a crash course in world religions (and zoology) on the level of good beach (or cruise ship) reading. Martel's novel begins with a brief and deliberately transnational frame in which an elderly man tells Martel, a Canadian on a walkabout in India, that he has "a story that will make you believe in God. . . . It starts right here in Pondicherry just a few years back, and it ends, I am delighted to tell you, in the very country you came from" (x). Most of the novel is given over to the interpolated tale in which this Scheherazadean power is said to reside, that of Piscine Molitor Patel, "Pi," whose family owned the Pondicherry zoo. After selling the zoo to North American buyers, family and animals set sail for Canada on a Japanese ship registered in the Philippines. The boat sinks somewhere in the Pacific and launches Pi's improbable 227-day voyage aboard a lifeboat with Richard Parker, a 450-pound Bengal tiger. Pi's sincere forms of devotion and omnivorous spirituality—in modes unthreatening to national security but heretical from the perspective of any religious orthodoxy—embody a vision of pluralistic religious harmony afloat in shallow theological waters. It is, moreover, highly dependent on private, textualized concepts of religion dominant among North Atlantic forms of Protestant Christianity but largely alien to observant Catholics, Jews, Hindus, and Muslims.

The novel depends in large part on the charisma of its youthful protagonist, as do intertexts like Rudyard Kipling's *Kim* and Salman Rushdie's *Midnight's Children.*[35] Born into what he describes as a secular family of the "New India—rich, modern and secular as ice cream," "[Pi] owe[s] to Hinduism the original landscape of [his] religious imagination" (50). In his words, he "was fourteen years old—and a well-content Hindu on a holiday—when [he] met Jesus Christ" (50). Through Pi, Martel unfolds a provincializing account of Christianity and the physical structure of a Christian church as seen through Hindu eyes: "I advanced and observed the inner sanctum. There was a painting. Was this the murti? Something about human sacrifice. An angry god who had to be appeased with blood" (52). But when Father Martin tells him the story of Christianity, "or rather, since Christians are so fond of capital letters, a Story" (53), he "spent three solid days thinking about Him . . . And the more [he] learned about Him, the less [he] wanted to leave Him" (57). The Christian message of love compels Pi, and "Islam followed right behind" (58); though he initially sees Islam as "nothing but an easy sort of exercise," Pi adopts Islam as well (60). Pi's spirituality is defined by nonexclusive logic and personal devotion, much to the dismay of his parents and religious authorities. Even after his priest, imam, and pandit clash ("This was my introduction to interfaith dialogue," he notes of a public dispute), Pi remains secure in his love of God (70). Against the desires of the three religious leaders (and, incidentally, his atheist biology teacher), who agree on nothing but that "he can't be a Hindu, a Christian *and* a Muslim. . . . He must choose," Pi asserts that, as "Bapu Ghandi said, 'All religions are true,'" before blurting out to his skeptical audience an attenuated mantra of religious universalism and spiritual essentialism: "I just want to love God" (69).[36]

Thinking back on his sea voyage, Pi reflects, "Alas there was no scripture in the lifeboat" (207). For Pi, ideal encounters with religion would be mediated by text alone: "I cannot think of a better way to spread the faith. No thundering from a pulpit, no condemnation from bad churches, no peer pressure, just a book of scripture quietly waiting to say hello, as gentle and powerful as a little girl's kiss on your cheek" (207). This is a gentler version of religion, one that Slavoj Žižek might have indicted as evidence of "the false tolerance of liberal multiculturalism" characteristic of New Age spirituality in his essay "Passion in the Era of Decaffeinated Belief." Pi may crave a connection with the divine in the visionary tradition, but his is a sanitized spiritualism that rejects ecstatic union or the surge of communal ritual.

This seeming paradox is held together by the novel's sharp distinctions between public and private and the relegation of religion to the latter sphere. Like his survival on the lifeboat, Pi's subsequent life in Canada confines religiosity to the domestic sphere: "his house is a temple" filled with religious artifacts that stage the proximity of Qur'an, Ganesh, and a suffering Christ, as the narrator observes in a journalistic interchapter (43). There is always, however, a wall of separation—or, more aptly, an ocean—between religion and the public sphere and, even more radically, between Pi's individual experiences of religion and communitarian forms of religiosity that define most people's experience. Belief-centered, narrative, private forms of religiosity mesh well with the way members of religious minorities are expected to perform their piety within the politically secular Canadian public sphere.[37]

The epistemological importance of belief in the novel raises the stakes of the plagiarism allegations in which Martel became entangled in late 2002. Trouble arose over the similarities between *Life of Pi* and *Max and the Cats*, a Portuguese novel by Moacyr Scliar, whom Martel credits with giving him "the spark of life" (xii). Whatever their ultimate legitimacy, the allegations are limited to what Pi calls the "story with the animals," not to the plot of Pi's romance with a trinity of world religions that is my focus here.[38] In the early 2000s, people around the world overwhelmingly chose what the narrator calls the "better story" over a "dry, yeastless factuality" (80). Among them was President Obama, who sent a brief, handwritten note on White House letterhead to Martel: "My daughter and I just finished reading *Life of Pi* together. Both of us agreed we prefer the story with animals. It is a lovely book—an elegant proof of God, and the power of storytelling. Thank you" (Stewart). Martel's novel rocketed up the best-seller lists; it won prizes around the world, including the Booker in 2002; and a Hollywood film version, directed by Ang Lee, was released in 2012 to critical and commercial acclaim. In its reception and circulation, and as a site of common reading, *Life of Pi* serves as a reminder of how thin the rhetoric of pluralism and spirituality can be, even as it signals a deep desire for substantive interfaith dialogue in a climate of conservative religious revival. The novel has not, however, lived up to its promise to make readers believe in God—because its false dichotomy of choosing the "better story" over "factuality" ultimately has little, if anything, to do with being religious or even with the nature of religious beliefs.

The second critique of textually mediated encounters with religion is best articulated by William Connolly in *Why I Am Not a Secularist*: "Modern secularism—in the main and for the most part—either ignores [the visceral] register [of human experience] or disparages it. It does so in the name of a public sphere in which reason, morality, and tolerance flourish. By doing so it forfeits some of the very resources needed to foster a generous pluralism" (3). Reading, it seems, suffers from a similar estrangement from the corporeal, just as textual encounters with alterity offer only a shadow of the knowledge gained by living in common with real others. Nadine Gordimer—a writer of terse and unforgiving political novels about injustice, and of thought experiments about love across race lines for over half a century—offers a dark reflection on the limits of reading as a vector of encounter in *The Pickup* (2001), a novel whose unresolved ending and ambivalent self-criticisms come as welcomed frictions after the symmetries of *The Kite*

Runner and the "decaffeinated" religiosity of *Life of Pi*.[39] Through its conception of creatural encounter, *The Pickup* explores the limits of reading as a mode of knowledge production and, more radically, of "knowledge" or "production" as goods in themselves.

In *The Pickup*, Gordimer engages for the first time with divisions produced by religion and globalization rather than those of apartheid and race. Longlisted for the 2001 Booker Prize and winner of the 2002 Commonwealth Writer's "Best Book from Africa" award, the novel benefited from an aura of prophetic salience in terms of theme and geography upon its post-9/11 publication. At the beginning of the novel, Julie Summers, a young white liberal in postapartheid South Africa, asks the young mechanic who fixes her car out on a coffee date. She is following the ethic of her mixed social set that meets in a Johannesburg café: "To be open to encounters, that was what she and her friends believed, anyway, as part of making the worth of their lives," as well as her own erotic instincts (10). Her pickup—a man she first saw "lying on his back half-under the belly of a car" and recognized as neither black nor white (invoking the color lines around which the concept of difference is constructed in South Africa) but as "young . . . [and] glossy dark haired with black eyes blueish-shadowed"—turns out to be an illegal immigrant from an unnamed and impoverished Muslim nation who gives his name as Abdu (7). When he is deported (for the second time, and with no hope of redress), Julie decides to marry Ibrahim ibn Musa (his real name) largely on the basis of their erotic bond and to emigrate with him to live among his family. About the allegorical nation of Ibrahim's birth, Julie knows next to nothing: "He named a country she had barely heard of. One of those partitioned by colonial powers on their departure, or seceded from federations cobbled together to fill vacuums of powerlessness against the regrouping of those old colonial powers . . . one of those countries where you can't tell religion apart from politics, their forms of persecution from the persecution of poverty" (12). Even the oil, readers learn, is "over the border" (25). Rather than an exposé of the injustice of the Muslim world or a fantasy of life behind the veil, the novel plots how, over a period of months, Julie becomes accepted among the women of Ibrahim's extended family and comes to find deep satisfactions in the traditional rhythms of Islamic life in a village at the edge of the desert.

Before she met Ibrahim, Julie did not know any Muslims; after a year of performing the rituals and routines of daily life as a daughter-in-law in a pious and traditional extended family, she is reshaped by a new habitus.[40] Though she does not formally convert, Julie observes the Ramadan fast, learns to dress according to local mores, and synchronizes her life around the call to prayer. Gordimer underscores the power of routine and temporality: "The first adjustment to any change must be to the time-frame imposed within it. . . . The other demarcations of the day set by that particular society follow, commuter time, clock-in time. . . . Five times each day the voice of the muezzin set the time-frame she had entered" (12). One of Julie's first realizations on her arrival in the village is that gaining proficiency in Arabic is essential. In addition to teaching English to school-age children and working with women conversationally, "She was studying the language out of primers" (191). Julie, however, hungers for a more private vocabulary than book learning can provide, but the women with whom she conducts "friendly exchange[s] of languages over tea also thought it respectful of theirs to teach her only its conventional formulations" (191). Before their lovemaking, Julie once queries Ibrahim, awkwardly, to open Arabic to her as an erotic language: "What are the names—I don't know, the, the . . . you know . . . the love words. . . . I'd like to hear them. You've never said them to me"—but he refuses (151).[41]

Julie's "readings" of Islamic holy texts, particularly of the Qur'an, are conditioned by the physical habits and forms of sociality of Ibrahim's family. As a reader, she is emotionally invested but naive and uncritical: while Ibrahim "reads as if his life depends on what is there," "the book she has been reading [Dostoyevsky's "A Gentle Creature"] lies on her breasts, open face-down at a page where she has come upon a sentence, a statement, that seems to have been written for her long before she came into existence" (35). Julie, with her book "on her breasts, open face-down," is a sensual knower, a characteristic she identifies as integral to her character and to the sexual chemistry that holds her relationship with Ibrahim together. Julie reflects that "they made love beautifully; she so roused and fulfilled that tears came" (27), while from Ibrahim's perspective, "This foreigner makes him whole," and sex with her brings them to "another country, a country of its own, not yours or mine" (96). For Julie, physical attraction and an impulse toward religion are intertwined: "There is something beguiling about submission, for someone who has believed she has never submitted. Something temptingly dangerous, too" (239).

Gordimer's valorization of the physical, like Julie's, is an attempt to guard against the paradigms of colonialism: "Hester Stanhope . . . and the man Lawrence," she says, serve as nothing but "English charades in the desert, imperialism in fancy dress with the ultimate condescension of bestowing the honour of wanting to be like the people of the desert" (198).[42] These adventurers, Julie thinks, whose memoirs stake their authority on intrepid travels to exotic lands, have "nothing to do with her; she wrapped herself in black robes only when it was necessary for protection against the wind" (198). Julie also gives up a vision of life in the village modeled on development discourse, a Peace Corps–inspired dream, derided by Ibrahim as nothing but a "rich girl's ignorance, [and] innocence," of using her family's capital to drill an irrigation well and start a viable farm in the desert (216). In privileging embodied knowledge and small-scale forms of sociality there is, for Gordimer, a critique of global economies and the large-scale public spheres that they imply.

In the village, Julie attempts to read the Qur'an in her trade paperback translation, but not in the manner of a theologian or an ethnographer, or primarily with a literary eye to textual aesthetics: "*Suras*, the footnotes said they were called. She read aloud to herself as if to hear the natural emphases of delivery which had been the passages come upon—for life—in these choices out of so much advice and exhortation, inspiration, consolation people find in religious texts. She read at random; the verses did not come in the order in which Maryam had happened to name them" (144). Julie seeks out the quotations frequently invoked in the course of daily domestic life by Ibrahim's mother, asking Maryam, Ibrahim's youngest sister, to identify the names of the verses. By default, Julie encounters the Qur'an in a way that Sells reminds us is unavailable to "a large section of American society," namely "the Qur'an as it is experienced in Islamic communities worldwide, that is, the Qur'an in Arabic recitation" (xiii). Julie searches for an ordering principle based on use-value and social context at once distant from the narrative arrangement of Suras in the Qur'an as a codex (in which longer verses appear earlier) and from traditional modes of exegesis (in which the context of revelation occupies the foreground). As Gordimer portrays it, embodied action and forms of sociality constitute the primary source and ultimate horizon of religious meaning—a compatibility in no small part responsible for the pleasures the village affords Julie. Like Sells, Gordimer strives to replicate the uses of Islamic texts in daily life, where the Qur'anic verses used in prayer and invoked in conversation are not those cited in approaches to Islamic theology routed through blatant Islamophobic attacks, international relations theory, or security studies.

In Gordimer's novel, religious differences do not prove as significant a barrier to relationships as do the new economic and political divides of capitalist globalization. Like fluencies with languages, for Julie, religion is something that can be learned and practiced without the necessity of being something to be "believed" in. Instead, the novel emphasizes the vast asymmetries in social and geographic mobility between the throngs of *sans-papiers* like Ibrahim, who constitute the true underclass of the global economy, and migrants of privilege, like Julie, a white English speaker with a South African passport, who "may move about the world welcome everywhere, as they please" (49). By privileging dwelling over reading, Gordimer casts an ironic light on her own project even as she challenges those who see religions primarily as systems of text and creedal commitment. Her embrace of the corporeal does not, however, mean that *The Pickup* celebrates embodied experience as a more authentic site of knowledge, or even that Gordimer is optimistic about romantic relationships as successful bridges across religious difference. While Julie and Ibrahim place too much faith in eros as a form of universal reason, Gordimer does not. The novel concludes, opening more questions than it resolves, with Julie's decision to stay on among the women in the village when Ibrahim, after the other Anglophone postcolonies have rejected his bids, obtains a visa to work in the United States. "I am not going—coming to America," she tells her astonished husband (248). Though she refuses to ask for monetary assistance from her family, reason or fidelity to belief is not Julie's primary motivator. Instead, like the sister-in-law's decision to remain behind when her husband left for work in the oil fields, her staying on is not a text to be read.

COMMON READING

While Americans were reading *The Kite Runner*, *Life of Pi*, and perhaps *The Pickup*, the best-selling novel in Arabic was Alaa al Aswany's 2002 novel *Imārat Yaʻqūbīān* (*The Yacoubian Building*), which was made into a celebrated Arabic film in 2006 and a television series in 2007.[43] Through interwoven narratives focalizing the lives of the mixed-use building's many occupants—from those who dwell on its rooftop "street," part slum, part liminal space, to the affluent and once-affluent residents of apartments, offices, and retail spaces below—*The Yacoubian Building* provides a vertical cross section of Egyptian life in robust social realist prose. Translated into English by Humphrey Davies, an award-winning writer based in Cairo, the novel was praised in the original and in its many translations for capturing the economic stagnation, political corruption, and erotic life (straight and gay) of a particular historical moment—Cairo in the early 1990s—that would become particularly salient in the subsequent decade. As a reading of Islam, the novel assumes an Arabic-speaking audience and a Muslim social context; its reflections on the specific trajectories of Islamic religiosity and the politics of secularism in recent Egyptian history are thus a critique both of the secular nationalist ideologies that have failed to live up to their promises and of the forms of religious resurgence to which they have given rise.

The Yacoubian building itself comes to symbolize the diversity and vitality of Cairo in the 1920s and 1930s under King Faud:

> In 1934, Hagop Yacoubian, the millionaire and then doyen of the Armenian community in Egypt, decided to construct an apartment block that would bear his name. . . . The cream of the society of those days took up residence in the Yacoubian building—ministers, big land-owning bashas, foreign manufacturers, and two Jewish millionaires (one of them belonging to the famous Mosseri family). . . . In 1952 the revolution came and everything changed. The exodus of Jews and foreigners from Egypt started, and every apartment that was vacated by reason of the departure of its owners was taken over by an officer of the armed forces. (11–12)

To Aswany's nostalgic eye, Nasser's secular nationalism and its subsequent dictatorships destroyed Cairo's cultural and ethnic pluralism. With a broad historical flourish, Aswany writes: "Then came the 1970s, and the downtown area started gradually to lose its importance. . . . An inexorable wave of religiosity swept Egyptian society" (33). Vestiges of ancien régime, Eurocentric secularity endure in characters like Zaki el Dessouki, an aging playboy and dilettante, and in the "few, scattered, small bars, whose owners had been able to hang on in the face of the rising tide of religion and government persecution" (33). Embodied by Zaki Bey and Maxim's, the restaurant at which Zaki el Dessouki "feels at home," cosmopolitan secularity, like an aging dandy, "bears the stamp of the elegant past in the same way as do old Rolls-Royces, ladies' long white gloves, hats decorated with feathers" (107).

If secularism is an aging dandy, the novel's face of Islamism is Taha, the son of the Yacoubian building's doorkeeper. When he begins to radicalize religiously and politically in his late teens—around the time of the first Gulf War—romance and socioeconomics are to blame. More specifically, when his relationship with the daughter of a neighbor runs aground on the twin shoals of her rising economic aspirations and his failure to gain enrollment in the police academy, he turns fully to the company of the pious young men he meets in the local mosque and, through it, the Muslim Brotherhood. His trajectory from law enforcement to violence against the state is rapid: "In less than a month, Taha had become friends with the whole mosque group" and, in the narrator's ironic summary, had "benefited greatly" from discussions where "he learned for the first time that Egyptian society was at the same stage that had prevailed before Islam and it was not an Islamic society because the ruler stood in the way of the application of God's Law" (92).[44] Over Taha's shoulder, readers listen to Sheikh Shakir's sermon, in which he preaches an ascetic vision of Islamic purity against the "times of decadence" that prevailed before the golden age of Islam and that reigns again in their "unhappy country . . . governed according to French secular law, which permits drunkenness, fornication, and perversion . . . benefits from gambling and the sale of alcohol . . . and torture[s] innocent people" (95).

The novel is clear, however, that what is behind Taha's radicalization is outrage over purely immanent concerns—political corruption, injustice, and inequality—rather than "religious" reasons. Like Taha, the other members of the mosque group are "country boys, good-hearted, pious, and poor" (92). While the secular state has failed to ensure prosperity or secure basic rights, Taha's religious revival and membership in Gamaa Islamiya allow him to overcome his low-class origins: "He was changed totally, as though he had swapped his former self for another, new one. It isn't just a matter of the Islamic dress that he has adopted in place of his Western clothes, nor of his beard, which he has let grow. . . . Now he faces them [the building's wealthy tenants] with self-confidence" (115). Finally, personal vendetta and failure in love inspire his acts of suicidal terror, not faith in ideology or divine will.[45]

In *The Yacoubian Building*, religion is politics by other means. While Taha's sheikh plots the overthrow of the Mubarak administration, Sheikh Samman supports the Gulf War and trades fealty to the reigning political dispensation for material and social gains: "[Sheikh Samman] organized lectures and seminars and wrote lengthy articles in the press to explain the legal justification for the war to liberate Kuwait. The government brought him to speak on television . . . [and] present to the people all the legal reasons for the correctness of the Arab rulers' position inviting American troops to liberate Kuwait from the Iraqi invasion" (171). The question is not whether there are, as Sheikh Samman argues, "legal reasons for the permissibility of seeking the help of the Western Christian armies to save the Muslims from the criminal unbeliever Saddam Hussein," or whether it is every Muslim's duty, as Sheikh Shakir argues, to turn "their weapons on the Zionists who have usurped Palestine and befouled the el Aqsa mosque" (171, 141).[46] Instead, the novel's heteroglossic approach to Islam emphasizes the way a particular secularist ideology has, by keeping religious agents and reason out of the political process, created specific forms of licit and illicit religiosity. As part of a multisited analysis, *The Yacoubian Building* reveals how secular dictatorships ironically established the conditions for the rise of modern Islamism and created the Muslim Brotherhood as its inverted mirror.

This chapter's attempt to offer a thicker description of what, how, and when discourses about Islam circulate in and through sites of common reading brings me to three overlapping conclusions. First, and most generally, it is clear we need better ways of talking about the traffic between modes of religiosity and secularity, both in the public sphere and in literary studies. At present, interfaith dialogue provides the best circumstances for discussions regarding religious differences. Despite a rich history and the productive work currently conducted under its auspices, however, participants in interfaith encounters have often entered them with the tacit or explicit goal of proving the superiority of their own confession. They allow little room for meaningful variation of beliefs or the presence of nonbelievers, and they often reduce participants to symbolic religious figures.

Second, a multisited analysis is needed to move beyond the static binaries that undergird ethnographic and postcolonial approaches to reading and religious difference. By *multisited* I mean to emphasize that a triadic (rather than dialogic or contrapuntal) comparative approach is the minimum necessary threshold for substantive discussions of religion in Anglophone literature, particularly regarding questions of religion and secularity. At what I would hazard to call a political level, reading representations of Islam, their sites of consumption, and their modes of circulation in this way can be an important part of broader efforts to break down reductive and politically debilitating binaries. While multisitedness risks drifting into groundlessness, geographically and intellectually—as it does when adrift on Martel's multifaith lifeboat—global fictions can play a significant role in cultivating what Connolly calls an "ethos of engagement" "made up of intersecting and interdependent *minorities* of numerous types and sorts who occupy the same territorial space" through encounter and translation (92).[47] As heteroglossic texts, novels are particularly efficient cultural containers; the sustained imaginative investment required to read novels, meanwhile, fosters diverse forms of ethical modeling. In terms of the canons we reflect and shape in our scholarship and teaching, the lesson to be drawn is not to eschew best sellers—as sites of common reading, prize-winning and widely circulated texts are locations of cultural exchange, encounters with difference, and knowledge production—but rather to revisit how we read in addition to seeking out novels that internally model multisitedness.[48]

Finally, when conceptualizing differences between human beings, these novels suggest that we should guard against binary concepts of alterity. The idea of the Other, which features so prominently in postcolonial theory (and in political theory, where it enters through the secularized door of Carl Schmitt's friend/enemy distinction, in which alterity is framed in "a specially intense way, [as] existentially something different and alien"), contributes to intellectually and morally reductive—though often politically useful—binary groupings (27). Reviews, book club guides, pedagogic practices, and paratextual materials reveal that readers overwhelmingly approach texts about Islamic societies as semitransparent containers for ethnographic content. The dominant academic account, often responding to the ubiquity of these naive ethnographic readings, argues that images of Muslims, and of Islam more generally, in contemporary Anglophone literature constitute only the most recent turn of a very old Orientalist screw. "Negative images of Islam are very much more prevalent than any others," Said wrote in *Covering Islam*, a statement that remains as accurate today as it was thirty years ago (136).

Part of the task for the critic in a profoundly Islamophobic society remains uncovering the relationships between the construction of knowledge about Islam and the exercise of hegemony over the Muslim world. But it is equally as important, if not more so, to frame the contexts for comparison more broadly. An awareness of the limits of reading means recognizing that building fluencies with religions, as with languages, is an ongoing project best realized through immersion, often best gained in foreign study. Even the "deep familiarity with three or more languages" (4) that Haun Saussy advocates as the litmus for robust comparison, however, will not address the necessary scale and diversity of world literature, in part because the fluencies necessary to undertake such projects are only partially linguistic.[49] While the value of multilingualism is self-evident, it is equally clear that we must cultivate new fluencies with religious and secular vernaculars around the world.

Coda: The Novel and the Secular Imagination

Writers and critics of fiction commonly believe that there is something inherently antireligious about the novel as a genre. There are many reasons why this view has maintained the widespread credence it has commanded for over a century. First, unlike other literary genres that predate the written word, the novel as a genre, in its origins and rise, formal characteristics, thematic concerns, and historical development, closely parallels European secularization. Second, it is precisely the question of immanence that prompts scholars to differentiate novels from other prose forms. Novels tell the stories of ordinary individuals amid their material and social relationships, repudiating the transcendental frames of reference within which allegories, romances, and epics forge their meanings. No critic would deny the existence of religious novels, but according to the dominant lines of reasoning, works of religious fiction achieve their religiosity *despite* the form, structure, and history of the genre. Finally, in terms of style, novels tend to be rhizomatic, presenting a multitude of voices and styles through which the active reader must negotiate—all characteristics at odds with secularist ideas about religious dogmatism and the monolingualism of a divinely authored text.

For many eminent Victorians, and later for the modernists, the retreat of religion promised to open new territory for the literary, a medium that could conserve religious textuality, retain the church's role as ethical guide, and replace the consolations of a lost faith in

God with a faith in fiction. Matthew Arnold's "The Study of Poetry" (1880) distills such replacement narratives: "More and more mankind will discover that we have to turn to poetry to interpret life for us, to console us, to sustain us. Without poetry, our science will appear incomplete; and most of what now passes with us for religion and philosophy will be replaced by poetry" (47).[1] Identifying and tracing the evolution of the novel's purported secularity—the motif of the novel against God—brings into view some key features of secularization theory's cultural effects. In his "Reflections on the Novel," the Marquis de Sade is among the first to emphatically assert the relationship between the novel and what he calls "secular customs." Novels, Sade suggests, are "for the philosopher who wishes to understand *man*, as essential as is the knowledge of history" (109). A sense of moral purpose has long inhered in the notion that the novel is an agent of secularization, thus endowing secularism and the novel with a kind of existential heroism visible in Sade's substitution of man for the divine as the ultimate object of inquiry.

The consensus on the novel's secularity offers a rare point of agreement across an influential range of critics, novelists, and public intellectuals. During the days leading up to the First World War, for instance, Hungarian philosopher and literary critic Georg Lukács famously asserted, "The Novel is the epic of a world that has been abandoned by God" (88). For Lukács, convinced of the bankruptcy of both individual heroism and transcendence, the novel offers a twisted form of catharsis for an orphan's grief. The ironic mode he associates with the genre refracts freedom from God through a nihilistic lens; the novel's "psychology," he writes, "is demonic" (203). Though Lukács later clarified the historical contingencies that produced *The Theory of the Novel*, the work remains a potent symbol and touchstone for discussions of the novel's secularism. In Mikhail Bakhtin's *The Dialogic Imagination*, the novel's formal indeterminacy, its "semantic open-endedness," its carnivalesque qualities, and its heteroglossic structure constitute a further development in the evolution of the idea that the novel is inimical to the sincere conviction associated with religious belief (7).

It is on religious grounds that Ian Watt, in *The Rise of the English Novel*, divides John Bunyan's novelistic allegory *The Pilgrim's Progress* from Daniel Defoe's properly novel work. Both *Robinson Crusoe* and *The Pilgrim's Progress* meet Watt's standard that a novel must be a fiction in which "an ordinary person's daily activities are the center of continuous literary attention" (74). For Watt, the crucial difference between the two lies in the fact that the ultimate significance of Bunyan's (allegorical) work "depends upon a transcendental scheme of things," while "in Defoe's novels . . . although religious concerns are present they have no such priority of status" (80). Watt believes that secularization's *Homo economicus* is symptomatic of the novelistic worldview: "The novel requires a world view which is centered on the social relationships between individual persons; and this involves secularization as well as individualism, because until the end of the seventeenth century the individual was not conceived as wholly autonomous" (84). The novel's connection to modernity in Michael McKeon's historicist account consists in large part of the genre's mediation between scientific and religious "truth" during what he calls "the early modern secularization crisis" (xxii). According to McKeon, the novel's unique ability to ease the crisis of status indeterminacy brought on by progressive capitalist and Puritan ideologies is directly tied to its nonhierarchical production of meaning. In light of its mediation, the novel helps bring about the spiritualization of religion, in which religiosity comes to be measured in terms of faith. For McKeon, as for many sociologists of religion, this new measure sets in motion the retreat of religion from the public sphere and the erosion of confidence in traditional claims about divine authority characteristic of subtraction theories of secularization.

In *The Broken Estate*, novelist and literary critic James Wood observes, "There is something about narrative that puts the world in doubt. . . . It was not just science but perhaps the novel itself which helped to kill Jesus' divinity, when it gave us a new sense of the real" (xxii). In his role as a reviewer for publications like the *New Yorker* and the *Guardian*, Wood makes assertions that are often more normative than descriptive, especially when his prose style leans toward that of the sermon: "Despite its being a kind of magic, it [the novel] is actually the enemy of superstition, the slayer of religions, the scrutineer of falsity" (xx). Like McKeon, Lukács, and Watt, Wood asserts the causal connection between the rise of the novel and the retreat of religion, though he sees substitution where the others see revolution: "At the high point of the novel's triumph [in the nineteenth century] the Gospels began to be read, by both writers and theologians, as a set of fictional tales—as a kind of novel. Simultaneously, fiction became an almost religious activity" (xxi). In these familiar accounts of genre formation, novels are claimed as both the chronicle and the cause of secularization as a historical process.

As for contemporary fiction, critics from Brian McHale and Linda Hutcheon to Fredric Jameson and Jean-François Lyotard emphatically align postmodernity with a culture of simulacra and neoliberal capitalism, while repudiating religion as an anachronistic vestige of defunct metanarratives.[2] Jameson, writing in the conclusion of *Postmodernism, or, The Cultural Logic of Late Capitalism*, notes that "one of postmodernism's ultimate achievements is the utter eradication of all forms of what used to be called idealism," including spirituality and traditional religions, which "seem to have melted away without a trace" (387). For Jameson, new religious movements thrive, to be sure, as symptoms of capitalist materialism, but "the very concept of belief" is a casualty of postmodern culture (388). As John Milbank, the architect of the Radical Orthodoxy movement, argues, the major assumption of postmodernism is the denial "both of depth and height in favor of surface, or a self-forming 'plane of immanence'" (34). Thus, while postmodernity is "constituted through the erection of a new version of transcendence," it shares little with received religiosity (34). In contrast, it is perhaps not surprising that scholars of postwar American literature, where religious writers like Flannery O'Connor, Marilynne Robinson, and Ron Hansen occupy a more prominent role than their European counterparts, have been more alert to the religious inflections of experimental fiction. John McClure cites a series of examples in novels by Thomas Pynchon, Don DeLillo, Leslie Marmon Silko, and Toni Morrison that plot what he sees as the return of secularist characters to religion and spirituality. According to McClure, American fiction in the late twentieth century celebrates a "radically pluralistic, exuberantly reenchanted universe" but refuses fealty to "any single school of spiritual formation as an exclusive source of possibility" (48, 55). Surveying a similar range of writers, Amy Hungerford offers a more rigorously historicized account of how writing and reading become available as modes of rapture as form effaces content; for Hungerford, "postmodern belief" is a belief in meaninglessness.

The conceit of the novel's constitutive secularity can be sustained, however, only on the scaffold of a thin and retrospective account of religion, one produced by a secularist ideology that identifies belief as the defining feature of religious experience and the transcendent as its primary object. As those like Asad, Taylor, and Connolly have argued, this perspective marginalizes the embodied and communal aspects of religiosity, from its devotional to its dietary practices. The tendency toward sermonizing that characterizes the "novel against God" motif is a symptom of an underlying problem: the idea of secularism on which the motif depends achieves meaning only in opposition, obscuring the way secularism produces knowledge in its own right. The idea that the novel form opposes religion merely appropriates those aspects of religiosity that privilege questioning, debate, and polyvocalism and grafts these branches onto an expanding secularist ideology of literary production.

"If there be a God," Cecil Rhodes infamously asserted, "I think that what he would like me to do is to paint as much of the map of Africa British red as possible" (98). Rhodes's pronouncement is merely a bald statement of the complicity and interdependence of Western Christianity and the logic of imperialism, both of which enforce as necessary and universal the contingent historical products of a particular group. This interdependence constitutes the indisputable ground from which postcolonial critical theory has engaged and continues to engage the subject of religion. Religion has so long wielded the sword of empire or been appropriated by colonial adventures that religious questions have often been anathema to postcolonial criticism in general, despite the gratitude expressed by many African and Caribbean writers for the education they received in missionary schools.[3] To understand the continued occlusion of religion from the serious work of postcolonial criticism, however, we must consider the complex legacy of Edward Said's argument that Orientalism and religion are structurally analogous as agents of prejudice and closure. In *The World, the Text, and the Critic*, Said sets out to combat the self-marginalizing trajectory of a trend toward "textuality" in critical theory, which he sees as a retreat from the "worldliness" of texts. Said advocates instead for a humanist practice of culturally and historically situated skeptical analysis that he calls "secular criticism."[4] Grand narratives like Orientalism, Said argues, "have something in common with religious discourse" because "each serves as an agent of closure, shutting off human investigation, criticism, and effort in deference to the authority of the more-than-human, the supernatural, the other-worldly" (290). The task of the critic, on the other hand, must be to ground oneself in a worldly, critical posture that is both open and pluralist in nature and that challenges closure and authority at every turn.[5] Though Said claims that his target is not religion as such but rather the forces of nationalism and empire, his use of the term *secular* fosters inevitable, if unfortunate, occlusions of the dynamic interplay of religious and secular modes of thinking and feeling.[6]

Said has in mind the idea of secular "worldliness"; it is in this sense that the *Oxford English Dictionary* defines *secular* as "of or pertaining to the world," a term that specifically denotes "members of the clergy . . . living 'in the world' and not in monastic seclusion . . . civil, lay, temporal," and thus framed not in opposition to religion but in opposition to world-renouncing forms of monastic life. However, as Vincent Pecora notes in his critique of Said's secular criticism, "What we may complacently understand as 'secular' about such criticism comes with certain historical and religious strings attached, and these are awfully hard to get rid of" (2). Said's work summons critics toward ethical and political engagement but does so through a fundamental misreading of the secular, contributing to the occlusion of "religion"—and with it concepts like belief, faith, and universality, as well as bodily practices, social institutions, and communities—from critical consciousness.[7] Religion, assumed as the site of self-authenticating ideologies of conservatism, particularism, and exclusion, has thus become increasingly marginal to and unthinkable within the most fertile trends of postcolonial literary and cultural criticism.

Several consequences emerge from this exclusion. By deploying religion as a negative limit against which liberal critique constitutes itself, critical theory unintentionally perpetuates the myth of secularization that supports celebratory narratives of globalization. In doing so, Said's "secular criticism" inadvertently contributes to the perceived crisis within postcolonial studies by closing off avenues of inquiry oriented toward religion, leading Simon Gikandi to conclude in a *PMLA* editor's column that "postcolonial studies, for all its achievement and promise, throws limited light on the world we face now" (636). Without a sufficiently nuanced and mobile theory of religiosity as compatible with liberal critique, the critical community abdicates its role in contesting the terms, texts, and ideologies of religious debate. Moreover, as Gil Anidjar argues, "To uphold *secularism* (or, for that matter, religion) as the key word for critical endeavors and projects today is, I am afraid, not to be that worldly" (50). To recapture a properly worldly sense of the text as, in Said's words, "a part of the social world, human life, and of course the historical moments in which they are located and interpreted," we must, ironically, move beyond secular criticism toward the cultivation of interepistemic fluencies (*World* 4).

While direct and indirect attempts by the United States and its client-state allies to assert hegemony in parts of the Islamic world have, if anything, increased since the explicit mandates of the Carter Doctrine, much has also changed since the 1980s, dating the methodological model Said developed and undermining its relevance to contemporary cultural production. Multilingual, global news organizations like Al Jazeera, the unfolding events of the Arab Spring, the varied sites of knowledge production about Islam in new and old media forms, and the growing prevalence of diasporic Muslim communities across Europe and North America cannot be usefully brought into focus by the lens of Cold War Orientalism. While the intent of contrapuntal analysis, as Said develops the term in *Culture and Imperialism*, is to interweave internal readings of texts with those generated from the multiple perspectives and histories they exclude, the "double vision" of a postcolonial perspective long focused on the colonizer/colonized dyad is similarly inadequate to the irreducible pluralism of the world's modes of being, both religious and secular. Consequently, many of those keenest to critique the "new Orientalism," "neocolonialism," or "neoimperialism" of representations of Islam in post-9/11 politics and culture can offer a no more viable way out of the dialectic they name than does Samuel Huntington's "clash of civilizations" or George Bush's "why do they hate us" rhetoric.

In Ian McEwan's novel *Black Dogs*, the conflict between transcendent conviction and immanent atheism is staged through the dysfunctional marriage of the protagonist's in-laws, Bernard and June Tremaine. For Bernard, the faith-versus-reason debate seems to have generated little more than "statements and counterstatements. . . . Each proposition blocked the one before or was blocked by the one that followed. It was a self-canceling argument, a multiplication of zeros" (96). While McEwan himself comfortably inhabits a public persona of robust atheism, I have argued that novelists like Rushdie, Coetzee, Pamuk, McEwan, Gordimer, and others move beyond secularism to advance more complex points about the way "secular reason" excludes certain faiths while invisibly privileging others. The task of wrestling with the human capacity for violence and the manifest horrors of our history (evoked in *Black Dogs* by the titular animals left behind by the Gestapo in France that attack June and provoke her mystical epiphany) demands a more subtle conceptual paradigm than either Bernard's "invincible atheism," on the one hand, or June's spiritual universalism, too much the province of "California professionals and dazed hippies," on the other (xxiii, 37). It is my hope that this book will help develop just such a perspective.

Notes

INTRODUCTION

1. Pamuk ("Frankfurt") describes his novel as "deliberately political" in an oft-cited interview with *Der Spiegel* in 2005.

2. The secularity of the Turkish Republic is one of the so-called "irrevocable" characteristics of the Republic in the constitution ratified on November 7, 1982.

3. Secular nationalism was intended to buttress Turkish nationalism while serving as a bulwark against pan-Islamic transnational attachments to the Islamic *ummah*, but since the end of single-party rule in 1946, maintaining a secularist hegemony has required military and juridical coups d'état, repeated disbandment of democratically elected parties, and the frequent implementation of penal code.

4. The key passage of article 1, cited here from the current (1958) constitution, reads: "La France est une République indivisible, laïque, démocratique et sociale. Elle assure l'égalité devant la loi de tous les citoyens sans distinction d'origine, de race ou de religion. Elle respecte toutes les croyances" (Conseil Constitutionnel) ("France shall be an indivisible, secular, democratic and social Republic. It shall ensure the equality of all citizens before the law, without distinction of origin, race or religion. It shall respect all beliefs"; French National Assembly). For a brief, incisive discussion, see Balibar, esp. 353–60.

5. See, for example, Bhadrakumar.

6. For anthropological accounts of the head-scarf issue, see Göle, *Forbidden Modern*, and Mahmood, *Politics of Piety*. For a lively discussion of the head-scarf controversy and the AKP in 2008, see "Headscarf Controversy," a collection of posts by various authors on the Social Science Research Council's online forum, *The Immanent Frame*, especially the contributions of Jenny

White, Markus Dressler, Nilüfer Göle, and Joan Wallach Scott. As a site devoted to essays and debates on religion and the public sphere, *The Immanent Frame* has played a central role in shaping the contours of what we might call the new secularity studies.

7. White's ethnography of the Ümraniye district of Istanbul, *Islamist Mobilization*, explores in great detail the increasing prominence of covered women in Turkish political culture. For White and others, new styles of piety have facilitated, rather than restricted, women's prominence in the public sphere.

8. As several of Weber's most capable readers argue, much depends upon the translation of Weber's term *Entgötterung*, a term that he borrows from Schiller, and that might more accurately be translated as "dedivinization" in order to avoid the overwhelmingly positive connotations of the term *enchantment* in English and French. See Robbins, "Enchantment?"

9. See Mathewes and Nichols; Lilla; and Gauchet.

10. As Talal Asad writes, "Where faith had once been a virtue, it now acquired an epistemological sense. Faith became a way of knowing supernatural objects, parallel to the knowledge of nature (the real world) that reason and observation provided" (*Formations* 321).

11. For a comparative engagement with political secularism in the United States, Turkey, and France, see Kuru. Jacoby offers a more celebratory assessment of the separation of church and state.

12. As a testament to these developments, "secular studies" programs and institutes have emerged in various universities. See Mangan.

13. In very different ways, the world literature rubrics advocated by Moretti and Damrosch offer compelling ways to approach literary production and patterns of circulation. For Damrosch, the category of world literature usefully denotes not a canon but a process whereby literary works "circulate beyond their culture of origin, either in translation or in their original language" (4). In this way, world literature describes "a mode of circulation and of reading, a mode that is as applicable to individual works as to bodies of material, available for reading established classics and new discoveries alike" (5). As he elaborates, "A work enters into world literature by a double process: first, by being read *as* literature; second, by circulating out into a broader world beyond its linguistic and cultural point of origin" (6). In "Conjectures on World Literature," *Graphs, Maps, Trees*, and elsewhere, Franco Moretti in contrast argues that the scope of world literature—with its hundreds of different languages and millions of titles published annually—requires that newly designed reading strategies render large-scale patterns visible.

14. This is especially true of Coetzee, who draws on not only his personal diasporic narrative but also on a tradition of diasporic literature including examples like Irish migrants Beckett and Joyce and domestic exiles like Dostoyevsky.

15. I sympathize with Weber's famous refusal to offer a definition of religion; it is likewise not my intention here to offer a transhistorical definition. Charles Taylor wisely restricts his understanding of religion to the cultural milieu of the North Atlantic world. He defines religion in terms of an immanent/transcendent distinction, supplemented by the idea that religious notions of human flourishing imply something outside what he calls "exclusive humanism." My

understanding of religion also draws variously on Émile Durkheim's practical anthropology of religion as a social phenomenon grounded in collective representations, Rudolph Otto's *Mysterium Tremendum*, Mercea Eliade's sacred/profane dialectic, and René Girard's exploration of violence and the sacred.

16. One of the main problems with "religion" as a category is that definitional projects tend to take one religion's standards for what constitutes religion and generalize them. Moreover, many of the early anthropologists of religion, Otto included, saw their scholarship as part of the project of identifying the superiority of Christianity over other faiths. We need to be especially suspicious of the category of religion in part because Christianity claims the status of exemplar in this category.

17. Asad is particularly instructive on this point in *Genealogies of Religion*, in which he problematizes "the very idea of an anthropological definition of religion by assigning that endeavor to a particular history of knowledge and power (including a particular understanding of our legitimate past and future) out of which the modern world has been constructed" (54). Similarly, he writes, "The insistence that religion has an autonomous essence—not to be confused with the essence of science, or of politics, or of common sense—invites us to define religion . . . as a transhistorical and transcultural phenomenon. . . . This definition is at once part of a strategy (for secular liberals) of the confinement, and (for liberal Christians) of the defense of religion" (28). The present work draws on Asad and Connolly's attentiveness to questions of embodiment but is cautious of Asad's tendency to discount the role of the supernatural in religious experience as well as his marginalization of specifically literary questions about language, rhetoric, and style in his effort to destabilize the centrality of belief.

18. The conflation of secularization and disenchantment, derived from Weber's influential postulate, can be seen most clearly in Bennett.

19. When I started working in 2005 on the project this book has become, I agreed with the hypothesis that the contemporary moment was "postsecular." However, the term *postsecular* was increasingly being used in problematic, often opposing ways by During ("Toward the Postsecular"), McClure, Habermas ("Notes"), and others. Especially given Taylor's description of the secular as a "frame" or ground, the "postness" of the "postsecular" seemed to become "something of a red herring," as Calhoun and Warner argue ("Secularism" 78). In light of Taylor's work, "In order to believe that we are post-secular, one must have a narrow and inadequate conception of what it means to be secular" ("Editors' Introduction" 22).

20. As Mahmood argues, the coherence of Taylor's "Latin Christianity" must be tempered with an awareness of "encounters [with religious difference that] did not simply leave Christianity untouched but transformed it from within" (285). See also Göle, "Civilizational, Spatial, and Sexual Powers."

21. Cardinal Jean-Louis Tauran, "Interreligious Dialogue—a Risk or an Opportunity?" Speech at Heythrop College, London, May 28, 2008. http://www.zenit.org/en/articles/cardinal-tauran-s-address-at-university-of-london

22. My point is not to criticize interfaith initiatives as such. Substantive sites of interfaith dialogue have emerged, including most prominently the open letter from Muslim leaders, *A Common Word between Us and You* (Muhammad).

23. Controversies like those sparked by the *Jyllands-Posten* cartoons of 2005 and Pope Benedict XVI's September 2006 lecture on faith and reason,

which offended many Muslims by seeming to endorse misleading criticism of Islam, led to a surge in post-9/11 interfaith initiatives.

24. Alternately, claims about religious homogeneity in a given society might be better read as signs of a poor survey or as evidence of tyranny; it is helpful to remember that evidence of homogeneity most easily achieved through bad testing or by bloodshed.

1. SALMAN RUSHDIE'S WOUNDED SECULARISM

1. For a thorough bibliographic description of *The Satanic Verses*, see Maxwell's account of its publication history.

2. Roger Clark—writing on behalf of the skeptical majority in his monograph on Rushdie's use of mythology and mysticism, *Stranger Gods*—finds Rushdie's later fiction "disappointing in various ways" that center on the overly rigid religious/secular binary that informs his post-fatwa thinking. For Clark, the "latest novels lack any profound or provocative religious challenges. . . . He no longer delves very far into the paradox of religion in the secular and postmodern world, be it that of London or Bombay. . . . It is as if Rushdie has given up on a more difficult literary exploration, and fallen back on some general anti-religious view, one that his earlier fiction examined within a larger panoply of belief, disbelief, and doubt" (182–83).

3. Ironically, as Talal Asad argues of the fatwa affair, "The political mobilization of Muslim immigrants in Britain to get *The Satanic Verses* banned produced an emotional reaction on the part of the liberal elite which was out of all proportion to what actually happened. It also produced an unprecedented statement from a government minister about British identity that was directed at the Muslim minority, a statement that was warmly welcomed as representative of liberal elite opinion" (*Genealogies* 248).

4. At the same time, Rushdie's rhetoric also participates in the discourse of neomedievalism I discuss at greater length in chapter 3 below, "Time and Terror."

5. For an introduction to the history of political secularism and social secularization in India, see Nandini Chatterjee; Needham and Rajan; and Bhargava. For a study with a literary focus, see Srivastava.

6. On Indian state secularism and the uniform civil code, see Galanter, esp. pt. 5, and Jacobsohn, esp. pt. 2.

7. The religion/politics distinction, confusing in itself, becomes particularly difficult to sustain when Rushdie writes, later in the essay, that "the religious revivals of the world are continuations of the political process by other means" (*Imaginary Homelands* 389).

8. For the sake of consistency, I refer to India Ophuls/Kashmira Noman as "Kashmira" throughout unless otherwise mandated by context or quotations.

9. For a history of this period, see Hasan (50–116).

10. In his essays, Rushdie accepts the consensus view that in its emphasis on the distinction between spirit and law, early Christianity set the stage for what has become Western secularism: "The *render unto Caesar* formula is, obviously, significant here. . . . From earliest times we see in Christianity a

willingness to separate the Church and State, and admission that such a separation is possible and maybe even desirable. In the world of Islam, no such separation has ever occurred at the level of theory" (*Imaginary Homelands* 380).

11. I argue this case at greater length in Neuman, "Religious Cosmopolitanism?"

12. I use the term *strong religion* in the sense articulated by Gabriel Almond, Appleby, and Sivan.

13. *Cosmopolitan* was a pejorative term throughout much of the twentieth century—especially when used to modify Jews, communists, and homosexuals—and as a concept was ignored or derided in the era of decolonization when hopes ran high for the emancipatory potential of postcolonial nationalism. By 1996, in the words of American literature scholar Eric Lott, the "new cosmopolitanism" had already become "the Next Big Thing," even in the nationalist discipline of American studies (108). Lott focuses here on the new meanings of the cosmopolitan in American studies; for early accounts of this shift in adjacent fields, see Brennan, *At Home*, and Cheah and Robbins, *Cosmopolitics*.

14. For other attempts to renovate the Stoic/Kantian lines of cosmopolitan thought in socially and politically trenchant directions, see the introduction to Breckenridge, Pollock, and Bhabha; Robbins, *Feeling Global*.

15. The aesthetic of rooted or vernacular cosmopolitanism can further be seen in *Camino Real*, Kashmira's documentary film about the diasporic subjects and labor conditions that constitute the inverted double of Max's own success. Kashmira's film investigates the consequences of transnational capitalism deliberately ignored by her father: "She was after . . . the changing gang culture of the barrios, the trailer-park families in the shadow of the freeways, the swarming immigrant armies that fed the housing boom, the new pleasantvilles being built in the firetrap canyons to house the middle-class arrivistes, the less-pleasantvilles in the thick of the urban sprawl filling up with the Koreans, the Indians, the illegals; she wanted the dirty underbelly of paradise, the broken harp-strings, the cracked haloes, the narcotic bliss, the human bloat, the truth" (333).

16. Working within Nussbaum's Kantian tradition, Seyla Benhabib has recently argued for approaching cosmopolitanism descriptively as the set of practices that best characterize the emergence of a global human rights regime: "Since the UN Declaration of Human Rights in 1948, we have entered a phase in the evolution of global civil society, which is characterized by a transition from *international* to *cosmopolitan* norms of justice" (*Another Cosmopolitanism* 16; italics in original). As Benhabib uses the term, it neither signifies an attitude toward humanity as a whole nor describes transnational cultures. Instead, cosmopolitanism indexes a specific system of norms that governs interpersonal and international relations—cosmopolitan law—that trumps the will of sovereign states. For Benhabib, contemporary cosmopolitanism begins, very plainly, with genocide and the notion of crimes against humanity; the crime of genocide and the transnational legal order with reference to which genocide is defined establishes the coherence of cosmopolitan norms as a system.

17. In their essays for Nussbaum and Cohen's *For Love of Country?* Benjamin Barber, Gertrude Himmelfarb, and Charles Taylor all specifically cite this problematic "thinness."

18. Appiah's insights regarding globalization and fundamentalism echo those of international relations theorists. Terrorism specialist Audrey Cronin put the general case well in 2003: "The current wave of international terrorism, characterized by unpredictable and unprecedented threats from nonstate actors, not only is a reaction to globalization but is facilitated by it" (30).

19. The apocryphal flight of the "Bugatti Racer" and indeed Max himself exemplify Rushdie's metafictional historiography: Ettore Bugatti did in fact design and build just such a prototype racer, though the plane was never flown.

20. Again, Rushdie offers a relatively accurate history; his account of "the Panther" appears to quote from Jacqueline Bromberger's testimony about the resistance movement. She writes: "The Clermont-Ferrand antenna was directed by Paul Blumenkampf, assisted by his very powerful secretary Ursula Brandt. We knew them soon: Blumenkampf played the jovial fellow. As for Ursula Brandt, she was soon nicknamed 'the Panther,' not that she was particularly cat-like (she was rather short indeed), but she wore a coat made of the skin of this animal, a coat which she never took off, even when the temperature reached 100°F."

21. Rushdie insists that an effective "war on terror" would require a far more materialistic resistance than the glamorous rearguard actions undertaken by Max in the struggle against the Nazis; as he wrote in October 2001, "We must agree on what matters: kissing in public places, bacon sandwiches, disagreement, cutting-edge fashion, literature, generosity, water, a more equitable distribution of the world's resources, movies, music, freedom of thought, beauty, love. These will be our weapons. Not by making war but by the unafraid way we choose to live shall we defeat them" (*Step* 338).

22. To put Max's reported wealth in perspective, his billionaire status in 1992 would place him among the 233 richest people in the world ("The Billionaires").

23. For specific commentary on Rushdie's satire, see Brennan, *Salman Rushdie*, esp. 84–95, and Israel, *Outlandish*, esp. his chapter "The Place of Rushdie." For a compendium of criticism skeptical of Rushdie's use of satire, see Ahsan and Kidwai.

24. For Walkowitz, who reads Rushdie's modernism as an integral part of his "cosmopolitan style," Rushdie's prose "emphasizes the aleatory, the trivial, and the playful, modernist strategies that [she associates] with Joyce. Like Joyce," Walkowitz maintains, "Rushdie proposes that ordinary social and semantic mistakes—mix-ups—can create opportunities for effective, if sometimes impermanent agency" (133). The various ways modernist novelists, heirs to Victorian crises of faith, sought to use the literary to substantiate values no longer supported by institutionalized religion have been cogently discussed by Pericles Lewis.

25. Robbins ("Enchantment?") has shown that the term *disenchantment* is, in fact, a misleading translation.

26. The misogynistic implications of Rushdie's portrayal of women, a common refrain in the scholarly responses to his work, here achieve a fevered pitch; for a sexually desirable woman like Qara Köz, "poets reached for their pens, artists for their brushes, sculptors for their chisels" (275)—which is to

say "that when you lay eyes on the pair of witches [Qara Köz and the mirror] the desire to fuck them comes upon you like swine fever" (237).

2. J. M. COETZEE'S PROPHETS OF ASCETICISM

1. Using eco-critic Rob Nixon's term, we might call asceticism a form of "slow violence," that, like climate change, is particularly difficult to recognize from the temporal vantage point of an average news cycle better equipped to cover spectacles of sudden violence. I have in mind here images like that of the self-immolation of the Vietnamese monk Thich Quàng Duc on June 10, 1963, which was famously captured by photojournalist Malcolm Browne of the Associated Press. As Browne notes in his autobiography, the monks themselves were keen architects of media spectacle: members of the monastic community experimented with different ratios of gasoline and diesel fuel before finding a ratio that would "produce a fire that was both intense and sufficiently long lasting" (9). The Tunisian protests of late 2010 that gave birth to the movements known as the Arab Spring were similarly sparked, as it were, by the self-immolation of Mohamed Bouazizi, who set himself alight in protest of government extortion and poor economic conditions.

2. While hunger strikes by charismatic leaders or among organized groups of inmates can present obvious threats to prison security, the state recognized that in this case the death of the inmate, a man convicted of aggravated sexual assault who testified that he saw his pain as a form of penance for a life of misdeeds, would provoke no riots in the prison or mobs of outraged citizens.

3. In *McNab v. Department of Corrections*, the Supreme Court of Washington ruled similarly: "The State's interests in orderly administration of the prison system" justified giving broad license to the state when rights of prisoners conflict with the goals and aims of the penal system.

4. In an ironic inversion of Carl Schmitt's famous dictum "Sovereign is he who decides on the exception" (5) the case made by the government of the United States that detainees lack constitutional rights, the protections of the Geneva Conventions, and the privileges of habeas corpus rests in large part on the denial of sovereignty. The denial of territorial sovereignty over Guantanamo is mirrored in the classification of detainees as enemy combatants—a term first applied broadly to any person engaged in hostilities against the United States or its allies and later formalized under the Military Commissions Act of 2006 to distinguish between "lawful" and "unlawful" combatants. In a series of rulings beginning with *Rasul v. Bush*, decided on June 28, 2004, US courts began to issue judgments supporting claims made by the detainees imprisoned at the Guantanamo Bay naval base in Cuba. Writing for the narrow majority in *Rasul*, Justice Kennedy rejected the state's denial of sovereignty—"In every practical sense Guantanamo is not abroad; it is within the constant jurisdiction of the United States" (38–39)—and added that "the laws and Constitution are designed to survive, and remain in force, in extraordinary times" (51). The plaintiffs in *Rasul*, Asif Iqbal and Shafiq Rasul, along with other petitioners of Australian and Kuwaiti origin, denied wrongdoing and, alleging that they were being held illegally, invoked the writ of habeas corpus, a procedural demand

that a court rule on the legitimacy of their detention. While the lower courts had refused to hear their case, citing a lack of jurisdiction, the Supreme Court ruled six to three that the federal judiciary indeed has jurisdiction to hear the habeas claims of Guantanamo detainees, giving foreign nationals held in Cuba the right to challenge the conditions of their confinement and the lawfulness of their detention. Rasul and several others were released without charge on March 9, 2004; subsequent decisions would be required to address the merits of detainees' habeas claims, culminating in *Boumediene v. Bush* (2008). In the intervening years, however, the Department of Defense continued to refuse independent oversight of the camps and, under the aegis of the Military Commissions Act of 2006, instituted a system of military tribunals to hear the cases of the Guantanamo detainees, a system deemed unconstitutional in the 2006 Supreme Court case *Hamdan v. Rumsfeld.*

5. A literary genealogy history of twentieth-century ascetics might begin with the Mahayana Buddhist Lama in Rudyard Kipling's *Kim* (1901), follow another guru with Somerset Maugham in *The Razor's Edge* (1944), and, remaining on the subcontinent, track Gandhi's renunciatory disciplines to Naipaul's Nietzschean genealogy of Brahmin self-denial in *Half a Life* (2001), or to the world-renouncing narrator of the second part of Geoff Dyer's *Jeff in Venice, Death in Varanasi* (2010). Alternately, an investigation of Judeo-Christian ascetics might begin in 1922 with the publication of Kafka's short story "The Hunger Artist," move through the midcentury with Simone Weil's ideas about mystical self-fashioning and her infamous self-starvation, and conclude with Don DeLillo's minimalist novella *The Body Artist* (2001), in which the performance artist Lauren Hartke sands, shaves, and starves herself in preparation for a performance piece entitled *Body Time*, which "begins with an ancient Japanese woman on a bare stage, gesturing in the stylized manner of Noh drama, and . . . ends seventy-five minutes later with a naked man, emaciated and aphasic, trying desperately to tell us something" (105). An Islamically inflected account of asceticism, *zuhd* in Arabic, might focalize Nawaal Sadaawi's *Woman at Point Zero* (1973), with its world-renouncing heroine Firdaus, along with the protagonist of Elias Khoury's *Yalo* (2002), and, perhaps most powerfully, Tahar Ben Jelloun's *This Blinding Absence of Light* (2003), a novel based on historical events and survivor testimony that recreates the experience of the narrator's eighteen-year internment in the secret Moroccan prison of Tazmamart, where framing hunger as part of a project of religious self-fashioning enables his survival.

6. Most of humankind, for Nietzsche, falls into the class of "degenerating life," a form of existence he describes as "a self-contradiction" in which "a most extraordinary resentment prevails,—the resentment of an insatiate instinct and will to power" (161).

7. Coetzee engages the question of his debt to Kafka in his 1990 interview with David Attwell and the critical essay "Time, Tense, and Aspect in Kafka's 'The Borrow,'" which appeared two years before the publication of *Life and Times of Michael K.* "There is no monopoly on the letter K," writes Coetzee (Interview 199), but the direct allusion of Michael K's asceticism to Kafka's "Hunger Artist" and "The Borrow," as well as more pervasive similarities in

style and tone, are unmistakable and have captured the notice of several critics. For a more thorough examination of Coetzee's engagement with Kafka, Attwell's interview and Coetzee's own essay offer the most suggestive starting points. Merivale pursues numerous subtle references to Kafka while arguing broadly for their relevance to Coetzee's literary project.

8. Barnard explores Coetzee's multifaceted critique (*White Writing*) of the pastoral mode in South African white writing, concluding with Coetzee that "an aesthetic appreciation of the African landscape" is often little more than "an alibi for a more fundamental heard-heartedness and inhumanity" (200)—but given that K is a member of apartheid's underclass, his identification with the landscape, though it shares the idiom of the pastoral, defies its politics.

9. While a thorough account of the concentration camp system the British Empire developed in response to the protracted campaigns of Boer guerrilla fighters is beyond the scope of this book, the history of the South African camps offers a suggestive intertext to *Life and Times of Michael K*. After a series of initial defeats, the British army successfully occupied the two independent Boer republics but faced a stubbornly elusive and disruptive resistance. To break the back of the guerrilla movement, British forces erected a system of camps in which to "concentrate" the civilian Boer population thought to be providing aid to guerrilla fighters, as well as the population of Black Africans. Like those in Coetzee's novel, the camps were justified as a "humane alternative to leaving the women and children on the 'desert veld'" but were in reality sites of disease, starvation, and death on a massive scale (Spies 185). In all, of the estimated 160,000 (Spies 194–96) people detained in the camps, at least 26,000 white and 12,000 black Africans perished (Raath 12). For extensive English-language primary source material on the concentration camps, consult Raath and Spies.

10. Although K is identified as "CM," or colored male, the unreliability of the narrator combined with the ad hoc nature of many racial designations in South Africa encourages our skepticism. With Michael's paternity an open question (though we never encounter his siblings, Michael is the fourth of Anna's children, all of ambiguous parentage), Anna's intensely isolated life and history of domestic employment (cooking and cleaning for white families) warrants the speculation that miscegenation is as likely a source of the "smiles" with which people insult Anna K as Michael's cleft palate.

11. A rather perverse irony haunts this teaspoon, an item that reemerges on the novel's final page reclaimed as a symbol of sustenance and minimal agency. The spoon of the opening page, in contrast, like the "life and times" of the novel's title, parodies the biographies of the famous and influential whom Coetzee satirizes. Though the spoon is not silver, Michael K is, essentially, "born with a spoon in his mouth." The proverbial "silver spoon" serves as potent metonymy for economic privilege, family lineage, and religious history. Michael K's spoon, in contrast, ironically recasts both the proverb and the genre.

12. In addition to being labeled "CM" or colored male by the hospital, K is called "Michaels" by the medical officer, the name with which he is identified in camp records.

13. As Agamben suggests in *Homo Sacer*, the supposed sacredness of life, upon which much human rights discourse rests, arises, not in opposition to sovereign violence, but from the unique structure of the state of exception. This structure is evident in the juridico-political definition of *homo sacer* offered by Roman historian and etymologist Pompeius Festus: *homo sacer* is that which is excluded from both human and divine law.

14. It is interesting to note that Coetzee frames K's renunciation of reproduction not through questions of sacrifice and the expiation of guilt, as do characters in Faulkner or Dostoevsky for instance, but in non-normative terms.

15. No entirely adequate etymology explains the term *muselmann*, though many Holocaust survivors and scholars hazard an account that usually alludes to the similarity between the crouched posture of the *muselmann* and the image of a Muslim in prayer. The most complete account of the condition of the *muselmann* in the camps can be found in Langbein's chapter of that title, where he cites prisoners' descriptions of these haunting figures: "You could see *Muselmänner* everywhere: skinny, dirty figures, their skin and faces blackened, their gaze gone, their eyes hollowed out, their clothes threadbare, filthy and stinking" (168).

16. Pleasure was thus doubly problematic: first for the active member of sexual partnership as they construed it, because ejaculation was linked to exhaustion, excretion, and death; and second, especially, for the boy, who "could not and must not identify with [his] role" (221) because the pleasure of the passive agent is of a fundamentally different order—it is an "*Anteros*" (189). Attaining virtue required both pleasure and the careful constrainment of those pleasures, resulting in a "medical regimen [that] proposes, then, a sort of animalization of the epithumia; that is, a subordination, as strict as possible, of the soul's desire to the body's needs; an ethics of desire that is modeled on a natural philosophy of excretions; and the tendency toward an ideal point where the soul, purified of all its vain representations, no longer gives its attention to anything but the austere economy of organic function" (*Care* 136).

17. Attridge, one of Coetzee's strongest readers, argues that the novel's shifting narrative modes and stylized voice serve as potent reminders of K's otherness and his resistance to representation from within dominant modes of discourse. As he argues, Coetzee's novels "can be read as a continued, strenuous enterprise in acknowledging alterity, a project which is at once highly local in its engagement with the urgent political and social problems of South Africa . . . and widely pertinent in its confrontation of the ethical demands of otherness, and its investigation of the relation of otherness to language, culture, and knowledge" (12). Marais has similarly staked a claim on ethical interpretations of Coetzee's novels in several essays that read Coetzee with Blanchot and Levinas. In his analysis of *Life and Times of Michael K*, for instance, Marais seeks to "establish the relevance of Emmanuel Levinas's notion of an ethics that is grounded in the subject's self-substituting responsibility for the other to Coetzee's understanding of the possibility for renegotiating the subjectivity that inheres in the act of writing" (108). An ethics of love rather than of obligation to the other defines the contributions of Gilbert Yeoh, another of Coetzee's prolific critics, while Spivak ("Ethics") reaches conclusions about

the ethical structure of a reader's encounter with Coetzee's fiction similar to those of Attridge.

18. In the essay "Secularization and Hunger," a meditation far more deeply invested in the latter idea than the former, Levinas attempts to ground the ethical obligation to preserve and protect the life of the other (as outlined in the face-to-face encounters of *Alterity and Transcendence*) in the creatural and somatic register of physical hunger. He writes, "Under the banal term 'compassion,' we are not astonished enough by the force of transference which goes from the memory of my own hunger to the suffering and the responsibility for the hunger of the neighbor"—but in the case of ascetic figures like Michael K, the Levinasian injunction to care for the starving would, it seems, participate in the very logic deployed by defenders of force-feedings ("Secularization" 11).

19. The relationship between Christianity and apartheid, like the relationship between Christian missionary work and European imperialism more generally, warrants a more thorough investigation than I can offer here. A useful starting point in this field is Elphick and Davenport.

20. Sulk follows a similar etymological line, while Kossew notes that Coetzee "never mentions Vercueil's color—he could conceivably be either a white derelict or a Cape Coloured, like K" (*Pen and Power* 202); in any event, both in Coetzee's novel and in colonial or diasporic contexts more broadly, the name given by or to a white master is not necessarily the name by which one knows oneself.

21. A love that regards all human beings as equally deserving and that distributes care accordingly will necessarily be rather "professional" in its ministrations, an idea I develop more fully in my subsequent discussion of nursing in the third section of this chapter.

22. Given the importance of Petrus's, and later David's, self-identification as the "dog man" in *Disgrace*, careful readers should also note that Elizabeth repeatedly identifies Vercueil as the "dog man" (56).

23. In the Latin Vulgate Bible, the normative definition of *caritas* derives from the Apostle Paul: "*Nunc autem manet fides spes caritas tria haec maior autem his est caritas* ("And now there remain faith, hope, and charity, these three: but the greatest of these is charity" (1 Cor. 13:13). The English translation cited above is drawn from the Douay-Rheims edition, which preserves the distinction between *caritas* and *agape* obscured in the New Revised Standard Edition. The 1611 King James Bible also translates "caritas" as "charity" ("And now abideth faith, hope, charity, these three; but the greatest of these is charity"), while the New Revised Standard Edition translates both *agape* and *caritas* as "love" ("And now faith, hope, and love abide, these three; and the greatest of these is love"). As Jackson writes in *Love Disconsoled*, "'*Agape*' is the New Testament Greek word for the steadfast love God has for human beings, as well as for the neighbor-love humans are to have for one another" (11). See also Aquinas's *Summa Theologiae* II-II, and Kierkegaard's *Works of Love.*

24. The *Oxford English Dictionary* insists that *care* is "in no way related to [the] L[atin] *cura*," or to *caritas.*

25. In Jackson's analysis, a rigorously Christian understanding of charity resolves the paradox of the unworthiness of charity's recipients and its

seemingly illogical nature through an appeal to the suprarational. He explains that "*agape* is neither the undervaluation nor the overvaluation of someone or something's worthiness, since it is self-consciously indiscriminate and other-enhancing. Love of the neighbor need not be irrational, in short, though it requires suprarational resources" (64).

26. Coles continues, "The profoundest goals, meanings, and textures of the generous act emerge from a receptive encounter with the other that risks . . . transgressing the self-enclosures of one's own narrative in ways that might transfigure the moment of giving" (3).

27. For an alternate critique of confession, see Foucault, *Introduction*.

28. A policeman who sees Elizabeth and Vercueil together reverts to Afrikaans to express his disgust: "'*In Godsnaam*,' said the detective," prompting Elizabeth to wonder whether his exclamation was "mere fulmination, or a curse on the pair of us?" (173).

29. Elizabeth presents her imitation of Mary (*pace* the "imitation of Christ") as a highly mediated event. In particular, her imagistic vocabulary for Mary and her breast-offering comes from the Italian painter Correggio, born in 1494, whose painting Elizabeth cites. Elizabeth invokes Correggio's Virgin Mary, "who delicately raises her nipple with her fingertips so that her baby can suck," as she describes her own "blessing": "What was going on revolved around . . . breasts and breast-milk" (144). Though Elizabeth does not name the painting she has in mind, the most likely seems to be Correggio's 1523 *Madonna del Latte*.

30. In Coetzee's echoing phraseology, to "give up" evokes, perhaps "cites," the famous closing vignette of *Disgrace* where the reader finds David and Bev Shaw—the recipient of something on the spectrum of David's "erotic charity"—"engaged in one of their sessions of *Lösung*": euthanizing dogs (218). The scene is attentive, tender, and sacred. When they come, at the end of the day's work, to his favorite dog, David calls to the dog to "come" and, "bearing him in his arms like a lamb," carries him to the table (220). "Are you giving him up?" Bev asks, to which David responds, "Yes, I am giving him up" (220).

31. Letters are themselves a rather problematic genre in *Elizabeth Costello*; many readers stumble over the novel's ending, which concludes with a cryptic postscript in the form of the "Letter of Elizabeth, Lady Chandos, to Francis Bacon," dated "This 11 September, AD 1603" (230). Though it is beyond the scope of this project, an engaged reader must explore this unsettlement, pushing the boundary of this strange "text" to pursue its referential horizon out into the world through digital media. As Coetzee pursues questions of ethics to the plane of textuality, he frequently disperses the sources and sites of authorship.

32. At least since French anthropologist Marcel Mauss's *Essai sur le don* in 1924, the idea of the gift has preoccupied the field of anthropology and percolated through the critical consciousness of other disciplines. While a genealogy of the role of the gift in essays by Mauss, Levi-Strauss, Bourdieu, Derrida, Bataille, and others is beyond the scope of this project, considering Elizabeth's act of sexual charity in terms of gift and mercy helps to triangulate

my analysis. For feminist approaches to the gift, see Hélène Cixous, especially "The Laugh of the Medusa," and Carol Gilligan's *In a Different Voice*.

33. For those looking for greater purchase on the growing body of work on the gift, Schrift's edited volume *The Logic of the Gift* compiles seminal essays by Ralph Waldo Emerson, Mauss, Derrida, Cixous, and others, as well as a selection of secondary materials and a suggestive introduction. See also Wyschogrod, Goux, and Boynton's *Enigma of Gift and Sacrifice*, which features essays by John Caputo and Mark Taylor and a comprehensive introduction by Wyschogrod.

34. As before, Elizabeth's actions resonate more with the ideas Bataille develops in *Consumption* (vol. 1 of *The Accursed Share*), that excess wealth that must be consumed in meaningless displays of luxury or sexuality lest it find release in war, than they do with Mauss's gift. While the lack of any possible reciprocity continues to echo Bataille's squandering, the commodity-driven sense of expenditure central to Bataille (and modeled on the concept of potlatch described by Mauss and others) runs counter to the logic of Elizabeth's act, which does not dispose of any "excess" energy despite the similar "magical" properties Mauss identifies in the gift.

35. The narrator's repeated use of "Nurse Naidoo's" full name and title deserves parenthetical attention. Like the name Vercueil, the name Naidoo carries palimpsestic ethnic, religious, and national implications. The name Naidoo is a version of the word *Naidu*, a title used by Hindu Tamils in Southeast India meaning "leader" or "protector." Moreover, the ethnic heritage of nurses becomes a subject of marked significance in Coetzee's *Slow Man*, in which Elizabeth also appears as a main character.

36. For those who lived or came of age in the postwar years (like Coetzee and Costello, though to a lesser extent than American nationals), the essays written for *This I Believe* and read by their authors to the nation, transect theistic and nontheistic orientations to build the foundations of what Jean-Jacques Rousseau called a "civil religion."

37. Wood's compelling review of the novel takes Elizabeth's claim to "believe in what does not bother to believe in me" in the following manner: "She means the frogs, but Coetzee probably has in mind Spinoza's blankly chilling proposition that 'He who loves God cannot endeavor that God love him in return.' He may also be thinking of Aristotle's notion of the poet as one who lavishes love on those—his characters—who cannot return it" (1).

3. TIME AND TERROR

1. As of June 20, 2013; see the video at Improv Everywhere, *Frozen Grand Central*.

2. See, for example, Evans for the RAND Corporation's modeling of the likelihood of such an attack, and McNeill, Carafano, and Zuckerman for the Heritage Foundation's analysis of Najibullah Zazi's alleged plot to attack trains at Grand Central on the ten-year anniversary of 9/11.

3. Redfield offers a sustained meditation on the "double movement of inscription and effacement" performed by the name-date "9/11" (15; also. esp.

16–22). Perhaps the most noteworthy and insightful commentary on the significance of the naming of 9/11 was offered by Jacques Derrida, who suggests in *Philosophy in a Time of Terror* that "pointing toward this date, the bare act . . . the minimalist aim of this dating also marks something else. . . . 'Something' took place, we have the feeling of not having seen it coming . . . repeating it endlessly, as a kind of ritual incantation, a conjuring poem, a journalistic litany or rhetorical refrain that admits to not knowing what it's talking about" (Habermas, Derrida, and Borradori 86). The endless repetition of the name-date, for Derrida, also signals that the truly traumatic nature of the event derives less from the destruction inflicted on September 11, 2001, than the possibility of its future repetition: "Traumatism is produced by the *future*, by the *to come*, by the threat of the worst *to come*" (97). I return to this concept of futurity in my discussion of the preemptive logic of the war on terror.

4. Bruce Holsinger describes this phenomenon in terms of the "9/11 premodern," a discursive regime through which "medievalism became a dominant journalistic and political paradigm for comprehending the identity, culture, and motivations of America's perceived enemy" (v).

5. Henry Perowne's secular heroism—the distinctive conjunction of worldly success, physical confidence, and haughty atheism that defines his character—evokes both Ayn Rand's objectivism and Nietzsche's Zarathustra.

6. For a sample of McEwan's interviews in which he discusses his personal atheism, see McEwan, "TNR Q&A"; McEwan, interview by Whitney.

7. The contrast with Bloom is striking and says much about why *Saturday*'s tone conveys such arrogance: where Bloom is the cuckold, the counter of coins, the wanderer, Henry Perowne is possessed of what he admits is an ungenerous share of the world's goods. He defeats his attacker with the help of his son, performs lifesaving surgery on the same man, and returns home to have sex with his wife for the second time that day.

8. Richard Dawkins (a friend of McEwan's) explores the music of the same phrase in his recent book *The Greatest Show on Earth* (2009).

9. See, for instance, Bradley and Tate; Impastato's thorough investigation of McEwan's atheist convictions; and McEwan, interview by Dawkins.

10. Philosophers use the term *tensed* to refer to the way memories appear to us as marked by a particular order. As the *Stanford Encyclopedia of Philosophy* glosses in their entry on the perception of time, "Information . . . [that] is *metrical* in nature (e.g. 'the burst of sound was very brief') is derived from *tensed* information, concerning how far in the past something occurred. The question is how we acquire this tensed information" (Le Poidevin). For more on tensed theories of time, see Craig.

11. In one prominent review by Lee Siegel, for instance, Baxter is a metonymy for the "ethical challenge presented by poor, starving countries to the affluent West." Elaine Hadley echoes this view, writing in her article "On a Darkling Plain," "Baxter's attack is terrorism finally, almost relievedly, brought home to his thoughts" (95). In her otherwise insightful analysis of the theme of empathy and ethics in "Writing Fiction in the Post-9/11 World: Ian McEwan's *Saturday*," Magali Cornier Michael argues that "although unable to conceptualize terrorist violence on a large scale or his own complicity

within the vast complex networks of global politics, Perowne is forced to face a graspable form of such violence and his own participation in an inequitable system when an intruder enters his home and holds his family hostage" (39).

12. Though this understanding is unavailable to Henry Perowne, readers can see the proximity between McEwan's somatic specious present and Agamben's concept of the state of exception; see *State of Exception* and *Time That Remains*. The "End~~less~~ *This* War" bumper stickers ubiquitous on American roads in the later years of the Bush presidency offer an interesting counterpoint.

13. Much of the writing on *Falling Man* to date has focused on the Falling Man himself, including an excellent article by Frost. Abel offers an incisive commentary on DeLillo's two essays on 9/11.

14. Just as their images have haunted so many people, the subject of those who jumped from the World Trade Center on 9/11 has been the subject of intense debate in media and the law. The "Falling Man" commonly refers to the photograph taken by *Associated Press* photographer Richard Drew. See also Junod.

15. People who are slow to "make sense" of the world are precisely those most vulnerable to what Klein calls the "shock doctrine," because asserting complexity is not necessarily an adequate response to change. The spirit of this critique accounts for concerns about the political and ethical engagements of deconstruction more broadly construed.

16. Genette uses the term *transfer point* in reference to Marcel's insomnias in the discussion of Proust's fiction through which he advances his argument in *Narrative Discourse*. Pages 29–45 contain the relevant passages for this discussion, as well as his analysis of other crucial temporal experiences. The sense of plotlessness DeLillo conveys in *Falling Man* achieves its apotheosis in the recent and far less satisfying novella *Point Omega*, where order of events is easily understood but their significance is only gestural at best.

17. Michael offers a nuanced discussion of this passage in her essay on McEwan's *Saturday*.

18. In her discussion of DeLillo, Hungerford devotes sustained attention to the role of the Catholic Mass in DeLillo's novels, focusing specifically on the role of meaninglessness in ritual forms; see especially ch. 4.

19. Though it is beyond the scope of this chapter, it is interesting to note the similarities between the forensic style of the *9/11 Commission Report* and that of the equally time-obsessed narrator of Orhan Pamuk's *Snow*.

20. The premise of trauma's delayed onset and disruption of time sense determines the curative approaches of both Freudian psychoanalysis and contemporary behavioral therapy. See, for example, Foa and Rothbaum; National Child Traumatic Stress Network. Several thinkers drawing on trauma theory to discuss 9/11 fiction include Kaplan and Simpson. Kaplan notes the "difficulty of fully distinguishing trauma from vicarious trauma," while scholars like Berlant and Brown cite responses to 9/11 as evidence of an American cultural addiction to trauma.

21. Several thinkers drawing on this tradition to discuss 9/11 narratives include Kaplan; Kauffman, "World Trauma Center"; Rothberg; and Simpson.

22. The fractious nature of the 9/11 Commission and members' shared suspicion of being intentionally deceived by government agencies is the subject

of commission chair Thomas Kean and vice-chair Lee Hamilton's *Without Precedent* (Kean, Hamilton, and Rhodes).

23. For information concerning the 9/11 Commission and its findings in various media forms, see National Commission on Terrorist Attacks, Archive.

24. Regarding the commercial success of the *Report*, see Wyatt, who explores the implications of digital media and compares the energetic sales figures to those of the 1964 *Warren Commission Report of the Assassination of President Kennedy*.

25. The archived site of the 9/11 Commission contains a trove of archival material, including not only the full text of the *Report* but also an archive of videos and transcripts from the public hearings. See National Archives and Records Administration.

26. Butler follows a similar approach, writing, "My claim will be that thinking through the problem of temporality and politics in this way may well open up a different approach to cultural difference, one that eludes claims of pluralism and intersectionality alike" (3).

27. The popular (and topical) television series 24 capitalizes on a similar technique in which the show's race against the clock compresses an hour of "clock time" into the roughly forty minutes of broadcast time in a television hour.

28. For a thorough account of the state of counterterrorism efforts prior to 9/11, see *The 9/11 Commission Report*, especially ch. 8, "The System Was Blinking Red."

29. The CIA memo in question, declassified on April 10, 2004, after requests by the 9/11 Commission, is available with limited redactions in National Commission on Terrorist Attacks, *9/11 Commission Report* (261–62).

30. Dementia is a major theme in Jess Walter's work and features prominently in his 2009 novel *The Financial Lives of Poets*, where a senile grandfather is both the source of comic energy and the occasion to reflect on memory and time.

31. Despite her contacts with Saudis of various stripes, March Selios, as the narrator takes pains to explain, bears a "Greek surname" and is a second-generation American citizen.

32. This conception of consciousness as necessarily continuous signals an important difference between Husserl and the likes of Bergson and Proust, both of whom respond to the unpredictable nature of memory and retrospection. Bergson, sharing with Husserl the rejection of time as discrete moments, writes in *Time and Free Will* that "states of consciousness [unlike material objects], even when successive, permeate one another, and in the simplest of them the whole soul can be reflected. We may therefore surmise that time, conceived under the form of a homogeneous medium, is some spurious concept, due to the trespassing of the idea of space upon the field of pure consciousness" (98).

4. MESSIANIC NARRATIVE

1. The Jewish liturgical tradition of the Passover Seder, with its symbolic reenactment of Exodus and the injunction to inhabit the position of the

oppressed ("God . . . took *me* out of Egypt"), requires a similar commitment to the past (Exod. 13:8).

2. Under the aegis of concepts like testimony, witness, and postmemory, critics including Shoshana Felman, Dominick LaCapra, Geoffrey Hartman, and Marianne Hirsch have studied the narratives of genocide, arguing that literature is a privileged site from which to access trauma. For these critics, the Holocaust produces a crisis in witnessing, a crisis that paradoxically requires the performative act of bearing witness, of giving testimony that is an estranging transmission of fragments exceeding expressibility. On the crisis of witnessing across generations, see Abraham and Torok's discussion of the "transgenerational phantom." Henke coined the term *scriptotherapy* for the approach to which Caruth and Felman implicitly subscribe.

3. In addition to Gershom Scholem's seminal work, the corpus of research devoted to the question of the origin and history of messianic thought, particularly surrounding the contexts of the early Christian movement, is extensive, diverse, and well documented. The discovery and painstaking analysis of the Dead Sea Scrolls, as well as the recognition by scholars in recent decades that theological imperatives provided the impetus for many earlier studies that masqueraded as sound historiography and ethnography has yielded a plethora of excellent texts on the subject for the specialist and nonspecialist alike. For recent research addressing the origins of messianism in the Old and New Testament periods, consult Collins; Horbury; Porter; and, most recently, Fitzmyer. For nonspecialists in Islamic studies, Peters offers a sincere and substantive introduction to Shi'ite messianism in a section of his book devoted to the subject. See also Corbin and Nasr; Dabashi; and Nasr. Though slightly out of date—and for this reason pleasantly removed from either apologetic or "clash of civilizations" rhetoric—Sachedina is an excellent resource. From a more literary than theological perspective, Ajami offers an interesting account of Shi'ite messianism's failure to extend the Iranian revolution into a messianic Shi'ite alternative to Sunni pan-Arabism.

4. The year 2000, the Branch Davidians' crisis in Waco, Texas, and other apocalyptic reckonings from 9/11 onward, occasion a further profusion of work devoted to postbiblical messianic and millenarian movements: Schäfer and Cohen; Katz and Popkin; and Worth offer a good starting point for further reading. Within the messianic Marxist tradition, key points include work by Bloch, in particular *Spirit of Utopia*; Benjamin; Lukács, in particular his *History and Class Consciousness*, whose "messianic utopianism" he later regretted; and Derrida, in particular *Specters of Marx*. More recent contributors to the vein of messianic Marxism include Žižek's *Parallax View* and *Puppet and the Dwarf*. Fukuyama's "end of history" ruptural argument in *End of History* has unmistakable messianic overtones and serves as an important point of entry into the appropriation of messianic discourse on the American political right. Ultimately, one of the most interesting aspects of messianic thought is the way it cuts across substantive ideological distinctions to be claimed by thinkers on both sides of the political spectrum.

5. In his writings on the Frankfurt School, including *Walter Benjamin* and *Frankfurt School Revisited*, Wolin traces what he aptly terms "the Frankfurt

School's trademark theoretical pessimism" to Benjamin's explosive and explicitly messianic conception of revolutionary action and, beyond that, to Judaic sources.

6. It seems no accident that the religiously and ethically vexed question of abortion should provide occasion for the event Toru believes was the turning point in his relationship with Kumiko. In fact, sexual and familial "defilements" (as Kumiko describes them) are at the core of Murakami's interest in the pains of the other.

7. Pamuk made this now infamous statement during an interview for the Swiss paper *Tages-Anzeiger*, published on February 6, 2005 (qtd. in Kolbert).

8. When we first encounter Briony, she is busy writing a play for her elder brother, which she calls *The Trials of Arabella*—a reference, as many have observed, to Charlotte Lennox's wildly popular novel *The Female Quixote; or, The Adventures of Arabella* (1752). Among other things, Lennox's novel details the romantic adventures of Arabella, a heroine whose reading of Gothic novels leads her not only to adopt the chivalric ideals of such works but also radically to misinterpret the world around her. Eventually learning how to distinguish fact from fiction, she rejects the ridiculous Bellmour and marries the wise and loving Glanville. In addition to providing obvious commentary on the danger fiction poses of distorting reality, the Arabella allusion links McEwan to Jane Austen, whose *Northanger Abbey* was also modeled on the novel.

9. The overarching narrative conceit that governs *Atonement* (that the novel we have just read and assumed to be "true" is, in fact, a fiction) and that is exposed in the final section is quite similar to the device used by Yann Martel in *Life of Pi*, also published in 2001.

5. READING ISLAM

1. All references to UNC materials are to this page unless otherwise noted.

2. For a survey of common reading programs, see Ferguson; for the National Association of Scholars' more critical analysis of such programs, see Thorne.

3. Yacovelli, it seems, sees any reading of the Qur'an as what J. L. Austin would call a performative utterance with conversionary force.

4. For President Bush's most detailed remarks about Islam as a religion of peace, see George Bush, "Islam Is Peace." Despite their significant differences in their pursuit of national security, President Barack Obama consistently echoes this message; see in particular his remarks at Cairo University.

5. UNC's Muslim Students Association claims around a hundred active members according to Matthew Stevens, one of its officers.

6. Statistics on the population of Jewish Americans are equally contested but generally range between approximately seven million who self-identify as Jewish and four million according to the criteria of matrilineal *halakhic* descent.

7. As a positive term, *Judeo-Christian* gained traction only during concerted efforts to combat anti-Semitism in the 1940s; see Silk; Masuzawa (esp. 302–3).

8. Demographic statistics vary from the relatively low figures cited by the 2008 American Religious Identification Survey (just over one million; Kosmin

and Keysar) to high estimates from the Council on American-Islamic Relations (six to seven million).

9. While it should be noted that permanent Muslim communities have lived as minorities, often ruling ones, in India and elsewhere throughout South Asia since Islam's initial globalization, as John Esposito argues, "For the first time in history permanent Muslim communities exist as religious minority communities in nations around the globe" (163).

10. Muslim social integration in European societies has been extremely uneven, though generally more difficult than in the United States. In Britain, according to statistics gathered by the Office for National Statistics and endorsed by the Muslim Council of Britain, the vast majority (around 70 percent) of the nation's approximately two million Muslims (who constitute roughly 4 percent of the national population) originally hail from the Indian subcontinent. See especially UK Office of National Statistics, "Census 2001," and also Muslim Council of Britain. In the broader western European context, migrations from Anatolia and the Arab Middle East constitute the majority of a twenty- to twenty-five-million-person population.

11. The issue of Qur'anic translation has a long and vexed history, and a broad consensus among Muslims scholars—both classical and contemporary—insists that only the Arabic original is adequate for devotional uses, though fewer than 20 percent of Muslims worldwide are native Arabic speakers. For a general account of the debates surrounding Qur'anic translation, see Mohammed; Kidwai; and Sardar, "Eternal Present Tense." For a useful overview that endorses Muhammad A. S. Abdel Haleem's well-annotated Oxford World Classics edition, see Sardar, "Lost in Translation."

12. Along with the general rise in interest with Islam in the Anglophone world, works of fiction and literary memoirs set or produced in Muslim-majority nations have surged in number and popularity, and translations of Arabic novels into English have significantly increased in recent years. For an analysis of the surge in publishing books about Islam, see Blais.

13. As Prince Ghazi bin Muhammad of Jordan emphasizes, even "a cursory review of the world's biggest bookseller, Amazon.com, shows that Americans are buying more books about Islam written by vitriolic former Muslims now touted as experts and sponsored by Christian fundamentalist groups than written by serious Muslim or non-Muslim scholars" (Volf, Bin Muhammad, and Yarrington 5).

14. As I argued in the Introduction, Ka's expectations about Blue in *Snow* emphasize the prevalence of the "bearded fundamentalist" trope.

15. For a compelling account of the "Semitization of Islam," the process whereby "the zealously monotheistic, materially poor, mentally rigid, and socially illiberal desert Arab . . . has come to stand as the quintessential Muslim, thus displacing the earlier image of the 'Mohammedan' as an indolent Turk wallowing in opulent infidelity," see Masuzawa (26 and esp. 179–97). Massad, in his study of sexual desires and representational practices in the Arab world, anchors the trope of the decadent Muslim man to the 1798 French invasion of Egypt (see esp. 3–15).

16. The subgenre of first-person prose, glossed by Dohra Ahmad as "'oppressed Muslim women' narratives," satisfies a range of complex psycho-social desires

among European and American reading publics (105). For example, Azar Nafisi's status as both native informant and celebrant of "Western" modernity—and the circular pleasures of *Reading Lolita in Tehran*, a book about collective reading that is consumed in similar contexts—creates an ideal public face for the neoconservative movement and a case-study in bad ethnographic reading practices, as several critics have compellingly argued. The oppression of women became a central issue in garnering support for and legitimizing the "war on terror," as Laura Bush made plain in a November 17, 2001, radio address: "The fight against terrorism is also a fight for the rights and dignity of women."

17. On balance the novel has become an important site of knowledge production about Afghanistan, and the history of the Afghan people has become far more visible in the Anglophone public sphere because of it. Hosseini himself has become a goodwill envoy to the UN High Commissioner for Refugees, and a wide range of paratextual material has emerged to use the movie and the novel to remedy the widespread ignorance of an English-speaking world that sees Afghanistan as an alien and confusing land.

18. See Roy; Esposito and Tamimi; and Esposito and Mogahed.

19. In "Secularism," Mahmood points out that promoting religious reform within Islam has become a prominent feature of US foreign policy. She cites 9/11 as the proximate trigger for reformist efforts directed at Islam, noting that the United States "has embarked upon an ambitious theological campaign aimed at shaping the sensibilities of ordinary Muslims whom the State Department deems to be too dangerously inclined toward fundamentalist interpretations of Islam" (329). Rushdie offers a literary counterpart to this ethos in his 2002 essay "Step across This Line," delivered in the Tanner Lectures on Human Values at Yale University. Rushdie writes: "If Islam is to be reconciled with modernity, these [critical Muslim] voices must be encouraged until they swell into a roar. Many of them speak of another Islam, their personal, private faith . . . The restoration of religion to the sphere of the personal, its depoliticization, is the nettle that all Muslim societies must grasp in order to become modern . . . If terrorism is to be defeated, the world of Islam must take on board the secularist-humanist principles on which the modern is based and without which Muslim countries' freedom will remain a distant dream."

20. I am drawing on Apter's terms here to stress the vital role of translation both in my project here and in public culture.

21. As an immigrant in the United States, Baba maintains the rugged individualism and neoconservative disdain for the welfare state that were the hallmark of his entrepreneurial ethics in his native Afghanistan. Ironically, however, these values do not translate to success within the system he so thoroughly identifies as his own. In America, Baba finds work only in an Afghani-owned gas station. Nonetheless, on his first day of work he proudly walks into the social services office and returns the stack of food stamps his pride forbids him to use: "Fifteen years I been doin' this job and nobody's ever done this," the social services worker informs him (130–31).

22. As Michael Sells emphasizes, the Qur'an stresses a message of divine mercy and the importance of charity, often singling out the orphan as a

particular example. A prominent forum on IslamOnline ("Charity") addresses the centrality of charity as a Muslim duty.

23. See Sells, especially the section "Muhammad, the Qur'an, and the Poets."

24. Baba's "translation" of Islamic ethical precepts into immanent norms seems to be what Jürgen Habermas had in mind when he recently argued that the values of religious reason might be "translated" into the language of the public sphere; Habermas, "Political."

25. In another scene Baba risks his life to protect a female member of their convoy from rape at the hands of a drunken Soviet soldier and declares, "Tell him I'll take a thousand of his bullets before I let this indecency take place" (116).

26. Amir's ignorance of Islam (in forgetting the words of *salah*, Amir has forgotten a prayer spoken far more frequently by Muslims than Christians utter the Lord's Prayer or Jews the *Shema*) emphasizes his nonreligious upbringing.

27. From the earliest days of the Islamic community, the consensus of the *ulama*, the group of legal scholars and guardians of the sharia, was taken to represent infallibly the consensus of the larger *Ummah,* or global Muslim community.

28. Especially in the Anglophone world, interactive online portals like Hadith Collection (http://hadithcollection.com) have become increasingly important.

29. Soraya later confesses that her father, a former general, took a gun on his trip to bring his daughter home from their disgrace.

30. IslamOnline organizes fatwas on subjects like "Arts & Entertainment" and "Children & Family," while the askamufti.com interface of the Fatwa Center of America aims to provide an "Islamic perspective to queries and specific concerns" by answering "all questions . . . in light of the sacred Shariah of Islam."

31. Catholicism renders the relationship between confession and redemption with greatest clarity, with the sacrament of penance and the act of confessing one's sins to a priest the obligatory path to absolution.

32. In the English tradition, John Wycliffe (1328–84) was an early advocate for biblical translation. The advent of the printing press helped power the later, more successful sixteenth-century Protestant Reformation. See esp. Norton.

33. For an introduction to comparative theological issues in Islamic and Christian perspectives, see Renard. In eloquent defense of text-centric approaches to religion, Harvard professor of comparative theology Francis Clooney advocates the "reading of texts, preferably scriptural and theological texts that have endured over centuries and millennia . . . Reading can be primary even if religion is not lived only or mainly through books, and even if religious learning is not always a matter of book learning . . . The reader is as it were reconstituted in relation to the text . . . [through] prolonged study" (58).

34. Hanif Kureishi's *The Buddha of Suburbia* (1990) offers an interesting counterpoint to the way Martel commercializes exotic forms of religiosity.

Kureishi's eponymous Buddha is a nonpracticing Muslim-Indian immigrant named Haroon who transforms his workaday life as a government bureaucrat by marketing himself to posh London suburbanites as a Buddhist guru. Haroon's effective masquerade trades on the currency of a cultivated exoticism that substitutes the threatening difference of Islam and the Pakistani immigrant community for a thrillingly exotic but anodyne Buddhism. Like Haroon's disciples, Kureishi's novel affirms secularity not by denying religion but by exploring faiths shorn of threatening edges.

35. In this vein, it is easy to recognize in *Life of Pi*—begun by a Canadian writer traveling on the cheap for over a year in postcolonial India—echoes of E. M. Forster's *Passage to India.*

36. The narrator describes Pi's most profound religious experience, which occurs not on the lifeboat but before his departure, on his bike ride home after praying with Kumar, the Sufi Muslim baker: "I felt like the center of a small circle coinciding with the center of a much larger one. Atman met Allah" (62).

37. See, e.g., Boyagoda.

38. The thrust of the novel's allegorical structure appears to be at stake here: *Life of Pi* implies that one might have to believe in religious truth in the way one believes in a story that is, in some sense, derivative. Martel, for his part, did not improve his case when his initial response to the allegations, a formal essay posted by bookseller Powells.com and widely cited on the Internet, proved to contain significant factual errors and was interpreted by some as being openly disrespectful to the author and culture of the source-text. In another interview, however, he proves more eloquent: "No, not really, because my novel is about the line between fiction and fact. It is about how we interpret reality, right? Reality isn't just out there; it's how we interpret it. And to me, that's what religion is about, isn't it? It's an interpretation of reality. And since I want to blur that division, I didn't want to outright say, "By the way, I borrowed this premise from this novel," because that would make it more difficult for me to make the reader suspend his or her disbelief. So that's why I just tipped my hat by saying, "and the spark of life to Mr. Scliar" (Martel, "Conversation").

39. Gordimer began writing love plots across race lines in *Occasion for Loving* (1963).

40. For an analysis of the return to the veil in *The Pickup* and Leila Aboulela's *Minaret*, see Sizemore.

41. Ibrahim, who scorns the utility of Arabic language acquisition with the same fervency with which he derides the country of his birth, refuses to speak to Julie in his native tongue: "We must talk English. I need to speak English . . . only with English," he insists, despite the fact that "he is aware that he is in dialogue with himself in the language she has taken a fancy to learn, no use to her, to them, where they would go. But what use—cruelty—to tell her that in the life she's decided for herself, following him" (151).

42. While the novel is self-aware in its use of images tinged with imperialist desire, Julie—with her spiritualist connection to the desert and her "oriental prince"—is another story. As Kossew observes in a review of the novel, "There is some evidence in the novel of the kind of fetishistic Orientalism that

has Julie see Ibrahim as an 'oriental prince' while her Johannesburg friends describe him, less romantically, as a 'grease monkey.' . . . However, the frequent shifts in perspective . . . anticipate these kinds of criticism."

43. Statistics about book production in Arabic have been a popular source of evidence in arguments about "what went wrong," as Bernard Lewis puts it, with "Muslim civilization." The United Nations *Human Development Report*, based on comparative measure of literacy, offers sobering statistics. The *Arab Human Development Report 2002* put the matter frankly: "Arab countries have undoubtedly seen remarkable economic and social achievements during the past three decades. But with the advent of the twenty-first century, they have started to face deep and complex economic and social problems . . . [including] high illiteracy rates, the deterioration of education, the slow-down of scientific research and technological development . . . rampant poverty and mounting unemployment rates" (v). As Naaman notes in a recent article on the state of Arabic literary studies, when compared to the half-million books published annually in the United States, "not only does Arabic book production constitute as little as a 1.1 percent share of the international market," but the books produced are "limited largely to religious themes," and thus a smaller percentage are literary (447). According to data presented at the Abu Dhabi book fair of 2009, "7,230, 7,080, and 5,910 books [were] written originally in Arabic and published across the Arab world in 2006, 2007, and 2008 respectively. . . . [Additionally] 1,480, 1,880, and 1,650 works translated into Arabic came out over that same time period" (Post).

44. While it is beyond the scope of this chapter, Aswany's novel cites an eclectic range of Islamic revivalists, from Yusuf al-Qaradawi, the founder of IslamOnline and creator of Al Jazeera's popular "Shariah and Life" program, to the inspirational Islamist Sayyid Qutb, as well as classical figures like Abdu Hamid al-Ghazali. Only after this disparate reading is Taha introduced to Sheikh Shakir, whose ministry to the "Muslim youth today" aims to "reclaim the concept of gihad [*sic*] and bring it back to the minds and hearts of the Muslims" (96).

45. The novel describes how, after being arrested in a government crackdown on the Muslim Brotherhood, Taha is tortured by government agents: "They threw him facedown on the ground and several hands started to remove his gallabiya and pull off his underclothes. . . . Two thick hands reached down, grabbed his buttocks, and pulled them apart. He felt a solid object being stuck into his rear and breaking the tendons inside and he started screaming. He screamed at the top of his voice. He screamed until he felt that his larynx was being ripped open" (153). In a novel that addresses homosexuality and gay life in Cairo with care and obvious sensitivity, the violence of Taha's anal rape is particularly striking, and I include the passage here for the resonance it offers to the related scene in *The Kite Runner.* Thoughts of vengeance, directed primarily against the officer who ordered the rape, inspire his final act of suicidal violence.

46. Both sheikhs, the reader knows, are opportunists who use selective readings of the Qur'an and Hadith and the supposed tradition of "authentic legal opinions delivered by the great scholars of religion" to support a particular position (174).

47. It is also important to be attentive to the relativity of our own hermeneutical frames—whatever those may be. We should, in short, learn to read as others read.

48. By this logic, for example, *The Yacoubian Building* is a far better book than John Updike's *The Terrorist* (2006), despite the fact that both plot trajectories of Islamist radicalization.

49. In *Death of a Discipline* and elsewhere, Spivak has sharply criticized scholars who work on and teach texts in translation, for, among other things, evacuating the specificity of local idiom and dense cultural networks in which meaning emerges. In a similar vein, Lanser memorably warns of the resemblance "between tourists and comparatists: both 'cosmopolitans' . . . who dwell mentally in one or two (usually Western) countries, summer metaphorically in a third, and visit other places for brief interludes" (281). While taking such warnings seriously, in this study I have obviously chosen a different approach.

CODA

1. There is something like Matthew Arnold's substitution logic at work in the ethical turn in literary studies. For critics like J. Hillis Miller, Simon Critchley, Gayatri Spivak, and Derek Attridge, the polyvocalism, opacity, and undecidability of fiction, especially fiction of the demanding, experimental kind, can be seen as a supplement to moral philosophy. As Miller argues, "It is not because stories contain the thematic dramatization of ethical situations, choices, and judgments that they are especially appropriate for my topic [the 'ethics of reading'], but for a reverse reason, that is, because ethics itself has a peculiar relation to that form of language we call narrative" (3). Opening oneself to the alterity of the text, by Attridge's estimation, helps us see "the impulses and acts that shape our lives as ethical beings . . . [which] cannot be adequately represented in the discourses of philosophy, politics, or theology . . . because [literature is] capable of taking us through an intense experience" (60).

2. The defining question in postmodern fiction for McHale, "Which world is this?" (1), is essentially atheological, while Hutcheon argues that contemporary metafiction is "fundamentally contradictory, resolutely historical, and inescapably political"—but equally removed from questions of religiosity (4).

3. Extensive scholarship documents the ties between Christianity and European imperialism. Notable works that interrogate the collusion between Western scholars of religion and the colonial project include Lopez; Powers; and King.

4. As it relates to the academy, however, secularization describes the process of disestablishment whereby universities, principally religious in origin and educational mandate, came to conceive religion not as a pillar of academic knowledge but as the shackles from which knowledge must be liberated. Significant scholarship has been devoted to the secularization of the academy; see especially Smith; Marsden and Longfield; and Schmalzbauer and Mahoney.

5. Writing a decade after Said, Aijaz Ahmad shares his sense that academics overlook the need for engaged political criticism, privileging textuality over the material conditions of global society, a view for which he gives his most forceful articulation in *In Theory*.

6. As Anidjar observes, "It is either the case that, when using the word *secular* Edward Said did not mean to take an oppositional stance vis-à-vis religion . . . or, insisting on being an *oppositional* critic, he was in fact, and for a number of elaborate reasons, *against religion*" (39).

7. Indeed, as one postcolonial critic, Neelam Srivastava, puts it, the novel is a "secular genre" that, "because of its dialogic structure, emerges as the most versatile form for staging the conflict between secular and religious identity, because it allows for a heteroglot representation of conflicting worldviews and differing conceptualizations of the 'national' past" (1).

Works Cited

Abel, Marco. "Don DeLillo's 'In the Ruins of the Future': Literature, Images, and the Rhetoric of Seeing 9/11." *PMLA* 118.5 (Oct. 2003): 1236–50.

Abington Township School District v. Schempp. 374 U.S. 203, Abington Township School District v. Schempp, 374 U.S. 203 (1963). http://supreme.justia.com/us/374/203/case.html.

Abraham, Nicholas, and Maria Torok. *The Shell and the Kernel: Renewals of Psychoanalysis*. Trans. Nicholas Rand. Chicago: U of Chicago P, 1994. Act to Authorize Appropriations for Fiscal Year 2003 for Intelligence and Intelligence-Related Activities of the United States Government. Title VI. National Commission on Terrorist Attacks upon the United States. 116 Stat. 2408 (2002). www.archives.gov/research/9-11/public-law-107-306.pdf#page=26.

Adams, Lorraine. "Beyond the Burka." *New York Times* 6 Jan. 2008. www.nytimes.com/2008/01/06/books/review/Adams-t.html.

Adichie, Chimamanda Ngozi. *The Danger of a Single Story*. TED Talk. July 2009. www.ted.com/talks/chimamanda_adichie_the_danger_of_a_single_story.html.

Adorno, Theodor. *Minima Moralia: Reflections from Damaged Life*. London: Verso, 1978.

———. *Negative Dialectics*. Trans. E. B. Ashton. New York: Seabury, 1973.

Agamben, Giorgio. *Homo Sacer: Sovereign Power and Bare Life*. Trans. Daniel Heller-Roazen. Stanford: Stanford UP, 1998.

———. *Remnants of Auschwitz: The Witness and the Archive*. New York: Zone Books, 1999.

———. *State of Exception* [*Stato di eccezione*]. Chicago: U of Chicago P, 2005.

———. *The Time That Remains: A Commentary on the Letter to the Romans* [*Tempo che resta*]. Stanford: Stanford UP, 2005. Meridian: Crossing Aesthetics.

Ahmad, Aijaz. *In Theory: Classes, Nations, Literatures*. London: Verso, 1992.

Ahmad, Dohra. "Not Yet beyond the Veil: Muslim Women in American Popular Literature." *Social Text* 27.2 (2009): 105.

Ahsan, M. M., and Abdur Raheem Kidwai. *Sacrilege versus Civility: Muslim Perspectives on the "Satanic Verses" Affair*. Markfield: Islamic Foundation, 1991.

Ajami, Fouad. *The Dream Palace of the Arabs: A Generation's Odyssey*. New York: Pantheon, 1998.

Albright, Madeleine, et al. *Views of a Changing World: June 2003*. Washington, DC: Pew Research Center for the People and the Press, 2003. http://people-press.org/files/legacy-pdf/185.pdf.

———. *What the World Thinks in 2002*. Washington, DC: Pew Research Center for the People and the Press, 2002.

Almond, Gabriel Abraham, R. Scott Appleby, and Emmanuel Sivan. *Strong Religion: The Rise of Fundamentalisms around the World*. Chicago: U of Chicago P, 2003.

Almond, Ian. *The New Orientalists: Postmodern Representations of Islam from Foucault to Baudrillard*. London : I. B. Tauris, 2007.

Anderson, Benedict. *Imagined Communities*. 1983. Rev. ed. New York: Verso, 1991.

Anidjar, Gil. *Semites: Race, Religion, Literature*. Stanford: Stanford UP, 2007.

Appiah, Anthony. "The Case for Contamination." *New York Times* 1 Jan. 2006. www.nytimes.com/2006/01/01/magazine/01cosmopolitan.html?pagewanted=all&_r=0.

———. *Cosmopolitanism: Ethics in a World of Strangers*. New York: Norton, 2006. Issues of Our Time.

Apter, Emily. *The Translation Zone: A New Comparative Literature*. New Jersey: Princeton UP, 2005.

Arendt, Hannah. *The Human Condition*. Chicago: U of Chicago P, 1969.

———. "Total Domination." *The Portable Hannah Arendt*. Ed. Peter Baehr. New York: Penguin, 2000. 119–45.

Arnold, Matthew. *Selected Essays*. Oxford: Oxford UP, 1964.

Asad, Talal. *Formations of the Secular: Christianity, Islam, Modernity*. Stanford: Stanford UP, 2003.

———. *Genealogies of Religion: Discipline and Reasons of Power in Christianity and Islam*. Baltimore: Johns Hopkins UP, 1993.

Aswany, Alaa al. *The Yacoubian Building*. 2002. Trans. Humphrey Davies. New York: Harper Collins, 2004.

Attridge, Derek. *J. M. Coetzee and the Ethics of Reading*. Chicago: U of Chicago P, 2004.

Bakhtin, Mikhail. *The Dialogic Imagination: Four Essays*. Ed. Michael Holquist. Trans. Vadim Liapunov. Austin: U of Texas P, 1982.

Balibar, Etienne. "Dissonances within *Laïcité*." *Constellations* 11.3 (2004): 353–67.

Barnard, Rita. "J. M. Coetzee's *Disgrace* and the South African Pastoral." *Contemporary Literature* 44.2 (2003): 199–224.

Bataille, Georges. *Consumption*. Trans. Robert Hurley. New York: Zone Books, 1991. Vol. 1 of *The Accursed Share: An Essay on General Economy*.

Beigbeder, Frédéric. *Windows on the World: A Novel*. Trans. Frank Wynne. New York: Hyperion, 2004.

Benhabib, Seyla, with Jeremy Waldron, Bonnie Honig, and Will Kymlicka. *Another Cosmopolitanism*. Ed. Robert Post. Oxford: Oxford UP, 2006. Berkeley Tanner Lectures.

Benjamin, Walter. *The Arcades Project*. Ed. Rolf Tiedemann. Trans. Howard Eiland and Kevin McLaughlin. New York: Belknap Press, 2002.

———. "Theses on the Philosophy of History." *Illuminations: Essays and Reflections*. Ed. Hannah Arendt. New York: Schocken Books, 1969. 253–64.

Bennett, Jane. *The Enchantment of Modern Life: Attachments, Crossings and Ethics*. Princeton: Princeton UP, 2001.

Berger, Peter. *The Sacred Canopy*. 1967. New York: Anchor Books, 1990.

Bergson, Henri. *Time and Free Will* [*Essai sur les données immédiates de la conscience*]. Trans. F. L. Pogson. 1910. London: Swan Sonnenschein; New York: Macmillan, 1950.

Berlant, Lauren. *Cruel Optimism*. Durham: Duke UP, 2011.

Bhadrakumar, M. K. "Turkish Snub Changes Middle East Game." *Asian Times* 4 Feb. 2009. www.atimes.com/atimes/Middle_East/KB04Ak01.html.

Bhargava, Rajeev. *The Promise of India's Secular Democracy*. Oxford: Oxford UP, 2010.

Bilgrami, Akeel. "What Is Enchantment?" Warner, VanAntwerpen, and Calhoun, *Varieties* 145–65.

"The Billionaires." *CNNMoney*. 7 Sept. 1992. http://money.cnn.com/magazines/fortune/fortune_archive/1992/09/07/76826/.

Bin Laden, Osama, et al. "Al Qaeda's Second Fatwa." *PBS Newshour* 23 Feb. 1998. www.pbs.org/newshour/terrorism/international/fatwa_1998.html#.

Blais, Jacqueline. "People Want to Know, so Koran Is Best Seller." *USA Today* 18 Oct. 2001. www.usatoday.com/life/books/2001-10-18-koran.htm.

Bloch, Ernst. *The Spirit of Utopia*. Trans. Anthony Nassar. Stanford: Stanford UP, 2000.

Boumediene v. Bush. 553 U.S. 723 (2008).

Boyagoda, Randy. "The Life of Pi." *First Things* May 2003. www.firstthings.com/article/2007/01/the-life-of-pi-42.

Bradley, Arthur, and Andrew Tate. *The New Atheist Novel: Fiction, Philosophy and Polemic after 9/11*. London: Continuum, 2010. New Directions in Religion and Literature.

Breckenridge, Carol, Sheldon Pollock, and Homi Bhabha, eds. *Cosmopolitanism*. Durham: Duke UP, 2002.

Brennan, Timothy. *At Home in the World: Cosmopolitanism Now*. Cambridge, MA: Harvard UP, 1997. Convergences.

———. *Salman Rushdie and the Third World: Myths of the Nation*. Houndmills, UK: Macmillan, 1989.

Bromberger, Jacqueline. "University Resistance: File Testimony." 1993. Ch. 2. "Actions of Gestapo against the University. December 1942. Talks between Reichfuhrer Himmler and Minister for Foreign Affairs Von Ribbentrop." http://mapage.noos.fr/jibro/resistance-universitaire/en/Chapitre_Deux_partie1.html.

Brown, Wendy. *Edgework: Critical Essays on Knowledge and Politics*. Princeton: Princeton UP, 2005.

Browne, Malcolm. *Muddy Boots and Red Socks: A Reporter's Life*. New York: Crown, 1993.

Bush, George W. "Address to a Joint Session of Congress and the American People, Washington, DC." *White House Archives*. 20 Sept. 2001. http://georgewbush-whitehouse.archives.gov/news/releases/2001/09/20010920-8.html.

———. "Iran and the War on Terror: Address to the Military Officers Association of America, Washington, DC." 5 Sept. 2006. www.presidentialrhetoric.com/speeches/09.05.06.html.

———. "Islam Is Peace Says President: Remarks by the President at Islamic Center of Washington, DC." *White House Archives*. 17 Sept. 2001. http://georgewbush-whitehouse.archives.gov/news/releases/2001/09/20010917-11.html.

———. "National Day of Prayer and Remembrance for the Victims of the Terrorist Attacks on September 11, 2001." *White House Archives*. 14 Sept. 2001. http://georgewbush-whitehouse.archives.gov/news/releases/2001/09/20010913-7.html.

———. "National Security Strategy of the United States of America." *White House Archives*. Sept. 2002. http://georgewbush-whitehouse.archives.gov/nsc/nss/2002/.

———. "President Bush Delivers Graduation Speech at West Point." *White House Archives*. 1 June 2002. http://georgewbush-whitehouse.archives.gov/news/releases/2002/06/20020601-3.html.

———. "Statement by the President in His Address to the Nation." *White House Archives*. 11 Sept. 2001. http://georgewbush-whitehouse.archives.gov/news/releases/2001/09/print/20010911-16.html.

Bush, Laura. "Radio Address by Mrs. Bush, Crawford, Texas." *White House Archives*. 17 Nov. 2001. http://georgewbush-whitehouse.archives.gov/news/releases/2001/11/20011117.html.

Butler, Judith. *Frames of War*. London: Verso, 2009.

———. "Sexual Politics, Torture, and Secular Time." *British Journal of Sociology* 59.1 (2008): 1–23.

Bzostek, Rachel. *Why Not Preempt? Security, Law, Norms, and Anticipatory Military Activities*. Burlington, VT: Ashgate, 2008.

Calhoun, Craig. "The Class Consciousness of Frequent Travelers: Toward a Critique of Actually Existing Cosmopolitanism." *South Atlantic Quarterly* 101.4 (2002): 869–97.

———. "Secularism, Citizenship, and the Public Sphere." Calhoun, Juergensmeyer, and VanAntwerpen 75–91.

Calhoun, Craig, Mark Juergensmeyer, and Jonathan VanAntwerpen, eds. *Rethinking Secularism*. New York: Oxford UP, 2011.

Calinescu, Matei. *Five Faces of Modernity: Modernism, Avant-Garde, Decadence, Kitsch, Postmodernism*. 2nd ed. Durham: Duke UP, 1987.

Camus, Albert. *The Plague*. 1947. Trans. Stuart Gilbert. New York: Vintage, 1991.

Caruth, Cathy. Introduction. *Trauma: Explorations in Memory*. Ed. Cathy Caruth. Baltimore: Johns Hopkins UP, 1995. 3–12.

Casanova, José. "The Secular, Secularization, Secularisms." *Rethinking Secularism*. Calhoun, Juergensmeyer, and VanAntwerpen 54–74.

Center for Constitutional Rights. "The Guantanamo Prisoner Hunger Strikes and Protests: February 2002–August 2005." New York: Center for Constitutional Rights, 2005. http://ccrjustice.org/files/Final%20Hunger%20Strike%20Report%20Sept%202005.pdf.

"Charity (Sadaqah & Zakaah)." Forum. *IslamOnline*. www.islamonline.com/index.php?sub-section=119.

Chatterjee, Nandini. *The Making of Indian Secularism: Empire, Law and Christianity, 1830–1960*. New York: Palgrave Macmillan, 2011.

Chatterjee, Partha. "Fasting for Bin Laden: The Politics of Secularization in Contemporary India." Scott and Hirschkind 57–74.

Cheah, Pheng, and Bruce Robbins, eds. *Cosmopolitics: Thinking and Feeling beyond the Nation*. Minneapolis: U of Minnesota P, 1998. Cultural Politics 14.

Chow, Rey. "The Old/New Question of Comparison in Literary Studies: A Post-European Perspective." *ELH* 71 (2004): 289–311.

Ciorap v. Moldova. ECHR 2007/11. No. 12066/02. 19 June 2007.

Cixous, Helene. "The Laugh of the Medusa." *Signs* 1.4 (1976): 875–93.

Clark, Roger. *Stranger Gods: Salman Rushdie's Other Worlds*. Montreal: McGill-Queen's UP, 2001.

Clifford, James. "Mixed Feelings." *Cosmopolitics: Thinking and Feeling beyond the Nation*. Ed. Pheng Cheah, Bruce Robbins, and Social Text Collective. Minneapolis: U of Minnesota P, 1998. 362–70.

———. *Routes: Travel and Translation in the Late Twentieth Century*. Cambridge, MA: Harvard UP, 1997.

Clooney, Francis X. *Comparative Theology: Deep Learning across Religious Borders*. Chichester: John Wiley, 2010.

Coetzee, J. M. *Age of Iron*. New York: Penguin, 1990.

———. *The Childhood of Jesus*. London: Havrill Secker, 2013.

———. *Diary of a Bad Year*. New York: Penguin, 2007.

———. *Disgrace*. New York: Penguin, 1999.

———. *Elizabeth Costello*. New York: Penguin, 2003.

———. *Foe*. New York: Penguin, 1986.

———. "Interview" [on Kafka]. By David Atwell. *Doubling the Point: Essays and Interviews*. Ed. David Atwell. Cambridge, MA: Harvard UP, 1992.

———. *Life and Times of Michael K*. New York: Penguin, 1983.

———. *Slow Man*. New York: Viking, 2005.

———. "Time, Tense, and Aspect in Kafka's 'The Burrow.'" [1981]. *Doubling the Point: Essays and Interviews*. Ed. David Atwell. Cambridge, MA: Harvard UP, 1992. 210–32.

———. *Waiting for the Barbarians*. New York: Penguin, 1980.

———. *White Writing: On the Culture of Letters in South Africa*. New Haven: Yale UP, 1988.

Coles, Romand. *Rethinking Generosity: Critical Theory and the Politics of Caritas*. Ithaca: Cornell UP, 1997.

Collins, John. *The Scepter and the Star: The Messiahs of the Dead Sea Scrolls and Other Ancient Literature*. New York: Doubleday, 1995.

Commissioner of Correction v. William Coleman. 303 Conn. 800; 38 A.3d 84; 2012 (2012).

Connolly, William. *Why I Am Not a Secularist*. St. Paul: U of Minnesota P, 2000.

Conseil Constitutionnel. "La Constitution du 4 octobre 1958." www.conseil-constitutionnel.fr/conseil-constitutionnel/francais/la-constitution/la-constitution-du-4–octobre-1958/texte-integral-de-la-constitution-de-1958.5074.html.

Corbin, Henry. *History of Islamic Philosophy*. Trans. Liadain Sherrad. London: Kegan Paul International, 1993.

Council on American-Islamic Relations. "About Islam." 2013. www.cair.com/american-muslims/about-islam.html.

Craig, William L. *The Tensed Theory of Time: A Critical Examination*. Boston: Kluwer Academic Publishers, 2000.

Cronin, Audrey. "Behind the Curve: Globalization and International Terrorism." *International Security* 27.3 (2003): 30–58.

Dabashi, Hamid. "Native Informers and the Making of American Empire." *Al-Ahram Weekly On-Line* 1–7 June 2006: 1.

Damrosch, David. *What Is World Literature?* Princeton: Princeton UP, 2003.

Dawkins, Richard. *The Greatest Show on Earth: The Evidence for Evolution*. New York: Free Press, 2009.

DeLillo, Don. *Falling Man*. New York: Scribner, 2007.

———. "In the Ruins of the Future: Reflections on Terror and Loss in the Shadow of September." *Harper's* Dec. 2001: 33–40.

———. *Point Omega: A Novel*. New York: Scribner, 2010.

Derrida, Jacques. *Specters of Marx: The State of the Debt, the Work of Mourning, and the New International*. Trans. Peggy Kamuf. New York: Routledge, 1994.

Diogenes Laertius. *Lives of Eminent Philosophers*. Ed. R. D. Hicks. Perseus Project online ed. www.perseus.tufts.edu/hopper/text?doc=Perseus%3Atext%3A1999.01.0258.

Dunlap, David. "Extracting 'Survivors' Stairway' for a Home at the 9/11 Museum." *New York Times* 17 Jan. 2008. www.nytimes.com/2008/01/17/nyregion/17stairway.html?pagewanted=print&_r=0.

During, Simon. *Modern Enchantments*. Cambridge, MA: Harvard UP, 2004.

———. "Toward the Postsecular." *PMLA* 120.3 (2005): 876–77.

Elphick, Richard, and T. R. H. Davenport. *Christianity in South Africa: A Political, Social, and Cultural History.* Berkeley: U of California P, 1997.

Esposito, John L. *What Everyone Needs to Know about Islam.* 2nd ed. New York: Oxford UP, 2011.

Esposito, John L., and Dalia Mogahed. *Who Speaks for Islam? What a Billion Muslims Really Think.* New York: Gallup, 2007.

Esposito, John, and Azzam Tamimi, eds. *Islam and Secularism in the Middle East.* London: Hurst, 2000.

Evans, Leslie. "RAND Tries to Model Risks of Terrorist Attacks." UCLA International Institute. 25 Apr. 2003. www.international.ucla.edu/article.asp?parentid=3713.

Fabian, Johannes. "The Other Revisited." *Anthropological Theory* 6 (2006): 139–52.

———. *Time and the Other: How Anthropology Makes Its Object.* 1983. New York: Columbia UP, 2002.

Fearon, James D. "Ethnic Structure and Cultural Diversity around the World: A Cross-National Data Set on Ethnic Groups." Working paper. 3 Jan. 2003. www.stanford.edu/group/ethnic/workingpapers/egroups.pdf.

Felman, Shoshana. *Literature and Psychoanalysis: The Question of Reading: Otherwise.* Baltimore: Johns Hopkins UP, 1982.

Felman, Shoshana, and Dori Laub. *Testimony: Crises of Witnessing in Literature, Psychoanalysis, and History.* New York: Routledge, 1992.

Ferguson, Michael. "Creating Common Ground: Common Reading and the First Year of College." *Peer Review* Summer 2006. www.aacu.org/peerreview/pr-su06/documents/PRSU06_analysis2.pdf.

Fitzmyer, Joseph. *The One Who Is to Come.* Grand Rapids: William B. Eerdmans, 2007.

Foa, Edna, and Barbara Rothbaum. *Treating the Trauma of Rape: Cognitive-Behavioral Therapy for PTSD.* New York: Guilford, 1998.

Foer, Jonathan Safran. *Extremely Loud and Incredibly Close.* Boston: Houghton Mifflin, 2005.

Foucault, Michel. *The Care of the Self.* Vol. 3 of *The History of Sexuality.* Trans. Robert Hurley. New York: Vintage, 1988.

———. *An Introduction.* Vol. 1 of *The History of Sexuality.* Trans. Robert Hurley. New York: Vintage, 1990.

———. *The Use of Pleasure.* Vol. 2 of *The History of Sexuality.* Trans. Robert Hurley. New York: Vintage, 1990.

French National Assembly. "Constitution of October 4, 1958." www.assemblee-nationale.fr/english/8ab.asp.

Frost, Laura. "Still Life: 9/11's Falling Bodies." *Literature after 9/11.* Ed. Ann Keniston and Jeanne Follansbee Quinn. New York: Routledge, 2008. 180–206.

Fukuyama, Francis. *The End of History and the Last Man.* New York: Avon, 1993.

Galanter, Marc. *Law and Society in Modern India.* New York: Oxford UP, 1993.

Gallup Inc. *Muslim Americans: A National Portrait*. 2009. www.gallup.com/strategicconsulting/153572/report-muslim-americans-national-portrait.aspx.

Gass, William H. *Tests of Time*. New York: Knopf, 2002.

Gauchet, Marcel. *The Disenchantment of the World: A Political History of Religion*. Trans. Oscar Burge. Princeton: Princeton UP, 1997.

Genette, Gérard. *Narrative Discourse: An Essay on Method*. Trans. Jane Lewin. Ithaca: Cornell UP, 1980.

Geneva Convention Relative to the Treatment of Prisoners of War. 12 Aug. 1949. 6 U.S.T. 3316, 75 U.N.T.S. 135 (1949). www.icrc.org/ihl/WebART/365-570006.

Gikandi, Simon. Contribution to "Editor's Column: The End of Postcolonial Theory? A Roundtable with Sunil Agnani, Fernando Coronil, Gaurav Desai, Mamadou Diouf, Simon Gikandi, Susie Tharu, and Jennifer Wenzel." Ed. Patricia Yaeger. *PMLA* 122 (2007): 633–51.

Gilligan, Carol. *In a Different Voice: Psychological Theory and Women's Development*. Cambridge, MA: Harvard UP, 1993.

Goldziher, Ignác. *Introduction to Islamic Theology and Law*. Ed. Bernard Lewis. Trans. Andreas and Ruth Hamori. Princeton: Princeton UP, 1981.

Göle, Nilüfer. "The Civilizational, Spatial, and Sexual Powers of the Secular." Warner, VanAntwerpen, and Calhoun, *Varieties* 243–64.

———. *The Forbidden Modern: Civilization and Veiling*. Ann Arbor: U of Michigan P, 1996. Critical Perspectives on Women and Gender.

———. "A Headscarf Affair, a Women's Affair?" *The Immanent Frame*. 21 Feb. 2008. http://blogs.ssrc.org/tif/2008/02/21/a-headscarf-affair-a-womens-affair/.

Gordimer, Nadine. *The Pickup*. New York: Penguin, 2001.

Habermas, Jürgen. "Notes on a Post-secular Society." Signandsight.com. 18 June 2008. www.signandsight.com/features/1714.html.

———. "'The Political': The Rational Meaning of a Questionable Inheritance of Political Theology." *The Power of Religion in the Public Sphere*. Ed. Eduardo Mendieta and Jonathan VanAntwerpen. New York: Columbia UP, 2011. 15–33.

Habermas, Jürgen, Jacques Derrida, and Giovanna Borradori. *Philosophy in a Time of Terror: Dialogues with Jürgen Habermas and Jacques Derrida*. Chicago: U of Chicago P, 2003.

Hadley, Elaine. "On a Darkling Plain: Victorian Liberalism and the Fantasy of Agency." *Victorian Studies* 48.1 (2005): 92–102.

Hamid, Mohsin. *The Reluctant Fundamentalist*. Orlando: Harcourt, 2007.

Hartman, Geoffrey. *The Longest Shadow: In the Aftermath of the Holocaust*. New York: Palgrave Macmillan, 2002.

Hasan, Mohibbul. *Kashmir under the Sultans*. Calcutta: Iran Society, 1959.

"The Headscarf Controversy." Collection of posts by various authors. *The Immanent Frame*. 10 Feb.–23 Oct. 2008. http://blogs.ssrc.org/tif/category/exchanges/world-affairs/the-headscarf-controversy.

Henke, Suzette. *Shattered Subjects: Trauma and Testimony in Women's Life-Writing*. New York: St. Martin's Press, 1999.

Hirsch, Marianne. *The Generation of Postmemory: Writing and Visual Culture after the Holocaust.* New York: Columbia UP, 2012.

Hitchens, Christopher. "Civilization and Its Malcontents." *Atlantic* 1 Apr. 2005. www.theatlantic.com/magazine/archive/2005/04/civilization-and-its-malcontents/303841/.

Holsinger, Bruce W. *Neomedievalism, Neoconservatism, and the War on Terror.* Chicago: Prickly Paradigm, 2007. Paradigm 29.

Horbury, William. *Messianism among Jews and Christians: Biblical and Historical Studies.* New York: T&T Clark, 2003.

Hosseini, Khaled. *The Kite Runner.* Riverhead ed. New York: Penguin, 2003.

Hungerford, Amy. *Postmodern Belief: American Literature and Religion since 1960.* Princeton: Princeton UP, 2010. 20/21.

Husserl, Edmund. *On the Phenomenology of the Consciousness of Internal Time.* Trans. John Brough. Dordrecht: Springer, 1991.

Hutcheon, Linda. *A Poetics of Postmodernism: History, Theory, Fiction.* New York: Routledge, 1988.

Impastato, David. "Secular Sabbath: Unbelief in Ian McEwan's Fiction." *Commonweal* 23 Oct. 2009.

Improv Everywhere. *Frozen Grand Central. YouTube.* 31 Jan. 2008. www.youtube.com/watch?v=jwMj3PJDxuo. 15 Nov. 2010.

India. Ministry of Law and Justice. The Constitution of India. 1 Dec. 2007. http://lawmin.nic.in/coi/coiason29july08.pdf.

In re Joel Caulk. 480 A.2d 93 (NH 1984).

"Islam and Secularism in Middle East Governments." *IslamOnline* 22 Aug. 2011. www.islamonline.com/news/articles/103/Islam-and-Secularism-in-Middle-East-Government-s.html.

IslamToday. "Fatwa Archive." 2011. http://en.islamtoday.net/Fatwa-Archive.

Israel, Nico. *Outlandish: Writing between Exile and Diaspora.* Stanford: Stanford UP, 2000.

Jackson, Timothy. *Love Disconsoled: Meditations on Christian Charity.* New York: Cambridge UP, 1999.

Jacobsohn, Gary. *The Wheel of Law: India's Secularism in Comparative Constitutional Context.* Princeton: Princeton UP, 2005.

Jacoby, Susan. *Freethinkers: A History of American Secularism.* New York: Metropolitan Books, 2004.

James, Jamie. "East Meets West." *New York Times* 2 Nov. 1997.

James, William. *The Principles of Psychology.* 1890. New York: Cosimo, 2007.

Jameson, Fredric. *Postmodernism, or, The Cultural Logic of Late Capitalism.* Durham: Duke UP, 1991.

———. *Signatures of the Visible.* New York: Routledge, 1990.

Junod, Tom. "The Falling Man." *Esquire* Sept. 2003.

Kafka, Franz. *The Complete Stories.* Ed. Nahum Glatzer. New York: Schocken Books, 1971.

Kant, Immanuel. *Perpetual Peace* [*Zum ewigen Frieden*]. Trans. Lewis White Beck. New York: Liberal Arts Press, 1957. Library of Liberal Arts 54.

Kaplan, E. Ann. *Trauma Culture: The Politics of Terror and Loss in Media and Literature*. New Brunswick: Rutgers UP, 2005.

Katz, David, and Richard Popkin. *Messianic Revolution: Radical Religious Politics to the End of the Second Millennium*. New York: Hill and Wang, 2000.

Kauffman, Linda S. "The Wake of Terror: Don DeLillo's 'In the Ruins of the Future,' 'Baader-Meinhof,' and *Falling Man*." *Modern Fiction Studies* 54.2 (2008): 353–77.

———. "World Trauma Center." *American Literary History* 21.3 (2009): 647–59.

Kean, Thomas H., Lee Hamilton, and Benjamin Rhodes. *Without Precedent: The Inside Story of the 911 Commission*. New York: Knopf, 2006.

Kidwai, A. R. "Translating the Untranslatable: A Survey of English Translations of the Quran." *Muslim World Book Review* 7.4 (1987): 66–71.

King, Richard. *Orientalism and Religion: Postcolonial Theory, India and the "Mythic East."* London: Routledge, 1999.

Klein, Naomi. *The Shock Doctrine: The Rise of Disaster Capitalism*. New York: Picador, 2008.

Kolbert, Elizabeth. "Dead Reckoning: The Armenian Genocide and the Politics of Silence." *New Yorker* 6 Nov. 2006.

Kosmin, Barry, and Ariela Keysar. *American Religious Identification Survey (ARIS 2008)*. Hartford, CT: Institute for the Study of Secularism in Society and Culture, 2009.

Kossew, Sue. *Pen and Power: A Post-colonial Reading of J. M. Coetzee and Ándre Brink*. Atlanta: Rodopi, 1996.

———. Rev. of *The Pickup*, by Nadine Gordimer. *Quodlibet* Feb. 2005. http://fhrc.flinders.edu.au/ejournals/quodlibet/vol1/qv1_sk_gordimer.html.

Krog, Antjie. *Country of My Skull*. London: Jonathan Cape, 1998.

Kureishi, Hanif. *The Buddha of Suburbia*. New York: Viking, 1990.

Kuru, Ahmet. *Secularism and State Policies toward Religion: The United States, France, and Turkey*. New York: Cambridge UP, 2009.

LaCapra, Dominick. 1996. *Representing the Holocaust: History, Theory, Trauma*. Ithaca: Cornell UP.

Langbein, Hermann. *People in Auschwitz*. Chapel Hill: U of North Carolina P, 2004.

Lanser, Susan Sniader. "Compared to What? Global Feminism, Comparatism, and the Master's Tools." *Borderwork: Feminist Engagements with Comparative Literature*. Ed. Margaret R. Higonnet. Ithaca: Cornell UP, 1994. 280–300.

Lantz v. William Coleman. 978 A. 2d 164 (Conn. Super. Ct. 2009).

Le Poidevin, Robin. "The Experience and Perception of Time." *Stanford Encyclopedia of Philosophy*. 17 Nov. 2009. http://plato.stanford.edu/entries/time-experience/.

Levinas, Emmanuel. *Alterity and Transcendence*. Trans. Michael Smith. New York: Columbia UP, 2000.

———. "Secularization and Hunger." *Graduate Faculty Philosophy Journal* 20.2 (1998): 3–12.

Lewis, Bernard. *What Went Wrong? The Clash between Islam and Modernity in the Middle East.* New York: Harper, 2003.

Lewis, Neil A. "Guantánamo Prisoners Go on Hunger Strike." *New York Times* 18 Sept. 2005. www.nytimes.com/2005/09/18/politics/18gitmo.html?pagewanted=print.

Lewis, Pericles. *Religious Experience and the Modernist Novel.* Cambridge: Cambridge UP, 2010.

Lilla, Mark. *The Stillborn God: Religion, Politics, and the Modern West.* New York: Vintage, 2007.

Lopez, Donald S. *Curators of the Buddha: The Study of Buddhism under Colonialism.* Chicago: U of Chicago P, 1995.

Lott, Eric. "The New Cosmopolitanism: Whose America?" *Transition* 72 (1996): 108–35.

Lukács, Georg. *History and Class Consciousness: Studies in Marxist Dialectics.* Trans. Rodney Livingstone. Cambridge, MA: MIT Press, 1971.

———. *The Theory of the Novel: A Historico-Philosophical Essay on the Forms of Great Epic Literature.* Trans. Anna Bostock. Cambridge, MA: MIT Press, 1971.

Mahmood, Saba. "Can Secularism Be Other-Wise? (A Critique of Charles Taylor's *A Secular Age*)." Warner, VanAntwerpen, and Calhoun, *Varieties* 282–99.

———. *Politics of Piety: The Islamic Revival and the Feminist Subject.* Princeton: Princeton UP, 2005.

———. "Secularism, Hermeneutics, and Empire: The Politics of Islamic Reformation." *Public Culture* 18.2 (2006): 323–47.

Mangan, Katherine. "Secular Studies Gains Disciples." *Chronicle of Higher Education* 20 Nov. 2011.

Marais, Michael. "'Little Enough, Less Than Little: Nothing': Ethics, Engagement, and Change in the Fiction of J. M. Coetzee." *Modern Fiction Studies* 46.1 (2000): 159–82.

Marsden, George M., and Bradley J. Longfield, eds. *The Secularization of the Academy.* New York: Oxford UP, 1992.

Martel, Yann. "Conversation: Life of Pi." *PBS Newshour* 11 Nov. 2002. www.pbs.org/newshour/bb/entertainment/july-dec02/martel_11-11.html.

———. *Life of Pi.* New York: Harcourt, 2001.

Massad, Joseph Andoni. *Desiring Arabs.* Chicago: U of Chicago P, 2007.

Masuzawa, Tomoko. *The Invention of World Religions: Or, How European Universalism Was Preserved in the Language of Pluralism.* Chicago: U of Chicago P, 2005.

Mathewes, Charles, and Christopher McKnight Nichols, eds. *Prophecies of Godlessness: Predictions of America's Imminent Secularization from the Puritans to the Present Day.* New York: Oxford UP, 2008.

Mauss, Marcel. *The Gift: Forms and Functions of Exchange in Archaic Societies.* Trans. W. D. Halls. New York: Routledge, 2011.

Maxwell, Bryan. "*The Satanic Verses.* Assignment 2: Publication History." Assignment for University of Illinois–Champaign/Urbana course in library science and English, "20th-Century American Bestsellers," taught by John Unsworth. http://people.lis.illinois.edu/~unsworth/courses/entc312/s05/search.cgi?title=The+Satanic+Verses.

McClanahan, Annie. "Future's Shock: Plausibility, Preemption, and the Fiction of 9/11." *symploke* 17.1–2 (2009): 41–62.

McClure, John. *Partial Faiths: Postsecular Fiction in the Age of Pynchon and Morrison*. Athens: U of Georgia P, 2007.

McEwan, Ian. *Atonement*. London: Jonathan Cape, 2001.

———. "Beyond Belief." *Guardian* 12 Sept. 2001. www.ianmcewan.com/bib/articles/9-11-02.html.

———. *Black Dogs*. New York: Anchor, 1998.

———. "Henry Perowne's Fish Stew" [from *Saturday*]. n.d. www.ianmcewan.com/bib/articles/fishstew.html. 1 Nov. 2010.

———. Interview by Richard Dawkins. *Intelligent Life*. 15 Feb. 2012. http://myintelligentlife.wordpress.com/2012/02/15/ian-mcewan-interviewed-by-richard-dawkins/. Excerpt from *The Root of All Evil*, video, Channel 4 TV (UK), 2006 .

———. Interview by Helen Whitney. "Faith and Doubt at Ground Zero: Interviews." *Frontline*. Apr. 2002. www.pbs.org/wgbh/pages/frontline/shows/faith/interviews/mcewan.html. 1 Nov. 2010.

———. *Saturday*. New York: Random House, 2005.

———. "The TNR Q&A: 'Atonement' Author Ian McEwan on Bellow, the Internet, Atheism, and Why His Books Are Still Scary." Interview by Isaac Chotiner. *New Republic* 11 Jan. 2008. www.newrepublic.com/article/books-and-arts/the-tnr-qa.

McHale, Brian. *Postmodernist Fiction*. New York: Methuen, 1987.

McKeon, Michael. 1987. *The Origins of the English Novel, 1600–1740*. 15th Anniversary ed. Baltimore: Johns Hopkins UP.

McNabb v. Department of Corrections. 180 P.3d 1257 (Wash. 2008).

McNeill, Jena, James Carafano, and Jessica Zuckerman. "39 Terror Plots Foiled since 9/11: Examining Counterterrorism's Success Stories." Heritage Foundation. 20 May 2011. www.heritage.org/research/reports/2011/05/39-terror-plots-foiled-since-911-examining-counterterrorisms-success-stories. 30 June 2013.

Merivale, Patricia. "Audible Palimpsests: Coetzee's Kafka." *Critical Perspectives on J. M. Coetzee*. Ed. Graham Huggan and Stephen Watson. Basingstoke: Macmillan, 1996. 52–67.

Michael, Magali Cornier. "Writing Fiction in the Post-9/11 World: McEwan's *Saturday*." *From Solidarity to Schisms: 9/11 and After in Fiction and Film from Outside the U.S.* Ed. Cara Cilano. New York: Rodopi, 2009. 25–51.

Michaels, Anne. *Fugitive Pieces*. New York: Vintage, 1998.

Milbank, John. *Theology and Social Theory: Beyond Secular Reason*. 2nd ed. Malden, MA: Wiley-Blackwell, 2006.

Military Commissions Act of 2006. Pub. L. 109-366. 120 Stat. 2600. 17 Oct. 2006.

Miller, J. Hillis. *The Ethics of Reading: Kant, De Man, Eliot, Trollope, James, and Benjamin*. New York: Columbia UP, 1989.

Mohammed, Khaleel. "Assessing English Translations of the Qur'an." *Middle East Quarterly* 12.2 (Spring 2005): 58–71.

Moretti, Franco. "Conjectures on World Literature." *New Left Review* 1 (2000): 54–68.

———. *Graphs, Maps, Trees: Abstract Models for Literary History.* New York: Verso, 2007.

Muhammad, Ghazi bin. *A Common Word between Us and You.* Jordan: Royal Aal Al-Bayt Institute for Islamic Thought, 2009.

Murakami, Haruki. *The Wind-Up Bird Chronicle.* Trans. Jay Rubin. New York: Vintage, 1998.

Muslim Council of Britain. "How Many British Muslims?" 2003. www.mcb.org.uk/library/statistics.php.

Naaman, Mara. "Disciplinary Divergences: Problematizing the Field of Arabic Literature." *Comparative Literature Studies* 47.4 (2010): 446–71.

Nandy, Ashis. "An Anti-secularist Manifesto." *Secularism in Crisis* 22.1 (1995): 35–64.

———. "The Politics of Secularism and The Recovery of Religious Tolerance." *Secularism and Its Critics.* Ed. Rajeev Bhargava. Delhi: Oxford UP, 1998. 321–44.

———. "The Twilight of Certitudes: Secularism, Hindu Nationalism and Other Masks of Deculturation." *Postcolonial Studies* 1.3 (1998): 283–94.

Nasr, Seyyed Hossein, Hamid Dabashi, and Seyyed Vali Reza Nasr, eds. *Expectation of the Millennium: Shi'ism in History.* Albany: State U of New York P, 1989.

National Archives and Records Administration. "9/11 Commission Records." www.archives.gov/research/9-11/. 1 Nov. 2010.

National Child Traumatic Stress Network. *How to Implement Trauma-Focused Cognitive Behavioral Therapy.* Durham, NC: National Center for Child Traumatic Stress, 2004.

National Commission on Terrorist Attacks upon the United States. Archive. 2004. Available from http://govinfo.library.unt.edu/911/archive/index.htm. 1 Nov. 2010.

———. *The 9/11 Commission Report.* New York: Norton, 2004.

National September 11 Memorial and Museum. "Survivors' Stairs." 2010. www.national911memorial.org/survivors-stairs. 1 Nov. 2010.

Needham, Anuradha Dingwaney, and Rajeswari Sunder Rajan, eds. *The Crisis of Secularism in India.* Durham: Duke UP, 2007.

Neuman, Justin. "Religious Cosmopolitanism? Orhan Pamuk, the Headscarf Debate, and the Problem with Pluralism." *Minnesota Review* 77 (2011): 143–61.

Nietzsche, Friedrich. *A Genealogy of Morals.* Ed. Alexander Tille. Trans. William Hausemann. New York: Macmillan, 1897. Vol. 10 of *The Works of Friedrich Nietzsche.*

Nixon, Rob. *Slow Violence and the Environmentalism of the Poor.* Cambridge, MA: Harvard UP, 2011.

Nobel Foundation. "The Nobel Prize in Literature 2006." 2006. http://nobelprize.org/nobel_prizes/literature/laureates/2006/.

Norton, David. *A History of the English Bible as Literature.* Cambridge: Cambridge UP, 2000.

Nussbaum, Martha Craven. "Patriotism and Cosmopolitanism." *For Love of Country? Debating the Limits of Patriotism.* Boston: Beacon Press, 1996. 3–20.

Nussbaum, Martha Craven, and Joshua Cohen. *For Love of Country? Debating the Limits of Patriotism.* Boston: Beacon Press, 1996.

Obama, Barack. "Remarks by the President on a New Beginning, Cairo University." June 4, 2009. www.whitehouse.gov/the-press-office/remarks-president-cairo-university-6-04-09.

O'Rourke, Meghan. "'The Kite Runner': Do I Really Have to Read It?" *Slate* 25 July 2005.

Pamuk, Orhan. "Frankfurt Book Fair Special: Orhan Pamuk and the Turkish Paradox." Interview. *Der Spiegel* 21 Oct. 2005.

———. *Snow.* Trans. Maureen Freely. New York: Vintage, 2005.

Parwez, Ghulam Ahmed. *Islam: A Challenge to Religion.* Lahore, Pakistan: Idare-e-Tulu-e-Islam, 1968.

Pease, Donald. "The Global Homeland State: Bush's Biopolitical Settlement." *Boundary 2* 30.3 (Fall 2003): 1–18.

Pecora, Vincent P. *Secularization and Cultural Criticism: Religion, Nation, and Modernity.* Chicago: U of Chicago P, 2006.

Peters, F. E. *Islam: A Guide for Jews and Christians.* Princeton: Princeton UP, 2005.

Pew Research Center. Forum on Religion and Public Life. *Mapping the Global Muslim Population: A Report on the Size and Distribution of the World's Muslim Population.* Washington, DC: Pew Research Center, 2009.

Porter, Stanley, ed. *The Messiah in the Old and New Testaments.* Grand Rapids: Wm. B. Eerdmans, 2007.

Posner, Richard. "The 9/11 Report: A Dissent." *New York Times* 29 Aug. 2004. www.nytimes.com/2004/08/29/books/the-9-11-report-a-dissent.html.

Post, Chad. "The Arab Book Market: Facts and Figures." Abu Dhabi International Book Fair. n.d. www.adbookfair.com/the-arab-book-market-facts-and-figures/. 17 Mar. 2009.

Powers, Peter Kerry. *Recalling Religions: Resistance, Memory, and Cultural Revision in Ethnic Women's Literature.* Knoxville: U of Tennessee P, 2001.

Raath, A. W. G. *The British Concentration Camps of the Anglo-Boer War, 1899–1902: Reports on the Camps.* Bloemfontein: War Museum, 1999.

Rasul v. Bush. 542 U.S. 466 (2004).

Redfield, Marc. *The Rhetoric of Terror: Reflections on 911 and the War on Terror.* New York: Fordham UP, 2009.

Renard, John. *Islam and Christianity: Theological Themes in Comparative Perspective.* Berkeley: U of California P, 2011.

Rhodes, Cecil John. *The Last Will and Testament of Cecil John Rhodes.* Ed. W. T. Stead. London: "Review of Reviews" Office, 1902.

Ricoeur, Paul. *Figuring the Sacred: Religion, Narrative, and Imagination.* Ed. Mark Wallace. Trans. David Pellauer. Minneapolis: Fortress Press, 1995.

Robbins, Bruce. "Enchantment? No, Thank You!" *The Joy of Secularism: 11 Essays for How We Live Now*. Ed. George Levine. Princeton: Princeton UP, 2011. 74–94.

———. *Feeling Global: Internationalism in Distress*. New York: New York UP, 1999. Cultural Front.

Rothberg, Michael. *Traumatic Realism: The Demands of Holocaust Representation*. Minneapolis: U of Minnesota P, 2000.

Roy, Oliver. *Secularism Confronts Islam*. Trans. George Holoch. New York: Columbia UP, 2007.

Rumsfeld, Donald H. "National Defense Strategy of the United States of America." Department of Defense. Mar. 2005. www.defense.gov/news/mar2005/d20050318nds1.pdf.

———. "Quadrennial Defense Review Report." Department of Defense. 30 Sept. 2001. www.comw.org/qdr/qdr2001.pdf.

———. "Quadrennial Defense Review Report." Department of Defense. 6 Feb. 2006. www.defense.gov/pubs/pdfs/QDR20060203.pdf.

———. "Testimony of U.S. Secretary of Defense Donald H. Rumsfeld Prepared for Delivery to the National Commission on Terrorist Attacks upon the United States." 23 Mar. 2004. http://govinfo.library.unt.edu/911/hearings/hearing8/rumsfeld_statement.pdf.

Rushdie, Salman. "The Book Burning." *New York Review of Books* 2 Mar. 1989. www.nybooks.com/articles/archives/1989/mar/02/the-book-burning/.

———. *The Enchantress of Florence*. New York: Random House, 2008.

———. *Imaginary Homelands: Essays and Criticism, 1981–1991*. London: Granta, 1991.

———. *Joseph Anton*. New York: Random House, 2012.

———. "Now I Can Say, I Am a Muslim." *New York Times* 28 Dec. 1990. www.nytimes.com/1990/12/28/opinion/now-i-can-say-i-am-a-muslim.html.

———. *The Satanic Verses*. New York: Picador, 1988.

———. *Shalimar the Clown*. New York: Random House, 2005.

———. *Step across This Line: Collected Nonfiction, 1992–2002*. New York: Random House, 2002.

———. "A War That Presents Us All with a Crisis of Faith." *Guardian* 2 Nov. 2001. www.theguardian.com/books/2001/nov/03/afghanistan.terrorism.

Sachedina, Abdulaziz. *Islamic Messianism: The Idea of Mahdi in Twelver Shi'ism*. Albany: State U of New York P, 1981.

Sade, Marquis de. *The 120 Days of Sodom and Other Writings*. Trans. Richard Seaver and Austryn Wainhouse. New York: Grove Press, 1994.

Said, Edward W. *Covering Islam: How the Media and the Experts Determine How We See the Rest of the World*. London: Routledge and Kegan Paul, 1981.

———. *Culture and Imperialism*. New York: Knopf, 1993.

———. "Islam and the West Are Inadequate Banners." *Observer* 16 Sept. 2001. www.guardian.co.uk/world/2001/sep/16/september11.terrorism3.

———. *The World, the Text, and the Critic*. Cambridge, MA: Harvard UP, 1983.

Sardar, Ziauddin. "The Eternal Present Tense." Rev. of *The Qu'ran*, trans. Tarif Khalidi. *Guardian* 20 June 2008. www.guardian.co.uk/books/2008/jun/21/saturdayreviewsfeatres.guardianreview26.

———. "Lost in Translation." *New Statesman* 9 Aug. 2004.

Saussy, Haun. "Exquisite Cadavers Stitched from Fresh Nightmares: Of Memes, Hives, and Selfish Genes." *Comparative Literature in an Age of Globalization*. Ed. Haun Saussy. Baltimore: Johns Hopkins UP, 2006. 3–42.

Schäfer, Peter, and Mark Cohen, eds. *Toward the Millennium: Messianic Expectations from the Bible to Waco*. Boston: Brill, 1998.

Schmalzbauer, John, and Kathleen Mahoney. "American Scholars Return to Studying Religion." *Contexts* 7.1 (Winter 2008): 16–21.

Schmitt, Carl. *The Concept of the Political*. Trans. George Schwab. Chicago: U of Chicago P, 2007.

Scholem, Gershom. *The Messianic Idea in Judaism and Other Essays on Jewish Spirituality*. New York: Schocken Books, 1971.

Schrift, Alan, ed. *The Logic of the Gift: Toward an Ethic of Generosity*. New York: Routledge, 1997.

Scott, David, and Charles Hirschkind, eds. *Powers of the Secular Modern: Talal Asad and His Interlocutors*. Stanford: Stanford UP, 2006.

Sells, Michael. *Approaching the Qur'an: The Early Revelations*. 2nd ed. Ashland, OR: White Cloud Press, 2006.

Sen, Amartya. *Identity and Violence: The Illusion of Destiny*. New York: Norton, 2006.

Shephard, Michelle. "Is Force-Feeding Gitmo Detainees Ethical?" *Toronto Star* 20 July 2009. www.thestar.com/news/world/2009/07/20/is_force-feeding_gitmo_detainees_ethical.html.

Siegel, Lee. "The Imagination of Disaster." *Nation* 11 Apr. 2005.

Silk, Mark. "Notes on the Judeo-Christian Tradition in America." *American Quarterly* 36.1 (1984): 65–85.

Simpson, David. *911: The Culture of Commemoration*. Chicago: U of Chicago P, 2006.

Sizemore, Christine. "The Return to Hijab in Nadine Gordimer's *The Pickup* and Leila Aboulela's *Minaret*." *Journal of Commonwealth and Postcolonial Studies* 15.2 (2008): 70–83.

Smith, Christian. *The Secular Revolution*. Berkeley: U of California P, 2003.

Spies, S. B. *Methods of Barbarism? Roberts and Kitchener and Civilians in the Boer Republics, January 1900–May 1902*. Johannesburg: Jonathan Ball, 2001.

Spivak, Gayatri Chakravorty. *Death of a Discipline*. New York: Columbia UP, 2003.

———. "Ethics and Politics in Tagore, Coetzee, and Certain Scenes of Teaching." *Diacritics* 32.3–4 (2002): 17–31.

———. "Terror: A Speech after 9/11." *Boundary 2* 31.2 (2004): 81–111.

———. "Use and Abuse of Human Rights." *Boundary 2* 32.1 (2005): 131–89.

Srivastava, Neelam. *Secularism in the Postcolonial Indian Novel: National and Cosmopolitan Narratives in English*. New York: Routledge, 2008.

Stevens, Matthew. Pers. comm. 26 Sept. 2011.

Stewart, Jeanette. "Obama Sends Yann Martel *Life of Pi* Appreciation Letter." National Post (Canada) 4 June 2010.

Sulk, Kay. "'Visiting Himself on Me': The Angel, the Witness and the Modern Subject of Enunciation in J. M. Coetzee's *Age of Iron*." *Journal of Literary Studies* 18.2–4 (2007): 313–26.

Tang, Alisa. "*Kite Runner* Rape Scene Worries Boy Actor." *Huffington Post* 23 Sept. 2007. www.huffingtonpost.com/huff-wires/20070923/afghan-kite-runner/.

Tauran, Cardinal Jean-Louis. "Interreligious Dialogue—A Risk or an Opportunity?" 27 May 2008. www.acommonword.com/vatican-cardinal-discusses-the-risks-and-opportunities-presented-by-interreligious-dialogue-at-london-theological-college/.

Taylor, Charles. *A Secular Age*. Cambridge, MA: Belknap-Harvard UP, 2007.

Thorne, Ashley. "Beach Books: What Do Colleges and Universities Want Students to Read Outside Class? 2011–2012." Report by the National Association of Scholars. September 2011. www.nas.org/images/documents/BeachBooks.pdf.

Turkish Constitution. 2001. www.anayasa.gov.tr/images/loaded/pdf_dosyalari/THE_CONSTITUTION_OF_THE_REPUBLIC_OF_TURKEY.pdf. www.hri.org/docs/turkey/.

UK Office of National Statistics. "Census 2001: Key Statistics for Local Authorities." Table KS07. 2001. www.statistics.gov.uk/hub/people-places/people/identity#graphTabContent3.www.statistics.gov.uk/hub/index.html.

United Nations Development Programme. *Arab Human Development Report 2009: Challenges to Human Security in the Arab Countries*. New York: UNDP, 2009.

University of North Carolina–Chapel Hill. "Carolina Summer Reading Program 2002." 17 July 2002. www.unc.edu/srp/archive/srp2002/assignment.html. 5 Sept. 2011.

van der Veer, Peter. "Pain and Power: Reflections on Ascetic Agency." *The Anthropologist and the Native: Essays for Gananath Obeyesekere*. Ed. H. L. Seneviratne. Florence: Studio Editoriale Fiorentino, 2009. 201–16.

Vickroy, Laurie. *Trauma and Survival in Contemporary Fiction*. Charlottesville: U of Virginia P, 2002.

Volf, Miroslav, Ghazi bin Muhammad, and Melissa Yarrington. *A Common Word: Muslims and Christians on Loving God and Neighbor*. Grand Rapids, MI: W. B. Eerdmans, 2010.

Vries, Hent de. "On General and Divine Economy: Talal Asad's Genealogy of the Secular and Emmanuel Levinas's Critique of Capitalism, Colonialism, and Money." Scott and Hirschkind 113–33.

Vries, Hent de, and Lawrence Sullivan, eds. *Political Theologies: Public Religions in a Post-secular World*. New York: Fordham UP, 2006.

Walkowitz, Rebecca. *Cosmopolitan Style*. New York: Columbia UP, 2006.

Walter, Jess. *The Financial Lives of Poets*. New York: Harper, 2009.

———. *The Zero: A Novel*. New York: Regan, 2006.

Warner, Michael, Jonathan VanAntwerpen, and Craig J. Calhoun. "Editors' Introduction." Warner, VanAntwerpen, and Calhoun, *Varieties* 1–31.

———, eds. *Varieties of Secularism in a Secular Age*. Cambridge, MA: Harvard UP, 2010.

Watt, Ian. *The Rise of the Novel: Studies in Defoe, Richardson and Fielding*. 2nd ed. Berkeley: U of C Press, 2001.

Weber, Max. *The Protestant Ethic and the Spirit of Capitalism*. Trans. Talcott Parsons. 1930. New York: Routledge, 2001.

White, Jenny B. *Islamist Mobilization in Turkey: A Study in Vernacular Politics*. Studies in Modernity and National Identity. Seattle: U of Washington P, 2002.

Wolin, Richard. *The Frankfurt School Revisited: And Other Essays on Politics and Society*. New York: Routledge, 2006.

———. *Walter Benjamin: An Aesthetic of Redemption*. New York: Columbia UP, 1982.

Wood, James. *The Broken Estate: Essays on Literature and Belief*. 1999. New York: Picador, 2010.

———. "A Frog's Life." Rev. of *Elizabeth Costello*, by J. M. Coetzee. *London Review of Books* 23 Oct. 2003.

World Medical Assembly. "WMA Declaration of Malta on Hunger Strikers." Nov. 1991; rev. Sept. 1992 and Oct. 2006. www.wma.net/en/30publications/10policies/h31/.

———. "WMA Declaration of Tokyo: Guidelines for Physicians Concerning Torture and Other Cruel, Inhuman or Degrading Treatment or Punishment in Relation to Detention and Imprisonment." Oct. 1975; rev. May 2005 and May 2006. www.wma.net/en/30publications/10policies/c18/.

Worth, Roland. *Messiahs and Messianic Movements through 1899*. Jefferson, NC: McFarland, 2005.

Wyatt, Edward. "For Publisher of 9/11 Report, a Royalty-Free Windfall." 28 July 2004. www.nytimes.com/2004/07/28/business/media/28book.html?scp=1&sq=%2522royalty-free%20windfall%2522&st=cse. 1 Nov. 2010.

Wyschogrod, Edith, Jean-Joseph Goux, and Eric Boynton, eds. *The Enigma of Gift and Sacrifice*. New York: Fordham UP. Perspectives in Continental Philosophy.

Zelikow, Philip. Interview by author. 5 May 2011.

Žižek, Slavoj. "Neighbors and Other Monsters: A Plea for Ethical Violence." *The Neighbor: Three Inquiries in Political Theology*. Chicago: U of Chicago P, 2005.

———. *The Parallax View*. Cambridge, MA: MIT Press, 2006.

———. "Passion in the Era of Decaffeinated Belief." *Symptom* 5 (Winter 2004). www.lacan.com/passion.htm.

———. *The Puppet and the Dwarf: The Perverse Core of Christianity*. Cambridge: MIT Press, 2003.

Index